T0301735

SOLID GROWTH

Strategies of
Industrial Champions
in Global Markets

SOLID GROWTH

Strategies of Industrial Champions in Global Markets

Olaf Plötner
ESMT Berlin, Germany

Johannes Habel
University of Houston, USA

Bianca Schmitz
ESMT Berlin, Germany

World Scientific

NEW JERSEY · LONDON · SINGAPORE · BEIJING · SHANGHAI · HONG KONG · TAIPEI · CHENNAI · TOKYO

Published by

World Scientific Publishing Co. Pte. Ltd.

5 Toh Tuck Link, Singapore 596224

USA office: 27 Warren Street, Suite 401-402, Hackensack, NJ 07601

UK office: 57 Shelton Street, Covent Garden, London WC2H 9HE

Library of Congress Control Number: 2022056894

British Library Cataloguing-in-Publication Data

A catalogue record for this book is available from the British Library.

SOLID GROWTH

Strategies of Industrial Champions in Global Markets

ISBN 978-981-126-451-1 (hardcover)

ISBN 978-981-126-452-8 (ebook for institutions)

ISBN 978-981-126-453-5 (ebook for individuals)

For any available supplementary material, please visit
https://www.worldscientific.com/worldscibooks/10.1142/13091#t=suppl

Desk Editors: Nimal Koliyat/Nicole Ong

Typeset by Stallion Press

Email: enquiries@stallionpress.com

Printed in Singapore

Preface

"There are important problems and urgent problems. We work mainly on the latter."

This quote from a manager is symptomatic of the current situation in many companies. At a time when crisis follows crisis around the world, it is also unsurprising: The coronavirus, wars, and dramatic supply shortages in some industries are phenomena that have kept executives on their toes in recent years. But it is important not to lose sight of the big picture amid all the operational hustle and bustle — that is, the strategic perspective.

What are the sustainable changes in our industry? Where do we need to go in order to survive in the market beyond the next few months? How do we achieve solid growth? These questions are the focus of this book. Our point of interest is on industrial companies that operate internationally.

We want to sharpen the readers' understanding of critical challenges and help them to identify strategic options for corporate development. In doing so, we focus firstly on the possibility of establishing oneself in premium areas and successfully addressing customers with a willingness to pay. As a second option, we look at success in low-cost markets, which offer major growth opportunities, particularly in emerging and developing countries. Thirdly, we discuss strategic approaches in which the product portfolio of an industrial company is developed into complex service solutions with the help of digital technologies. Often, innovative business and pricing models are then introduced in parallel.

Many of our statements are based on scientific studies — all authors work at academic institutions and are involved in scientific research projects as part of their "Bringing Technology to Market" center. However, we make use of many practical examples, particularly with regard to our implementation recommendations. We were able to gain insights into these through countless discussions with executives from industrial companies, as all three authors work intensively with top managers from global industrial companies. Our special thanks go to these industry partners.

About the Authors

Olaf Plötner is a Professor at ESMT Berlin and the Director of ESMT's BTM Center. His research and teaching focus is on strategic management in global B2B markets. His work is reflected in his most recent book, *Counter Strategies in Global Markets*, published by Palgrave Macmillan, Springer, and SDX Shanghai. His research has been portrayed in journals such as *Industrial Marketing Management*, the *Journal of Business and Industrial Marketing*, as well as in leading international media such as *CNN, The Wall Street Journal Europe, The Times of India, Frankfurter Allgemeine Zeitung, China Daily Europe, People's Daily (China)*, and the *Financial Times*.

Johannes Habel is an Associate Professor of Marketing at the C. T. Bauer College of Business, University of Houston. His primary areas of interest are the digital transformation of the sales function and sales psychology. His research has been published in some of the world's most renowned academic marketing journals, such as the *Journal of Marketing* and the *Journal of Marketing Research*. Beyond academic research, Johannes has published case studies with Harvard Business Publishing and

The Case Centre as well as managerial articles with journals such as *Forbes, Harvard Business Manager*, and *European Business Review*.

 **Bianca Schmitz** is a Director of leadership development programs at ESMT Berlin and Director of knowledge transfer at the BTM Center. Her research has been published in journals such as *Industrial Marketing Management* and the *Journal of Family Business Management*. Beyond academic research, Bianca has published a number of case studies and managerial articles on hidden champions and digital transformation.

Contents

Abbreviations

AI	Artificial Intelligence
AM	Additive Manufacturing
ATTAC	Association for the Taxation of Financial Transactions and Citizens' Action
B2B	Business to Business
B2C	Business to Consumer
BCG	Boston Consulting Group
BDR	Business Development Representative
CIM	Computer-Integrated Manufacturing
CQ	Cultural Intelligence
CRM	Crew Resource Management
EU	European Union
EUV	Extreme Ultraviolet
FDI	Foreign Direct Investment
GE	General Electric
GRI	Global Revenue Index
HR	Human Resources
IT	Information Technology
MRI	Magnetic Resonance Imaging
PIMS	Profit Impact of Marketing Strategies
R&D	Research and Development
RCEP	Regional Comprehensive Economic Partnership
SDR	Sales Development Representative
SHIG	Shandong Heavy Industry Group
SME	Small and Medium-sized Enterprise
TCO	Total Costs of Ownership

Chapter 1

The Essence of Business Strategy: Developing a Robust Planning Framework

Abstract

In this chapter, we discuss the role that business strategy planning plays in a company in addition to outlining the core components of a business strategy. We first present the most important factors that need to be determined prior to developing a business strategy before revealing the key global developments that affect multinational companies. In addition, we identify the main difficulties in implementing business strategies and reveal how they might be overcome. We conclude with an initial overview of the counter strategies that are examined in more detail in the other chapters of this book.

Misunderstandings

As an electrical engineering graduate, Roman Ley took his first step on the career ladder as a trainee at an international technology company. He worked there for three years as a sales engineer in the industrial turbines business unit, which was part of the group's energy division. After spending two years in Asia, he was promoted to the role of sales manager. Five years later, he became head of the industrial turbines unit. Shortly after that, the energy division welcomed in a new CEO, who asked Roman to outline his unit's business strategy in a half-hour presentation.

The meeting took place on a Monday morning. On the Sunday evening prior, Roman went through his PowerPoint presentation one more time and was confident that he had covered all the key aspects. On Monday morning, he met with the new CEO, the CEO's assistant, and the CFO of the energy division in a conference room. Roman started with the financial targets that he aimed to meet within the next five years. Bernd Jacob, the new CEO, interrupted him after a few sentences and asked him to move on, as the financial targets were due for revision by the Group's management. He added that he considered plans extending beyond three years to be pointless, considering the market's fast-paced dynamics.

Chastened, Roman moved on to the next point, addressing precisely those market dynamics and their trends. He assumed this would help him make up for his unfortunate false start. "Please don't," Jacob said. "I invited you to present your business strategy, not to list well-known results of market research. I'm not interested in the dynamics of your market — I want to know how you intend to act in this environment."

Perturbed, Roman clicked through to the slide summarizing the specifications for the latest turbine model. "This data is irrelevant to me," the CEO interrupted. "If anything, I would like to hear how our customers view this new development, which of its functions differ from rival products, and how significantly. Perhaps you could explain these aspects to me?"

Apologizing, Roman promised to submit this information after the meeting, as he did not have it available then and there. Nervous and confused, he moved on to the final part of his presentation and explained the communications campaign lined up for the new turbine model's launch on the market. Jacob sighed. "Excuse me, Mr. Ley, but these are operational issues. I do not want to get involved with these. I thought that you were going to enlighten me on your business strategy today," he said, looking at his watch. "Please arrange a new appointment with my secretary."

Roman went back to his office, slammed the door shut, and wondered what he had done all that work for. For his part, as he made his way to his next meeting, CEO Jacob was wondering whether Roman was really the right man to head the industrial turbines unit.

Unfortunate meetings like this occur in many companies throughout the world, in one form or another. The heart of the problem is misunderstanding. Although both parties want to discuss a business unit's strategy, they understand the task differently — whether it be planning the timescale for business strategies, deciding to what extent targets form part of a strategy, or finding the dividing line between operations and strategy. This means that they are approaching the issue from two different perspectives. As a result, both sides feel misunderstood, and they end up annoyed and disappointed with one another.

For this reason, we start this chapter by defining the basic terminology. A framework is then constructed for a business strategy that is both scientifically robust and proven in practice. This does not cover all of the support beams and crossbeams involved, but rather the load-bearing elements. We also examine new strategic growth opportunities and how to implement business strategies.

What Is Strategy?

In very general terms, strategy is a plan for achieving goals. It does not need to have anything to do with markets or companies. The term was first used in military circles. The pioneers in military strategy are considered to have been the Chinese General Sun Tzu and Prussian General Carl von Clausewitz. The term only migrated into business management during the 1960s, due primarily to the American economic historian and economist Alfred D. Chandler and his book *Strategy and Structure: Chapters in the History of the Industrial Enterprise.*[1] Chandler's key message was that organizational structures have to align themselves to strategies, not vice versa — a message that remains as relevant to practice as ever.

Our understanding of strategy is based on three key assumptions:

1. A target has already been set. The financial target for a business unit is generally defined by a company's owners or management. The strategy describes how this target is to be met.
2. It is a plan and, thus, an abstract concept. This is why Peter Drucker, one of the fathers of business administration studies, referred to strategy as "the theory of the business." The practical implementation of strategic measures, although important, does not form part of the strategy.
3. Strategy focuses on the key aspects that go toward reaching the target. It is limited, in other words, to a plan's most important elements.

---

[1]A. D. Chandler, *Strategy and Structure — Chapters in the History of American Industrial Enterprise* (Cambridge, MA: MIT Press, 1969).

For us, solid growth is the most important goal of a company. Growth is a developmental process beyond sales and profits, and it includes the interests of employees and society. Solidity is part of this goal and clarifies that these developmental processes shall have a long-term impact.

Strategic planning in a company can address different elements — the entire company, a strategic business unit, or a function. Here, we are primarily concerned with strategic business units. This is an area that operates in a defined market environment and is responsible for its own profits and losses. If a company operates in just one market environment, there is no difference between the corporate and business unit strategies.

The different levels and their respective strategies are interdependent (see Figure 1.1). The targets for lower levels are derived from the strategies of those above. Elements that represent a key strategic statement at a lower level might be too insignificant to play a role at a higher level.

This leads us to draw a distinction between strategic and operational planning. The former is less specific than the latter. In practice, the easiest way to distinguish between the two is to remember that the question "Are we doing the right thing?" refers to strategic matters, and "Are we doing it right?" refers to operations. Having said that, the answers often overlap, which means that they cannot always be clearly differentiated. Among other things, this depends on the specific level in the company's hierarchy, as well as on the different opinions of those involved as to what constitutes strategy. (See the following example of Messrs. Ley and Jacob, who

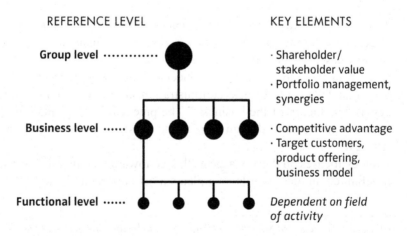

Figure 1.1:   Strategic hierarchy in a company.

each had very different opinions about whether the new communications campaign was a strategic or operational issue.)

When it comes to setting targets, which should always precede strategy development, the terms "mission" and "vision" are frequently used.

- A vision paints an inspiring picture for the future. It aspires to reach a target state that goes beyond financial figures. Famous examples include Bill Gates' vision to put a PC on each desk and in every household, or Wikipedia's desire to create a world "in which all knowledge is freely accessible to everyone."
- A mission explains the reason for pursuing this aim. It is the higher purpose behind an organization. The Red Cross has a very striking mission: "To serve the most vulnerable." So does the BBC: "To enrich people's lives with programs and services that inform, educate, and entertain."

Together, the vision and mission form a company's guiding principle.

Yet, this raises the question of why we should define a guiding principle and strategy in the first place? The answer is that both provide orientation. First and foremost, this orientational function is important to the managers of companies. They often have to make their business decisions under immense operational pressure, which can obscure their view of the company's overarching aims. In situations like these, a glance at the guiding principle and strategy can point them in the right direction. Henry Mintzberg likened strategy to setting course on a sailing ship.[2] The ship represents the company, and the strength of the wind the attractiveness of the market. The stronger the wind blows, the faster the boat moves. The captain — or management — not only sets the course but also steers the ship and navigates with the aid of the information available about the relative position, whereas the technical tools required for sailing a ship are a sextant or radar — in a business context these are financial controlling and market research.

A strategy's orientational function affects other employees in a company, not the least those whose interests extend beyond their immediate working environment to include the aim and purpose of their activities.

---

[2]H. Mintzberg, *The Rise and Fall of Strategic Planning* (New York, NY: The Free Press, 1994).

The strategy — along with the company's guiding principle — provides them with answers and boosts their motivation. It has a similar effect on the company's owners, motivating them to invest. A strategy helps them to estimate whether a business unit will be successful in its competitive environment in the future and whether it is worth investing capital. The motivation for publishing a strategy is not always obvious, given the general tendency to not disclose the plans for beating competitors. Yet, doing so shows other stakeholders, such as suppliers, customers, and political representatives, the direction that the company wants to take.

Is it still worth setting a specific course if the environment is in a constant state of change? Particularly in recent years, this question has cropped up a lot, as it is believed that major and rapid changes are shaping our lives. The acronym VUCA is often cited in this regard. It stands for volatility, uncertainty, complexity, and ambiguity — phenomena that seem to be on the increase in current times.

The situation is not quite as dramatic as this might imply. This is not the first time that market conditions have been subject to such extreme change. During the first half of the 16th century, for example, merchants in Europe had to grapple with an inflation crisis. At the same time, they had to deal with the rampant spread of power of the Fugger and Medici families, the prospects of a New World on the other side of the Atlantic, and the political turmoil caused by the religious uprising now known as Protestantism. The geopolitical, social, and economic upheavals during and after the World Wars show that these disruptive dynamics are not unique to the present.

Nevertheless, any changes in the market require reorientation. Changes that occur in rapid succession can put pressure on the planning time frame. They can require a greater readiness to modify plans on short notice. This does not eliminate the need for strategic planning. The battles that General von Clausewitz fought were fraught with uncertainty, referred to as "friction." They could not be solved by having plenty of information about the enemy, either. In any case, such information was unreliable in earlier periods. Thus, the strategies adopted by von Clausewitz required a great deal of flexibility from the commanders and the ability to identify, think through, and correctly assess the range of options for action based on extraordinary "mental prowess."[3] These very same requirements can be applied to present-day managers, especially

---

[3]C. von Clausewitz, *Vom Kriege* (Hamburg: Anaconda, 2010).

given that current forecasts being offered by economists and market researchers are about as reliable as the military intelligence was in the day of von Clausewitz.

Today, the ability to adapt to environmental conditions is often referred to as "agility." However, agility becomes meaningless if it is applied without a strategy or purpose. The maritime metaphor above illustrates this well. Sailing without setting a course would mean drifting haphazardly in the hope of reaching the desired destination by chance.

All the same, setting a course for a sailing ship does not guarantee reaching the intended destination. This applies equally to strategic planning. The first voyage Columbus undertook to find a nautical passage to India is a well-known example. Albert Einstein's words that "planning replaces coincidence by error" are also applicable in this case. There is more to be learned from mistakes than from coincidences.

Where Does Our Competitive Advantage Lie?

For business to take place, both the supplier and the customer must stand to benefit. Each party receives and gives something. In the broadest sense, it is a cost–benefit equation. Both the supplier and the customer assume that they are receiving more than they give. This can be portrayed in the form of two sets of scales (see Figure 1.2), on which the costs and benefits are placed in the opposing pans.[4] Before making a decision to buy or sell, both parties expect the benefits of the transaction to outweigh its costs, so that the scale tips in their favor.

The markets that we are interested in here are characterized by intense competition. It is therefore not enough for the supplier to offer the customer something that provides greater benefit than it had cost them. In addition, the customer must see it as being better than anything put forward by relevant competitors. If this is the case, then the supplier enjoys a customer advantage.

Suppliers can secure this advantage by keeping their prices lower than those of their competitors, thus reducing the weight in the pan containing the customer's costs. However, they must then consider how much this weighs down their own side of the scale. If suppliers agree to transactions

---

[4]W. Plinke, "Grundlagen des Marktprozesses," in *Technischer Vertrieb*, 2nd ed. (Berlin: Springer, 2000), pp. 3–99.

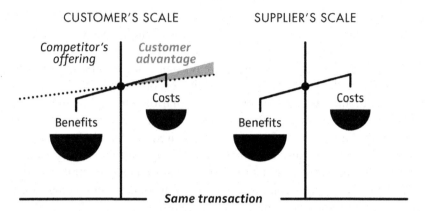

Figure 1.2:   The cost–benefit scale for the supplier and customer.

that do not cover their own costs over the long term, they will disappear from the market down the line. This means that suppliers not only have to keep offering customers as many benefits as possible, but they must also ensure that they remain profitable. Only then can it be said that the supplier in question enjoys a competitive advantage. In summary, a competitive advantage must fulfill the following three criteria:

- It must be important for the customer.
- It must be difficult for the competition to replicate.
- It must be profitable for the supplier.

Understanding the concept of competitive advantage is easy, but analyzing and implementing it in operational practice is difficult. The considerations in this context lead to the core entrepreneurial question as follows: "How is it that we make money?" To this, some managers have a quick answer ready without having penetrated the complexity of customer behavior, competitive developments, and their own profit drivers more deeply.

Achieving this competitive advantage is the key focus when considering a business strategy, and it has already been scrutinized in countless research projects. Michael Porter is well known in this field, particularly for his extensive empirical study into "PIMS": profit impact of marketing strategies. The study was commissioned by General Electric (GE) in the 1960s to examine how companies or individual business units can secure competitive advantages. One of the results that Porter achieved was to plot a U-shaped curve (see Figure 1.3) that portrays the relationship between a business unit's return on investment and its share of the market. As it turned out, successful companies' market shares were either particularly large or small. Business units with medium-sized market shares, on the other hand, were less successful.

With regard to business units with large market shares, this phenomenon surely stems from the lower production costs per item that result from economies of scale. In the 1920s, the aircraft industry discovered that doubling production volume reduced the costs per item by around 20–30 percent. This potential for reducing costs became prominent under the name "learning curve effect," coined by the Boston Consulting Group.

By definition, business units with small market shares cannot leverage economies of scale. Their success stems from the flexibility that their small size affords them, particularly when it comes to meeting customer requirements. Customers are prepared to pay higher prices for this reward, which has a positive effect on the supplier's profitability. By contrast, medium-sized business units risk being too small to benefit from economies of scale, yet they are already too large to be flexible. One example of this is Nordex, a European supplier of wind turbines and equipment with a workforce of approximately 5,000. Although the market for these products has grown worldwide, the company has lost some of its market share. On the one hand, it competes against larger suppliers such as Vestas, Siemens/Gamesa, and Goldwind. On the other hand, it competes against smaller specialist manufacturers, such as TetraSpar, which focus on floating offshore systems.

The results of this research led Porter to draw up three generic strategy options:

- A business unit can secure a competitive advantage with the quality of its products, which Porter terms a "differentiation strategy."
- A business unit can achieve lower unit costs through large sales volumes, so as to offer customers lower prices than the competition — a cost leadership strategy.
- A business unit can focus on a specific segment of customers by pursuing a niche strategy.[5]

---

[5]M. E. Porter, *Competitive Strategy* (New York, NY: The Free Press, 1980).

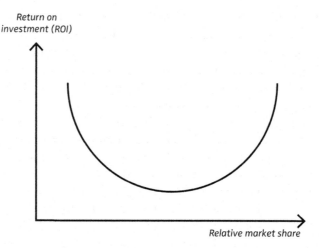

Figure 1.3:   Porter's U-shaped curve.

Xavier Gilbert and Paul Strebel then expanded these three strategies by adding a dynamic component.[6] They believe that competitive pressure forces companies to improve themselves over the long term with regard to both costs and customer benefits. This helps firms to always stay one step ahead of the competition. To start with, companies should focus for a certain period on just one dimension, which Gilbert and Strebel call "outpacing." Porter then ascertained that improvements in costs and quality cannot be continued indefinitely. A few decades ago, video recorders were big, heavy, and expensive when they first came on the market. Over the course of time, they became more compact and affordable, but the price never dropped below €10. Manufacturers reached the limit for optimizing the quality and costs of video recorders at some point. In this regard, Porter talks of the productivity frontier. In the best-case scenario, suppliers will occupy a point on the outside curve (see Figure 1.4).[7]

These trains of thought were further developed by W. Chan Kim and Renée Mauborgne under the heading "Blue Ocean Strategy."[8] They

---

[6] X. Gilbert and P. Strebel, "Strategies to Outpace the Competition," *Journal of Business Strategy* 8, no. 1 (1987): 28–36.

[7] M. E. Porter, "What Is a Strategy?" *Harvard Business Review*, November/December (1996): 61–78.

[8] W. C. Kim and R. Mauborgne, *Blue Ocean Strategy: How to Create Uncontested Market Space and Make the Competition Irrelevant* (Boston, MA: Harvard Business Review Press, 2005).

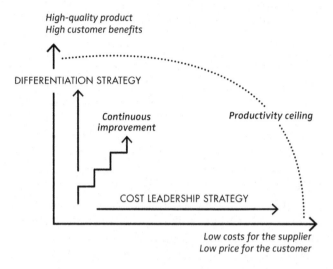

Figure 1.4: Outpacing and the productivity frontier.

argued that companies must strive for product and process innovations if they are to overcome the productivity limits and thus attain unique competitive positions. The idea is to use innovative offerings to generate new demand, thus rendering the previous interaction between costs and quality redundant. An example of this is how we can now use streaming technology to watch a film on a notebook more conveniently and cheaply than with a top-of-the-range video recorder 10 years ago.

The approaches adopted by Porter, Strebel and Gilbert, and Kim and Mauborgne set up the first rough decision-making framework for developing a competitive advantage. But before considering any other factors in the company, the market that the strategy is to address must first be defined. Consider Porsche as an example. Some see the success of this brand as evidence of the successful application of Porter's implementation strategy. Others view Porsche as implementing a successful cost leadership strategy. It depends on how you define the company's market. The first group views Porsche as the quality leader in the automotive market, whereas the second defines the relevant market more narrowly, comparing Porsche only with other suppliers of luxury sports cars, thus focusing on Porsche's much higher production volumes than Ferrari and Lotus.

This example shows that defining a division's competitive advantage raises further key questions, which need answering. The three most important of these are discussed as follows.

Which Customer Need Are We Addressing?

The supplier must determine which customer need it wants to address. In the B2B sphere, where products are often described as a solution to a problem, there is an additional question: What fundamental problem has generated the demand for a solution? For example, potential customers might be seeking to bond two materials, to transport goods from point A to point B, or to obtain certain chassis parts to manufacture a car. The question can thus focus more squarely on the solution: What function must an offering serve to meet the customer's need?[9]

A customer's problem — such as transporting goods — can be broken down into its specific components, in this case by asking the following: What distance needs to be covered? How quickly must the goods arrive? What safety regulations must be followed?

Customers have different expectations of the products that they buy. Nonetheless, some share certain similarities when it comes to the criteria they base their purchase decisions on and how they evaluate offers. These customers can be grouped into segments. In many markets, customers' willingness to pay is used to define a segment. For example, some passengers will pay 10 times more than others for the same flight to enjoy the perks of first class. Others are willing, or forced, to pare things down to the basics to secure a cheap ticket.

The more accurately a supplier defines and addresses the needs of a segment, the greater the benefits for the customers in question. Pharmaceutical companies such as Pfizer are currently adopting this approach. As sales of mass-market, blockbuster drugs are on the wane, Pfizer is successfully focusing on developing drugs that target the precise needs of small target groups. It is important for suppliers who concentrate on a specific market segment to not lose sight of their own needs. Kim and Mauborgne cite the example of the airline Song to illustrate this. In the United States, this company focused on female business customers,

---

[9]Derek Abell, the founding president of ESMT Berlin and previously professor at Harvard Business School and IMD, talks of the "function served" in this context. D. Abell, *Defining the Business: The Starting Point of Strategic Planning* (Englewood Cliffs, NJ: Prentice Hall, 1980).

Close to our approach of understanding the customer's demand is the concept of "job to be done" developed by Harvard professor Clayton Christensen and colleagues; see C. Christensen, T. Hall, K. Dillon, and D. S. Duncan, "Know Your Customer's Job to Be Done," *Harvard Business Review* 94, no. 9 (2016): 45–49.

offering organic meals and a targeted entertainment program, including in-flight workouts. However, Song was unable to survive on the market for long.[10] The authors thus recommend "desegmenting" customer groups, which means considering whether a strategy might be too tightly focused on a specific target group.

Suppliers decide whether to address single, several, or all customer segments in the market. McLaren Automotive, for example, only addresses the premium segment of purchasers in its market — that of extremely expensive sports cars. Volkswagen targets the same segment with its Bugatti and Lamborghini brands while simultaneously addressing lower customer price-bracket segments with 10 other brands. The only segment that Volkswagen has ignored so far is the large one of emerging economies, where the customers' price bracket for cars lies between €5,000 and €8,000, though the company is planning to close this gap.

Closely linked to customer segment considerations is a supplier's regional alignment: Customers' purchasing behaviors differ from country to country and according to traditional tastes and national legal frameworks. This proved a fatal pitfall for Starbucks in Israel and for Walmart in Germany. It is why no company in the alcoholic beverages sector would plan to set up an affiliate in an Islamic state, for example. In most markets, other customer segmentation criteria are more important than nationality, meaning that cross-border customer segments can be formed. Nonetheless, it is important for suppliers to consider which customers in a target segment are to be addressed in which regions of the world, since serving foreign markets consumes a lot of resources. Fundamental decisions on regional focus should therefore be made during the strategic planning.

What Is It That We Are Marketing?

We have seen that a product portfolio is determined by customers' needs. Next, the operating principles and technology that the supplier will require to solve a customer's problem must be decided during the strategic planning. This might be to bond two materials using screws or an adhesive; to transport goods by rail, truck, plane, or ship; or to manufacture car chassis parts from steel, plastic, or aluminum.

---

[10]W. C. Kim and R. Mauborgne, "Red Ocean Traps," *Harvard Business Review* 93, no. 3 (2015): 68–73.

A supplier's predominant technology is frequently used to specify its sector, such as in the automotive industry. Having said that, a supplier can apply several technologies to solve a customer's problem and thus fall into a broader category of sectors. For instance, current developments in requirements and technology are turning companies such as Daimler, General Motors, and Volkswagen into "mobility" rather than "automotive" operators. This means that they want to offer their customers a broader range of transportation technologies in the future.

Besides determining the technology that will be used to solve a customer's problem, the breadth of the portfolio should be defined during the strategic planning. For example, a truck manufacturer must decide whether to offer just standard versions of a vehicle or a wider range of models. It must also decide whether to include truck bodies in the portfolio and whether financing options should be offered or not. Closely related to this is customer individuality, which increases, for example, in cases where traditional industrial enterprises make the strategic decision to extend their product portfolios.[11]

In their quest to fulfill customers' every wish and leave no sales potential untapped, some companies are tempted to make their sales portfolios as broad as possible. Although one should bear in mind that a wider range of products does not automatically generate more demand. Konrad Wetzker and Peter Strüven cite an experiment in which supermarket customers were given coupons for jelly. As many as 10 times more customers used the coupons when only six jelly choices were offered instead of 30.[12] Suppliers sometimes overlook the fact that a wider range of products can incur high complexity costs, even if digitization promises savings in this respect. Furthermore, any supplier offering a wide range of products should be aware that they are competing against product specialists in certain fields who can offer customers greater benefits. To avoid losing the focus on competitive advantage, it should be decided during the strategic planning as to what is *not* part of the supplier's offering.

---

[11] We use the term "product" to cover both material and immaterial components, in other words both goods and services.
[12] K. Wetzker and P. Strüven, *Der enttarnte Stratege: Rationalisierte Irrationalität im Management* (Heidelberg: Springer, 2016).

What Business Model Are We Applying?

Finally, defining a business strategy should set the cornerstones of the commercial framework in which the supplier wishes to conduct business. In this context, we are referring to the business model. This defines which inputs and outputs are attributed to the supplier and the customer in a transaction. It also addresses how pain and gain are divided between the two parties along the value creation chain.[13]

Deciding on a business model can be a matter of determining who has which usage and property rights. Is a product going to be offered for sale, rent, or lease? Recently, the question has arisen as to who owns the data produced during the value creation process. The Italian rail company Trenitalia, for example, shares the data for its climate control units with SAP. By contrast, Deutsche Bahn keeps its product data under wraps for its own further value creation activities.

The business model must stipulate how any created value will be distributed between the supplier and the customer. For example, the aircraft turbine manufacture Rolls-Royce links its earnings to an airline's use of its products and charges customers based on "power by the hour". This means spreading the risk. By systematically applying this rule in this case, Rolls-Royce shares the sales loss risk with its customers, for example, if an airline's workers go on strike.

When it comes to service-oriented pricing schemes, there are even business models in which the supplier's risk goes beyond the customer's use of the product. For example, the business consultancy Bain & Company entered the market by offering to link its consultancy fees to its customers' stock exchange value. The actual course that the stock price takes, of course, depends on factors over which Bain has no influence.

---

[13]The term "business model" can be interpreted in very different ways. A good overview is provided in T. Bieger and S. Reinhold, "Das wertbasierte Geschäftsmodell — ein aktualisierter Strukturierungsansatz," in *Innovative Geschäftsmodelle*, ed. T. Bieger, D. zu Knyphausen-Aufsess, and C. Krys (Berlin/Heidelberg: Springer, 2011). It should be noted that here we interpret the term more narrowly than the now relatively popular definitions forwarded by Osterwalder, who understands a "business model" as basically covering all elements of what we think of as business strategy. See A. Osterwalder, Y. Pigneur, and C. L Tucci, "Clarifying Business Models: Origins, Present, and Future of the Concept," *Communications of the Association for Information Systems* 16 (2005): 1–40.

The design of a business model's core elements can determine which work processes in the value creation chain are to be performed by the supplier and which by the customer. Consider the furniture retailer IKEA. To save costs, the company made a name for itself by leaving the final product assembly to its customers.

Of course, these decisions are closely linked to the kinds of products on offer and the breadth of the portfolio. Yet, the elements of business strategy decisions always overlap. They are interdependent. Ultimately, everything is interlinked. It is nonetheless advisable to structure strategic decisions in the same way. This makes it easier to cope with the complexities that crop up in practice. With this in mind, the 3 + 1 key questions depicted in Figure 1.5 provide a useful guideline for devising a business strategy.

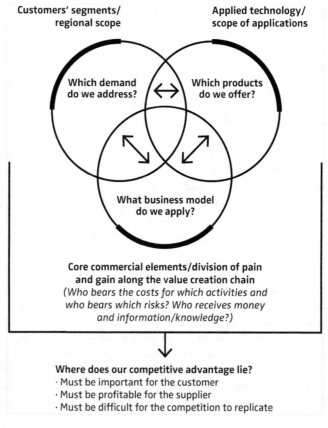

Figure 1.5:   3 + 1 key questions for devising a business strategy.

As stated above, strategic planning should focus solely on the key elements of business development. This restriction helps when it comes to explaining the strategy to others. Too many details can blur the overall picture. The key questions cited above can, of course, be subdivided. Consider, for example, a supplier as it determines a business model. If the supplier intends not to sell but rather to lease the product in question, it needs to decide how to set the leasing rate, the frequency of payments, and who is to be responsible for which kinds of product damage. The answers to these questions already encroach upon the operational planning, which exceeds the scope of strategic planning and goes into more detail.

The Starting Point

Companies are rarely on the green field when answering the 3 + 1 questions for devising a business strategy. Instead, their answers need to take into account both their unique starting points and the concept of "core competencies," which was developed by C. K. Prahalad and Gary Hamel and has become an established approach for doing so.[14] (Although designed in relation to companies, the concept can be applied to individual business units.) In contrast to market-centric approaches, in which strategic decisions are based primarily on market conditions, Prahalad and Hamel recommend focusing on the skills that exist in the company or business unit. However, only those skills that help the company maintain a lasting competitive advantage are considered relevant in terms of core competencies. Prahalad and Hamel illustrate their concept in the form of a tree, with the roots representing the core competencies, the branches the types of product, and the leaves and blossoms the products.

Besides core competencies, a company's financial resources are a variable that must be considered to determine a business unit's starting point. The first factors to be ascertained are sales and costs. These can be broken down further, for example, by product type or region. A comparison between income and expenditures then produces values that can be used to ascertain the economic starting point. These values can be broken down even further according to the specific goal of the analysis. This could include, for example, a focus on financial data (i.e., cash flow).

---

[14] C. K. Prahalad and G. Hamel, *Competing for the Future* (Boston, MA: Harvard Business School Press, 1996).

In recent years, profit levels have increasingly been set in relation to a company's capital factors, such as the return on capital employed, which compares pre-tax operating returns with operating assets. These and similar indicators are not compiled just to ascertain a business unit's current situation. They also help estimate the potential for raising the financial resources necessary to implement a specific business strategy. This potential is a key factor in the strategic decision-making framework.

Besides the available skills and resources, how the company applies them is of interest. A wide range of approaches exist for structuring these processes, of which Porter's value creation chain model (see Figure 1.6) is the best known.[15] This calls for recording the stages involved in the process used to transform the basic material into a ready-to-use product. This process is then divided into the primary activities directly related to providing the service (e.g., customer service) and the support activities used to perform the primary processes (e.g., human resources). The costs and effects of these activities in the company are then analyzed to evaluate their contribution toward creating competitive advantages. The goal is to identify the strengths and weaknesses of a company or business unit as accurately as possible.

The level of detail required in such an analysis varies from case to case. In general, benchmarks will be required to evaluate the results. It is

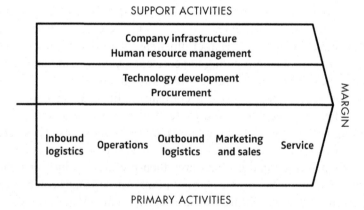

Figure 1.6:   Porter's value creation chain.

---

[15]M. E. Porter, *Competitive Advantage: Creating and Sustaining Superior Performance* (New York, NY: Free Press, 1985).

common practice to perform annual comparisons within each business unit. Comparisons with other companies' business processes are even more useful, although the information is more difficult to obtain. The most helpful comparison would be with a company that achieves the best cross-sector results for a specific activity. This is what is meant by the practice of benchmarking.

Market-specific Developments

We now return to the sailing analogy. Besides knowing your own position, you have to have an idea of how environmental conditions such as the weather will develop during the course of your journey. With regard to planning a business strategy, this means anticipating how the market environment will develop in the future as well as knowing your point of departure. In the following section, we compare and contrast the developments that relate to a business unit's particular market and the overarching developments relevant to strategic planning.

Numerous institutions and associations conduct studies to ascertain the current situation and predict developments in an industry. These efforts are supplemented by the market research that many companies conduct themselves. Porter's Five Forces model has become the established approach for sorting and understanding bundles of information better. This model was developed originally as a means of explaining how profitability differs between industries.[16] Porter discovered, for example, that profits in the aviation industry had been much lower than those of soft drink products for years.

A large number of subsequent studies confirmed large industry-related differences in profits. A 2018 study by McKinsey found that more than 50 percent of a company's financial success depends on the industry in which it operates — making the industry more important than the chosen business strategy. According to the study, mediocre companies in high-profit industries outperformed high-performing companies in moderately profitable industries. To illustrate the industry differences related to financial success, Bradley *et al.* refer to the incomes of the world's best

---

[16]M. E. Porter, "How Competitive Forces Shape Strategy," *Harvard Business Review* 57, no. 2 (1979): 137–145.

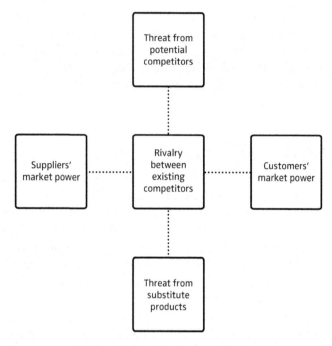

Figure 1.7:   Porter's Five Forces model.

players in badminton and tennis. The former earn many times less than the latter, even though they all train equally hard.[17]

Porter identified five sector-specific factors that were responsible for these differences: suppliers' and customers' market power, the threat of new entrants and substitute products entering the market, and intense competition from rivals (see Figure 1.7).

The more intense the competition is in a sector, the lower the suppliers' profitability will be, particularly if many rivals pursue the same strategy. If strategies differ — for example, because one company seeks its competitive advantage through low prices, whereas another focuses on providing quality — these suppliers can still be competitors despite

---

[17]C. Bradley, M. Hirt, and S. Smit, *Strategy Beyond the Hockey Stick* (Hoboken, NJ: McKinsey/John Wiley & Sons, 2018). The poor profitability of an industry can also lead to the analytical work of a company indicating that it should not change the business strategy within a certain industry, but instead change the industry right away, according to the saying "change your industry or change the industry".

targeting different customer segments. The reason for this is customers' inconsistent behavior, as they base their decisions on changing criteria. This is the context in which substitutes represent competition.

The power wielded by customers and suppliers depends primarily on the extent to which these market participants rely on each other. The supplier must therefore consider several important questions. Could a customer still manage without my products? Could they produce them themselves? Has the customer committed long term to purchasing from a certain supplier? If not, do other suppliers offer similar products to mine in their portfolios? In the latter case, the customer's costs for switching to a different supplier must be considered. The amount that a company would stand to lose if a customer or supplier were to end the business relationship — or the cost of finding a new partner — also plays a role. According to the logic of the Five Forces model, the more power that lies with a customer or a supplier, the lower the profitability for the company.

The threat presented by new competitors and substitute products is determined mainly by the costs associated with their entry into the market. These costs depend, among other things, on the capital that the new market entrant requires and the extent of the economies of scale available to competitors. Apart from this, the achievable profits, of course, play a role, as low profits in a sector can be a barrier to market entry.

Finally, government regulation can influence the number and profitability of suppliers in a sector. This can take the form of incentives for start-up companies or, equally, protection for well-established businesses, whose survival on the market would otherwise be under threat. One example of this is the steel industry, in which none of the major suppliers dropped out of the market in 2015, despite global production of approximately 1.5 billion metric tons versus global demand of just 800 million. The spectrum of state intervention measures is diverse and can range from subsidizing loss-making companies to introducing punitive tariffs for competitors. This aspect leads us to our next topic, which deals with the broader set of factors that extend beyond the sector.

Cross-market Developments

The number of people living in urban environments worldwide surpassed rural regions for the first time in 2008. This trend toward urbanization is international and affects companies from a wide range of sectors. An approach called the PEST analysis, which stands for "political, economic, socio-demographic, and technical", is frequently used to record cross-market developments. Of the numerous aspects covered in a PEST analysis, we focus on five points that are particularly important for global industrial companies:

1. The world's population keeps on growing, despite the reverse trend in industrialized countries. From an economic perspective, this growth is good news, as it means purchasing demand will grow as well. As most of the population growth is occurring in emerging economies and developing countries, the increase in demand is focused mainly on customer segments with a low willingness to pay. Prosperity is increasing in pockets throughout emerging economies and developing countries, and this boosts demand for products in the higher price ranges. Yet, over the medium term, higher sales potential is located in the lower price ranges.

2. Instead of international corporations, the financially weak customer segments in these emerging-markets are more often addressed by regional suppliers, whose lower-quality but more affordable products meet the requirements in these countries. Although most of the suppliers in question cannot maintain their success over the long term and disappear from the market over time, a number of them keep growing and reach levels that prompt them to seek new business opportunities. These suppliers have the chance to improve the quality of their offerings and address customer segments with a higher willingness to pay. At this point, they start to compete with the established premium companies and change the competitive landscape in their markets. This is how the Chinese companies Huawei and ZTE were so successful in ousting the US company Lucent Technologies and Germany's Siemens Public Networks from their commanding positions in the telecommunications network infrastructure market.

3. Rapid developments in state-of-the-art information and communication technologies are changing many customers' requirements, while the exchange of information between objects such as machines and products is becoming increasingly important. These new communication options are coupled with analysis and evaluation systems that are able to capture, analyze, and evaluate big data for the purposes of boosting the efficiency of processes and offerings. These developments are discussed under different slogans, depending on the region: "Internet of Things" in the United States, "Made in China

2025" in China, and "Industry 4.0" in Germany. A pertinent example of this big data is state-of-the-art aircraft turbines, which today are already equipped with more than 3,000 sensors. The information they provide can be continuously evaluated, for example, to alert the need for a replacement part before the fault causes an operational outage.

4. Because data management and the associated software play an increasing role in fulfilling customers' wishes, some companies in the IT sector are moving into markets that were previously dominated by industrial companies. For example, electricity grid operators are no longer restricted to well-established suppliers such as GE, Siemens, and ABB. Today, they can seek grid optimization from companies such as IBM. In general, it can be said that software companies are increasingly investing in hardware companies, whereas the abovementioned industrial companies have been investing very heavily in developing software expertise in recent years. For example, the stalwart industrial company Siemens is now one of the ten largest employers of software programmers in the world, and Google bought the room thermostat manufacturer Nest for more than $3 billion in 2014. Developments like these shake up the conventional competitive landscape.

5. Globalization is on the rise. By this, we mean the cross-border movement and exchange of people, goods, services, data, and money. Though it is true that international trade in goods is no longer showing the same rates of growth as in recent decades, and it has experienced a significant decline in 2020 due to the COVID-19 pandemic. But during this pandemic, it has become apparent that globalization was continuing to grow in other areas, particularly in the exchange of data. Between 2005 and 2014, cross-border data traffic increased to 45 times its prior volume (see Figure 1.8). In the upcoming years, the increase will be more and more exponential. It was set to increase again to nine times its current volume in 2021.

All of this affects economic globalization in many ways. Knowledge is now accessible around the clock, international teams of developers can work simultaneously on the same project, and machines coordinate production processes autonomously across borders. An aircraft turbine manufacturer no longer has to send entire spare parts to a customer. Instead, it can transmit information to a 3-D printer in the customer's country for local manufacture. This opens up new potential for globalization, particularly for small companies, as they no longer require a large administrative apparatus

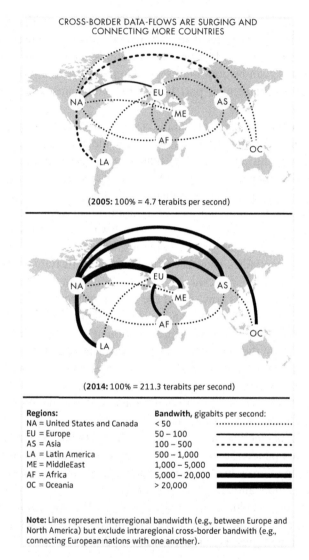

Figure 1.8:   Increase in cross-border data exchange 2005–2014.[18]

or contacts overseas to purchase or sell products worldwide. This makes it easier than ever for small companies to become "micro-multinationals."

---

[18]McKinsey Global Institute, "Digital Globalization: The New Era of Global Flows," February 24, 2016.

Internationalization

A business unit engages with foreign markets either to increase sales or to harness cost benefits. Smaller companies, such as the abovementioned micro-multinationals, initially have their sights set on boosting sales. They frequently use large international trade platforms such as Amazon and Alibaba to sell their products abroad. These platforms offer a number of advantages. They dispatch products to customers on the seller's behalf, assist with customs procedures and payment methods, and, above all, attract large numbers of potential customers to peruse the offers. This provides suppliers with access to customers in other countries without needing to be there on the ground. In this particular respect, the same goal can be achieved by appointing agents and distributors to perform marketing activities. If an industrial company wishes to outsource production to third parties abroad, it can award licenses. The German engine manufacturer MAN has been doing this for years with its ship engines. These diesel engines, which provide more than 100,000 hp, were too large to transport from German factories to its customers in Asia. Awarding licenses saved MAN the costs of constructing its own production facilities there.

If an industrial company does not wish to entrust its foreign activities to external partners, it must establish its own resources there instead. This is advisable, for example, with complex products that require explanation. External partners would be unable to easily acquire the requisite knowledge. That is why it is smarter for the supplier to dispatch a member of the company's own workforce to oversee sales. Alternatively, a representative office might be founded abroad for purchasing materials or other value-creating activities. Depending on the supplier's business model, multiple value creation activities can be performed abroad, right through to establishing an independent company that covers a similar spectrum of value creation as that in the home country. Some suppliers achieve this by acquiring a foreign company, as Chinese automaker Geely did when it purchased Volvo's private car division, or when the Indian automaker Tata Motors acquired Jaguar. The resulting advantages of the increasingly international division of value creation can be harnessed even better by leveraging synergies between networked foreign branches. The technologies developed under the heading "Industry 4.0" have greatly expanded these possibilities in recent years. Figure 1.9 depicts the different options for foreign business activity.

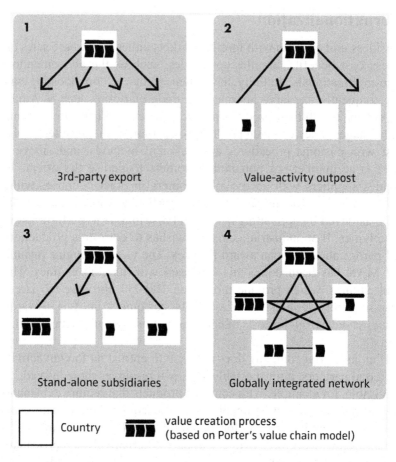

Figure 1.9:   Organizational options for foreign business activity.

The ordering of the options in Figure 1.9 indicates a process of glo-balization that industrial companies frequently use. After all, companies are rarely "born global." An exception to this in the consumer goods sec-tor is Airbnb, an international internet platform set up to provide travelers with private accommodations. Another example, this time from the B2B environment, is Upwork, an employment platform that lists workers in 180 countries (so it claims) and taps into the low-wage levels of emerging economies and developing countries. The business models for such born-global companies are based on the use of internet platforms to match business partners worldwide. Industrial companies should examine how to use this kind of sales potential, although their portfolios generally require much more extensive value creation activities in development, production, and sales.

If a company wishes to perform some of these value creation activities abroad using its own resources, this calls for investment. Economists often refer to foreign direct investment (FDI) in this regard. Whether FDI eventually pays off depends on the opportunities and risks that the host country has to offer, such as those that stem from political instability. The competition situation also plays a role. For example, some suppliers with small market shares worldwide make any new entry into a foreign market conditional upon the market leader's behavior, according to the principle "never attack a gorilla at his home." The risks attached to foreign investments not only relate to the market but can also arise from local management errors. The higher the ratio between suppliers' investment and their financial capacity, the greater the risk. To keep these risks better in check, small and medium-sized enterprises (SMEs) in particular prefer to carefully increase their foreign investments incrementally.

A good example is the German SME Wilo, which manufactures pumps for use in water supplies and climate technology. The company generates annual sales of €1.3 billion in more than 60 countries. When it wants to break into the market in a new country, Wilo starts off by looking for a "pioneer." This is usually a local who is familiar with German culture. After that, the company checks this potential pioneer's entrepreneurial spirit and sense of responsibility. If the person turns out to be suitable and is appointed, he or she starts off by focusing on selling Wilo's products. As soon as sales exceed €1 million, Wilo establishes a representative company in the related country. Once revenues reach €2 million, Wilo creates a subsidiary, which is preferably managed by the pioneer. After that, Wilo starts to consider whether third parties should take on certain assembly stages of the product in the host country, and if so, which ones. At the same time, warehouses are constructed to hold products and spare parts. As a rule of thumb, sales of €50 million warrant stocking around 70 percent of the Wilo product portfolio. If sales continue to increase, the company considers establishing country-specific product platforms and local production.

Following this approach, Wilo invests abroad primarily to increase sales of its products, thereby attracting new customers and encouraging repeat purchases by existing foreign customers. These sales increases are generated in no small part by the inventory held in the host country. This shortens delivery times, thus making the products more attractive.

The Global Revenue Index (GRI) can be used to acquire an overview of how far a company leverages the global sales potential in a given market. This index identifies the global distribution of sales according to sector and compares it with the supplier's own regional sales distribution. A low GRI indicates that a supplier focuses heavily on one region. A high GRI represents an even distribution of sales across regions worldwide.

Acquiring a foreign company increases a supplier's sales thanks to the new brand rights and the expertise that this secures. These factors play a key role. This is particularly true for suppliers from emerging economies who buy companies in industrialized countries, including the above-mentioned automakers Geely and Tata Motors. Another possible motive for companies to invest abroad is to gain access to subsidies. Foreign acquisitions, however, are more commonly made to save on import duties, taxes, and other government levies. This then relates to the supplier's costs rather than sales factors. FDI can achieve further cost savings thanks to the economies of scale generated by higher sales volumes and lower transportation costs. Furthermore, access to cheap resources abroad can have a positive effect on a company's cost structures. As with the business idea behind Upwork, international differences in wage levels are often the key factor.

In Western countries, the FDI is often limited to the cases of European and North American companies relocating jobs to Asia or South America, though other trends are now becoming evident. One example is Huajian Group, one of the world's largest manufacturers of shoes for women. In 2011, the company relocated some elements of its production to Ethiopia, where wages were only one-fifth of those in China.[19] In fact, China had lost much of its production cost advantage by 2014. This can be seen in Figure 1.10, which shows the results of a study on manufacturing costs in various countries. Besides personnel costs, this comparison factors in further components such as expenditures on energy. To illustrate the differences, production costs in the United States were given an index value of 100.

When it comes to marketing abroad, companies must decide on the degree to which their portfolios and business models need to be localized. Adaptations are necessary where differences exist between customers' requirements. For example, trucks with the driver's seat on the left can hardly be sold to customers in countries where people drive on the left side of the road, and vice versa. Differences in safety and emissions

---

[19] In 2019, the difference in salaries between the two countries has even grown to a factor of 10. See P. M. Barrett and D. Baumann-Pauly, *Made in Ethiopia* (New York, NY: NYU Stern Center for Business and Human Rights, 2019).

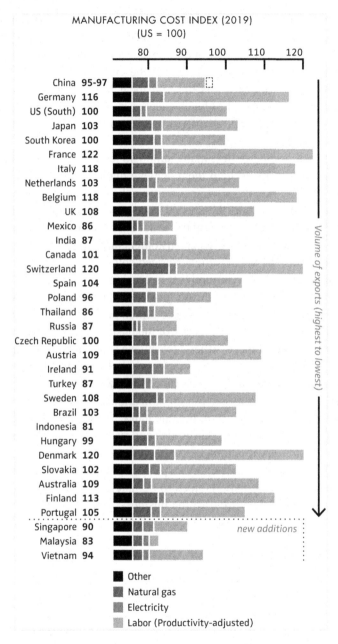

Figure 1.10: International comparison of production costs.[20]

Note: The index only covers four direct costs. No difference is assumed for other costs, such as raw material inputs and machine and tool depreciation. Cost structure is calculated as a weighted average across all industries.

standards also need to be considered with regard to production setup. Country-specific adaptations might be necessary with regard to sales channels. Western companies operating in Arab countries, for example, are frequently unable to sell directly to the customer company. Instead, they must conduct transactions through local brokers. A lot of country-specific idiosyncrasies need to be considered in communications measures, such as when a brand name is difficult to pronounce or has negative connotations in the target country.

In terms of pricing policy, many suppliers tend to make initial concessions in new countries to help them achieve market entry. This can cause problems if the market is very transparent on the demand side, and customers in other countries spot the special terms and conditions. It can cause customer dissatisfaction and — in the worst-case scenario — encourage the practice of arbitrage, which is when customers buy products in the cheapest country and transport them to higher-priced countries.

Suppliers have to bear in mind that increasing the number of adaptations to suit different countries complicates managerial tasks. If the brand names, distribution channels, and pricing and condition policies are different in each country, it is easy to lose the overview of the business. Any increase in product variations makes it more difficult to achieve cost synergies in purchasing and production. For this reason, suppliers should follow the formula "as much standardization as possible, as much localization as necessary".

In summary, the reasons for globalization can be divided into the potential for increasing sales on the one hand, and for cost savings on the other. This depends on the opportunities and risks in the target country. To harness the potential, it is thus better for industrial companies to increase their value creation abroad step by step. While doing so, the specific characteristics of the local markets need to be taken into account, along with any synergies with other areas of the business.

Planning a Strategy with Impact

According to a 2018 McKinsey study of 2,393 international, high-revenue companies, 70 percent of managers are unconvinced by their company's strategy. One wonders how this can be. Another result of this study is equally revealing — it states that even more managers reject planning

---

[20] J. Rose, I. Colotla, M. McAdoo, and W. Kletter, *A Manufacturing Strategy Built for Trade Instability* (Munich: Boston Consulting Group, 2020). Retrieved from https://www.bcg.com/de-de/publications/2020/manufacturing-strategy-built-trade-instability.

processes or do not consider them to be target-oriented. The following steps describe how many perceive this process:

Step 1 — CEO calls their group of senior executives
- Invitation to the annual strategy meeting.
- Request for "creative ideas for growth" and to have "lively discussions."

Step 2 — Annual strategy meeting
- Each senior executive has prepared about 100 slides for a 20-min. presentation.
- They include terms such as "digitization," "innovative business models," and "value chain resilience."
- They suggest a hockey-stick-based business plan (see Figure 1.11) for the next five years.
- But they do not substantiate any disruptive, strategic moves.

Step 3 — Budget negotiations for the upcoming year
- CEO welcomes plans for revenue growth.
- CEO rejects cost increases or shifts them to the future.

Step 4 — Implementation in the upcoming year
- 99% of last year's activities will be repeated.
- 1% of new plans are implemented and communicated as "new visionary path."

Step 5 — After the upcoming year
- Senior executives change positions.
- Strategic planning procedure does not change.

The planning of the hockey stick business plan mentioned in Step 2 means that initially a short phase of deterioration is forecast, followed by a long phase of steady growth. However, the latter rarely occurs. Instead, the planned hockey stick growth estimates are repeated annually until performance levels reflect a so-called hairy back. When planning and reality curves look like this, a company must say goodbye to the market, at least for the long term.

This strategic planning process is exaggerated, but it illustrates the problems that exist in many companies. These problems can be traced back to three main causes:

- Inadequate information base.
- Manipulation tactics.
- Unconscious bias.

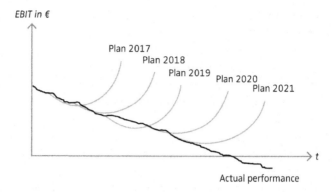

Figure 1.11:   Hockey sticks leading to a hairy back.

The inadequate information base is due to the challenge of having to consider a number of complex factors whose development is uncertain when making strategic decisions. In order to conceal this lack of knowledge, all kinds of information are used, including information that does not make a substantial contribution to the decision-making process. Accordingly, the presentations or decision documents are overloaded with information — see the 100 slides mentioned above — and obscure the view of what's essential. Important information, on the other hand, may be missing, such as the current competitive advantage of the initial situation.

If presenters are dependent on the agreement of others to make a strategic decision, they may suppress information that affects their argument or deliberately use information overload to confuse recipients. This leads us to the second problem: manipulation tactics. The personal interests of those involved in strategic planning often differ, and each wants to assert their own interests, if necessary by manipulating the other members of the meeting. Perhaps the person in charge of a business unit wants to create low expectations about the chances for future success among his group's board of directors. They might do this to come under less pressure to succeed, or perhaps to receive special recognition for surpassing expectations. It might also be done for budgetary reasons so they can deliberately raise the expectations of success to a level that would allow them to make larger investments in their area. However, corporate board members also use tactics to implement their personal interests, for example, when they argue against the strategic ideas of a business unit to avoid conflicts with those responsible for other business units. Such conflicts quickly arise when resources are allocated to one business unit in order to implement a strategic idea, whereas other business units are expected to cut costs. Manipulation tactics are conscious actions. In contrast, the third problem in strategic planning is that participants unconsciously perceive information and ideas in a distorted manner due to their own disposition. In this case, they are subject to an "unconscious bias." Thus, managers may misjudge the chances of success of a strategy, because they overestimate their own capabilities. This happens, among other times, when they transfer past successes to new problems. We examine this phenomenon in more detail using an authentic case study in Chapter 4.

At least as important as manipulation tactics is "unconscious bias", which leads people to overestimate risks due to their need for security. Daniel Kahneman's[21] experiments, for example, show that the chances of loss are overestimated, and the chances of gain are underestimated, even if they are objectively the same. If managers are subject to unconscious bias, disruptive changes in strategy will hardly find their way into a company, because they are always associated with risks. For industrial companies facing highly volatile market dynamics, such a risk-averse attitude endangers their existence, at least in the long term.

To avoid hairy backs and manager frustration in strategic planning, the three problems specifically identified here should be counteracted. To this end, we propose the following, while keeping in mind that an industrial company comprises several business units and strategic decisions require the approval of more than one business unit manager.

Significant strategic moves: If the market changes significantly — as is the case with most industrial companies — the companies operating there must also change significantly. Strategy proposals that contain only incremental changes — or even continue doing what has been done so far — are of no use here.

There is a long list of formerly successful companies that failed to address the changes in their markets by changing strategy. Kodak is a well-known example. Once the global market leader in photographic technology, the company fell victim to digital photography, even though Kodak itself had developed numerous digital camera elements. Other well-known examples are Nokia and BlackBerry from the mobile communications industry, both of which missed the leap into the era of the mobile internet.

---

[21]D. Kahneman, *Thinking, Fast and Slow* (New York, NY: Farrar, Straus and Giroux, 2011).

In order to be able to grow in a highly dynamic market, significant strategic moves should therefore be the goal of strategic planning. The planning process should be set up accordingly, that is, all stakeholders should be invited to make proposals on significant strategic moves. Since their implementation usually requires investment, and financial resources are a scarce commodity, it should be made clear to all stakeholders that only the most promising proposals will be implemented. These are the ones from which the company has the most to gain and which have the highest probability of successful implementation. In addition, everyone must be aware that, in places where significant strategic moves are not made, there must be improvements in efficiency.

Two-step approach: In the strategy development process, it makes sense to decouple the first presentation on the significant strategic moves from any detailed planning process or even precise budget planning. A presentation of 15 minutes must suffice to outline the core elements of a new strategy — after which there is time for questions, which should focus exclusively on the core elements of an idea. Only when others recommend pursuing a proposed significant strategic move should it be elaborated upon in more detail during a second presentation. In this second step, the business units that do not require the implementation of a significant strategic move present their plans for efficiency improvements.

Focus on key information: To demonstrate the meaningfulness of a significant strategic move, the person presenting the idea must be fully informed about the matter. When presenting their proposal to others, however, the information should be prepared in such a way that the key points are presented clearly and are easy to understand. If others are not familiar with the specifics of a business unit, the strategic starting position should be presented first — possibly with an image based on Figure 1.5. In addition, the central market developments should be pointed out to clarify the starting position. The "need for change" can then be derived from these developments, from which, in turn, the core elements of the strategic changes can be deduced. The core elements should also contain the desired goal and a rough estimate of the required resources. In addition, there must be an assessment of the greatest risks, their probability of occurrence, and the probability of the proposal's success. The projections about probabilities will inevitably be vague and unreliable — in principle, future problems cannot be solved. But the clear assessment of targets, risks, and probabilities of success represents the elements upon which strategic decisions must be based. In subsequent discussions, this constellation will consistently help to bring differences of opinion back to the essentials.

De-bias mechanism: In order to reduce the risk of bias when evaluating information and proposals, the first step is to ensure that everyone involved is aware of this risk and critically questions their own opinions. In addition, the bias of decision-makers or entire teams — keyword: collective operational blindness — can be counteracted by involving independent, external persons in the process. These can be trusted manager colleagues from another industry, for example. According to the McKinsey study mentioned above, Warren Buffet's investment team uses another interesting approach to achieve greater clarity on the arguments for or against a proposal in strategic decision-making processes: They designate one group to make a case for the proposal and another group to make one against it. The decision-makers then form their opinions by weighing the arguments against one another, in the role of judge, as it were.

However, the steps proposed here for designing the strategic planning process only make sense if the appropriate organizational culture exists. This applies in particular when dealing with business risks. If a significant strategic move has a 70 percent chance of success, this means that the move also has a 30 percent chance of failure, even if the managers responsible do their best. If such a failure means the end of career opportunities for these managers, they will always propose low-risk strategies to be on the safe side. For most industrial companies, this is likely to mean their demise in the long run.

From Planning to Implementation

Strategic plans are abstract in nature. Turning concepts like these into tangible success for the company calls for implementation. To do this, the strategy must first be broken down into increasingly specific steps, that is, strategic planning must be turned into operational planning. The level of specification continues to increase until all employees know what they have to do. This ideal scenario can be illustrated in Figure 1.12. Strategic planning (large arrow on the left in the diagram) sets the general direction for a business unit. It is then suitably translated into operations for all subdivisions (small arrows). Finally, strategic planning and operational planning are implemented appropriately (large and small arrows on the right).

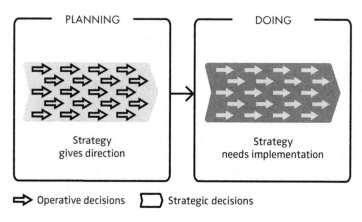

Figure 1.12:   From strategy to implementation.

So much for the concept. In reality, linking strategic planning, operational planning, and practical implementation does not always work in companies. There are four main reasons for this:

- Individual actions prove to be unsuitable.
- The actions have not been coordinated carefully enough between those involved.
- Some employees lack the skills required for implementation.
- Some employees lack the motivation required for implementation.

Unsuitable actions include anything that will not help a company achieve its goals. This would be the case, for example, if the target audience in a country was supposed to be wealthy, but the marketing or sales department focused on customers outside of this segment. Even more problematic is when it comes to a department implementing operational actions without their being sufficient interdepartmental coordination. This could happen if a purchasing department were to force price reductions from a supplier, but then production could no longer operate due to a lack of essential materials. Insufficient coordination between departments is often accompanied by a lack of mutual trust. In a survey conducted by Donald Sull *et al.*, 84 percent of managers said they felt that they could rely on their superiors or charges in their own department — compared to 9 percent in relation to coworkers in other departments.[22]

---

[22]D. Sull, R. Homkes, and C. Sull, "Why Strategy Execution Unravels — and What to Do About It," *Harvard Business Review* 94, no. 3 (2015): 58–67.

Even rigorous operationalization and cross-departmental coordination do not guarantee success if employees do not implement the plans. Among other things, this can be due to a lack of skills, which can be remedied with supplementary training programs as long as deficits are properly identified. This is simple if it is a matter of employees needing to learn a new language or software program. It is more difficult if an employee's social abilities need to be evaluated, such as leadership, teamwork, or stakeholder management skills.

If asked about the reasons for the unsatisfactory implementation of strategy, managers cite a lack of motivation on the part of employees more frequently than skills deficits. Above all, this applies to strategic decisions that require transformation in the company and behavioral changes from employees. The managers in question sometimes try to overcome resistance by asserting their authority and issuing orders — a principle known as top-down management, or "command and control." This approach ascribes different functions to the head and the hands of the company. Management does the thinking, makes the decisions, and issues orders. Employees simply do what they are told. Roger L. Martin is one of the many researchers to have shown that this approach has little hope of success in companies today.[23] However, when it comes to implementing strategy, managers like to run things from the top and, where possible, employ this approach even more rigorously in response to problems. This can lead them to ramp up the pressure on their employees and issue increasingly operational directions. As a consequence, they get bogged down in detailed project plans and long to-do lists.

Martin argues the case for including employees in the planning processes for implementing strategy. His research indicates that this boosts employees' motivation to become more involved. In addition, Stephen Bungay advises going beyond co-developing the individual stages of the process and working out the reasoning behind them, as in "each *what* needs a *why*". This inclusive form of managerial behavior has been subject to extensive academic debate under the heading "adaptive leadership". Research conducted by Ronald Heifetz and Marty Linsky indicates that the inclusion of employees even improves the resulting plans and is particularly advisable in cases where there are no established solutions to

---

[23]R. L. Martin, "Drawing a Line Between Strategy and Execution Almost Guarantees Failure," *Harvard Business Review* 88, nos. 7/8 (2010): 64–71.

the problems at hand.[24] Furthermore, it can ensure that employees are able to thoroughly understand the key statements in the strategy. This is not always the case with a top-down approach. Sull *et al.* cite a case in which 55 percent of mid-level managers were unable to repeat even one of the key statements of their business strategy correctly, despite senior managers reiterating them.

Having said that, even these inclusive "commitment through involvement"-style approaches to implementation planning have their limits. This might be due to legal restrictions, for example, if a growth strategy involves the takeover of another company, or if other confidentiality clauses prevent employee involvement. Other examples include plans to cut working hours, wage freezes, and redundancies. In situations like these, it can be assumed that employees' individual interests would compromise implementation planning. Finally, the differences between countries need to be taken into account. After all, openly discussing planning decisions can seem very foreign to employees in strictly hierarchical cultures. It could even be perceived as weakness on the part of the managers.

The individual characteristics of companies and their specific situations thus need to be taken into consideration when implementing strategy. The Congruence Model, created by David Nadler and Michael Tushman, presents a comprehensive picture of the relevant elements of strategy implementation.[25] In summary, it says that when implementing strategies, the four elements of employees, organizational culture, organizational structure, and work content must be harmonized with the company's environment (see Figure 1.13). This recommendation makes sense. If you wanted to construct the perfect automobile, it would be unwise to combine the design of a Porsche, the interior of a Rolls-Royce, the engine of a Ferrari, and the chassis of a Mercedes. Although these individual components might be excellent in their own right, they do not fit together. The four factors in question always need recalibrating if the company's strategic decisions require modification. Furthermore, the time and contents of any such changes need to be synchronized. In general, it can be

---

[24]R. A. Heifetz, A. Grashow, and M. Linsky, *The Practice of Adaptive Leadership: Tools and Tactics for Changing Your Organization and the World* (Boston, MA: Harvard Business School Press, 2009).

[25]D. Nadler and M. Tushman, *Strategic Organization Design: Concepts, Tools & Processes* (London: Longman Higher Education, 1988).

Figure 1.13:   The Congruence Model devised by Nadler and Tushman.

said that structures are easier to change than employees' behavior and corporate culture. However, if the corporate culture is not adapted to fall in line with changes in strategy, the much-cited phenomenon outlined by Peter Drucker will occur: "Culture eats strategy for breakfast."

To ensure that strategic decisions are steering the company in the desired direction and are being implemented on an ongoing basis, goal compliance must be continuously monitored. To achieve this, operational goals must be fixed on a timeline. If a pump manufacturer decides to address premium customers in Thailand in the future, the operational goals might be to hold acquisition discussions with 120 potential customers in the coming 12 months and generate incoming orders worth $6 million. Monitoring these goals can reveal any developments that might be running off track and help analyze the causes. Goals should therefore be defined in a way that makes progress measurable. The Balanced Scorecard, developed by Robert S. Kaplan and David P. Norton, is widely used for this purpose. It even includes operationalizing and quantifying factors such as customer focus and employee motivation.[26]

Goals can be missed if environmental factors change, so these must be checked continuously. Are new competitors copying a product? Do technical innovations place the need for a product in doubt? Have any new regulations been introduced that hinder access to foreign markets? Changes such as these might even mean that it no longer makes sense to continue pursuing the previous goals. Thus, we keep returning to the starting point of strategic planning and the observation that the process of planning and implementing strategy is a never-ending cycle (see Figure 1.14).

---

[26]R. S. Kaplan and D. P. Norton, *The Balanced Scorecard: Translating Strategy into Action* (Boston, MA: Harvard Business School Press, 1996).

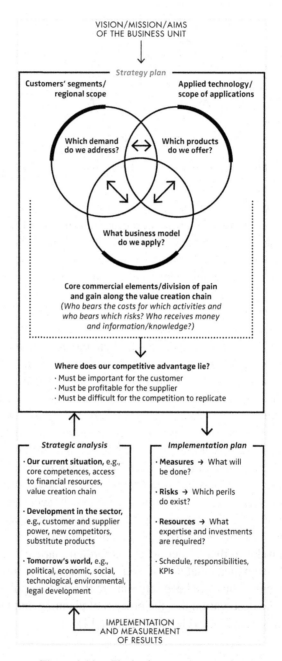

Figure 1.14: The business strategy cycle.

Counter Strategies

Advanced globalization is increasing the competitive pressure in many sectors. New competitors are breaking into industrial markets, which until now have been stable and sometimes even limited to one region. Cutting-edge communication and information technologies are accelerating this process. In addition, these technologies enable companies in the IT sector to advance into hardware markets, thus changing the previous processes that distributed value creation between suppliers and customers. Many established industrial companies see these developments as a threat and are searching for ways to defend their market positions. The concept of counter strategies, on the other hand, views market developments as opportunities for growth. Strategic options emerge for industrial companies to not only defend but also expand their market positions.[27]

Counter strategy options touch on all the categories in the afore-mentioned 3 + 1 key questions used for devising a business strategy. The following questions should be asked from the very beginning:

- What spectrum of services is to be offered, particularly in terms of innovative data-based services?
- How is the business model to be developed, particularly with regard to property rights and pricing?
- To what extent are high-price segments to be addressed? (This question is especially relevant for suppliers in emerging economies.)
- To what extent should low-price segments be addressed? (This question is particularly relevant for suppliers in industrialized countries.)
- In which parts of the world are certain services to be provided? How is value creation to be distributed around the world?
- To what extent must the organizational structure, processes, and leadership culture be changed if cutting-edge technologies are to be introduced in the company?

Counter Strategy 1: Advanced Premium Products

"Premium" means that this strategy is aimed at customers who are willing to pay high prices. "Advanced" indicates the use of state-of-the-art

---

[27]O. Plötner, *Counter Strategies in Global Markets* (New York, NY: Palgrave Macmillan, 2012).

technologies to create these products. Even though the marketing for this strategy option in industrial markets focuses on physical objects such as machinery, trucks, and turbines, it includes services related to the products, such as maintenance and repairs.

Although traditional markets for advanced premium products are found in industrialized nations, emerging economies and developing countries are gaining ground in this sphere. Some players in these regions are acquiring companies that deal in advanced premium products, such as the aforementioned automotive companies Geely and Tata Motors. In other cases, they break into markets for advanced premium products on their own, such as Huawei, the Chinese telecommunications company that registered the most patents worldwide in 2019.

Besides globally renowned technology groups such as Huawei, Philips, and Boeing, there are many less well-known, medium-sized, advanced premium product manufacturers. Hermann Simon coined the term "hidden champions" for the most successful ones.[28] The companies in question can provide the answers to the following questions:

- How can technical development expertise be expanded over the long term?
- How can products achieve high-quality standards?
- How can an appropriate brand image be established?

We return to these questions in Chapter 2.

Counter Strategy 2: No-frills Products

As we have noted, the global developments mentioned above generate the greatest growth potential in those customer groups with a low willingness to pay. It therefore makes sense to develop low-price, cost-effective offerings for these segments — known as "no-frills" products. Industrial companies used to serve these markets simply by providing older product types. This was the case in the truck market, where manufacturers supplied earlier vehicle models produced under license by companies in the emerging economies and developing countries. In many sectors, this no

---

[28] H. Simon, *Hidden Champions of the 21st Century: Success Strategies of Unknown World Market Leaders* (New York, NY: Springer, 2009).

longer meets the needs of the no-frills target customers. Just like everyone else, these customers now expect innovative products that have been tailored to meet their price-sensitive needs.

Obvious evidence that the demand for no-frills offerings is on the rise in industrialized countries can be found in the aviation sector. The business model innovations introduced by Southwest Airlines in the United States and Ryanair in Europe (e.g., using only online reservations for cheap tickets and charging extra for luggage) completely shook up the sector's competitive structures. This approach not only won them new customer groups but also individuals who were prepared to exchange standard comforts for a lower price. Budget airlines were formed in the no-frills markets of the emerging economies and developing countries, for example Gol Linhas Aéreas (Brazil), Lion Air (Indonesia), and China United Airlines (China). Many established airlines reacted to these rivals by targeting no-frills customers. British Airways' response was to set up an airline called Go. But these new companies enjoyed limited success. Despites its low prices, Ryanair generates above-average profits, whereas the results for Go were so unsatisfactory that British Airways closed it down.

It is apparent in other sectors that companies serving affluent target groups struggle to address no-frills customer segments successfully. The kinds of questions that arise are as follows:

- Which employees are most suited to developing no-frills products?
- Should we enter these markets by company acquisition, with strategic partners, or on our own?
- How can a cost level be reached that generates profitability from low prices?
- Which sales channels are suitable?

Besides numerous suppliers in emerging economies and developing countries, companies in industrialized countries found answers to these questions after acquiring first-hand experience — some of it painful. We present these in Chapter 3.

Counter Strategy 3: Complex Service Solutions

The first two strategy options involve suppliers who manufacture physical products that are standardized or contain numerous standard components. The sales process begins after production. By contrast, complex service solutions are produced to meet specific customer requirements. Large segments of their value creation are not physical but based on a pool of services. The supplier sells these services before they are performed in collaboration with the customer. Success depends upon many variables, leading to the term "complex" solutions.

Trumpf, for example, is a German global leader in laser machinery for processing metal. The company now offers to assist its customers in digitizing all their production processes. The portfolio covers both design and assistance with implementing new smart factories or individual modules, such as setting up customer-specific business platforms and introducing automated material flow controls.

Many complex service solutions like Trumpf's are now based on data management. Industrial companies combine their existing product and market expertise. Their combined potential — unleashed by cutting-edge information and communication systems — provides customer solutions with advantages that never existed before. For companies like Trumpf, this means performing activities that were previously done by the customers themselves. In this specific example, customers previously coordinated their own material flows and calibrated their own machines. This is

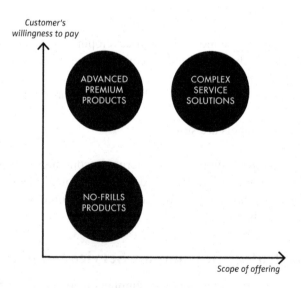

Figure 1.15: The three counter strategy approaches.

now done by Trumpf. Most industrial companies are navigating unknown waters with such offerings and should ask themselves the following questions:

- Which business model for these new complex service solutions is accepted on the market, and what revenue generation can be expected?
- What risks are associated with data-based service offerings?
- What skills are required for marketing them successfully?

We examine these issues more closely in Chapter 4.

These three counter strategies differ in two main respects: the scope of the offering and the customer's willingness to pay. Their relationship can be visualized in this way (see Figure 1.15).

The three strategy options are explored in more detail in the following chapters. The main focus is on industrial companies that established themselves on the basis of one of these strategy options and are now seeking growth. Some of them, such as GE and Siemens, adopted all three approaches. These companies then operate in different markets and think beyond the strategies for specific fields. This overarching perspective addresses the following questions:

- How can synergies be harnessed between different business units?
- To what extent should the head office be involved in the business units' decisions?
- How can cultural differences between the groups be bridged?

We address these questions in Chapter 5.

Chapter 2

Advanced Premium Products: Understanding the Success Formula of Hidden Champions

Abstract

In the following chapter, we introduce companies that have achieved sustained market success through outstanding product quality. It is often not large corporations, but rather lesser-known medium-sized enterprises — so-called hidden champions — that have reached a leading position in specific industrial market segments. We analyze these companies' success factors with a special emphasis on their technical expertise and ability to respond flexibly to customers' needs. In addition, we examine how to establish a positive brand image as a B2B company before highlighting the limitations that should be considered when developing unique competitive advantages in industrial markets.

Industrial Premium Products from China

Tongxian Guan, President of ZPMC, looked out of the window of his small, spartanly furnished office on the edge of Shanghai's eastern city limits. His closest colleagues had gathered behind him. He turned to them and said, "I will only be satisfied when we sell complete container cranes to American ports. If Americans buy equipment from a Chinese manufacturer, customers in other countries will also be convinced of our products'

47

quality." It only took a few years for Guan to receive ZPMC container crane orders from Miami and then Vancouver.

Guan founded ZPMC in 1992 when he was 59 years old. He led the company for 27 years with great personal commitment, sacrificing his private life in favor of the company's global expansion. Each year, he only allowed himself to take three days off from work, which he spent with his family in Beijing. Guan adopted a simple lifestyle. He made sure that ZPMC executive salaries, including his salary as president, did not exceed four times the salary of a skilled worker. Guan was generally considered to be very loyal to the Chinese Communist Party. That did not prevent him from occasionally criticizing individual party members — even in front of other people. This was especially the case when he felt that officials' behavior was working against the best interests of ZPMC.

The newly founded ZPMC initially produced spare parts for the cranes of established Western manufacturers such as Liebherr and Terex. ZPMC then sold these parts directly to the crane users. Although these customers were offered price savings of up to 85 percent, the business was highly profitable because of the high prices for established manufacturers' replacement parts and ZPMC's location-driven cost advantages. Yet, instead of paying out profits, Guan reinvested them into research and development (R&D) in the 1990s. The company was soon able to produce entire cranes independently.

ZPMC engineers ultimately developed the "double-container crane" (see Figure 2.1), which allowed just one crane to move two containers simultaneously. ZPMC patented this crane innovation. It proved to be a tremendous help in ship loading and unloading processes, and it served the interests of port operators and shipowners alike. ZPMC offered port operators another advantage. Because the company's cranes were delivered pre-assembled, they did not have to be assembled on site. This saved weeks of time for port operators, allowing them to earn more money with loading and unloading processes.

By 2007, ZPMC container cranes had a market share of more than 75 percent worldwide. The company has been able to maintain this dominant position to this very day. In the years following 2007, ZPMC diversified its portfolio of services, including the manufacturing of special-purpose vessels, steel bridges, and oil platforms.

For the purposes of this introduction, we intentionally chose an emerging-market company for our case example. It is important to emphasize that marketing premium industrial products worldwide is no

Figure 2.1: ZPMC harbor crane transport.

longer the privilege of Western companies. Today, we know that excellent wines can come from countries such as South Africa and Argentina. In the same way, the competitive landscape in industrial premium markets has become increasingly globalized.

When we refer to industrial products, we mean gas turbines, trucks, and lathes, just to name a few examples. These items are not purchased to be consumed. They are not business-to-consumer (or B2C) products. Instead, they are business-to-business (or B2B) products — items bought by business customers. Industrial products are used in business customers' value chains. The industrial product examples mentioned above are characterized by a high degree of materiality. They are "tangible," so to speak. In practice, we apply the same logic to product-related services such as installation, maintenance, and repair work.

Whether or not an industrial product belongs in the premium category depends on customers' willingness to pay. This means that customers are willing to accept higher prices for premium products than they would for similar products with the same technology and functional principles. The price for an internal combustion engine truck capable of carrying a 16-ton payload, for example, varies between €30,000 and €120,000 worldwide. Beverage bottling systems are available for €2.5 million. The most expensive ones cost up to €12 million. By contrast, the price differential for premium-priced combine harvesters can be 20 times higher than those of low-priced products.

Customers' greater willingness to pay for a premium product is based on the perceived quality advantage. However, the valuation is based on the customer's perspective rather than the seller's. For industrial goods, this type of quality advantage is usually linked to functional properties such as greater performance, operational convenience, or the greater durability of parts. Suppliers achieve quality advantages of this type through the use of state-of-the-art technologies, high-quality materials, and first-class workmanship. Quality advantages that go beyond technical and functional uses, such as attractive design and social status aspects, are less important for industrial products than they are for consumer goods. Although it is not frequently discussed, B2B markets do indeed have purchasing criteria that go beyond cost efficiency. We discuss this later in more detail.

Creating products that use state-of-the-art technologies or high-quality materials generates high costs. Customers' willingness to pay more for some premium products can more than compensate for these costs. In such cases, a premium supplier's profit per unit is much greater than for cheaper products, in spite of the higher manufacturing costs. The iPhone is a frequently cited example within the context of the consumer goods sector, where much more information is available on this topic than in the industrial sector. As a premium manufacturer, Apple has been able to achieve significantly higher margins in recent years than those of its competitors with cheaper products. Reports from 2017 noted that Apple generated 87 percent of the smartphone industry's profits, even though the company only produced 18 percent of the devices sold worldwide.[1]

As a result, many suppliers who sell to target markets with customers who have a lower willingness to pay now want to enter premium segments. Entering such markets may or may not be the right strategic

---

[1] P. Seitz, "Apple Rakes in 87% of Smartphone Profits, but 18% of Unit Sales," *Investor's Business Daily*, February 28, 2018.

decision, however. There is no automatic relationship between improved quality and increased profits. In fact, companies must consider a number of factors. Indeed, it is only with the right mix that they can succeed in the market. The most important success factors are presented on the following pages.

The Strong Focus of Hidden Champions

Hermann Simon conducted a key study on these success factors. He announced his findings by coining the term "hidden champions".[2] He did not focus on well-known global companies. Instead, he examined medium-sized companies with annual sales of no more than €5 billion. In addition to their relatively low profiles, these companies are characterized by the fact that they occupy a leading position in their markets (i.e., they are among the leading three vendors worldwide and/or number one on their respective continent). Most of them market premium products. It indicates, among other things, that the prices for their offerings are significantly higher than those of their competitors. Unlike other market leaders, hidden champions' high market shares are not based on price concessions. Rather, they are based on product offerings that customers value more than those of competitors.

Simon's study includes companies from around the world. His findings are interesting because most of the hidden champions he identified are found in industrial markets. Examples include EOS, a global leader in additive manufacturing (AM), and Rosen AG, which surpassed a corporation like GE to become the world leader in large pipeline maintenance. Another hidden champion is the company Heraeus. Its expertise in processing precious metals has already made it the market leader across a whole range of industries — whether it be the tiny carbide balls for ballpoint pen refills, the gold rims on high-quality beer glasses, or the silver pastes found in photovoltaic cells. We return to each of these company examples in the pages that follow.

When viewed within the framework of Porter's generic strategies concept, hidden champions focus on a quality leadership approach. They concentrate on a single market segment. (For narrowly defined markets,

---

[2]H. Simon, *Hidden Champions of the 21st Century: Success Strategies of Unknown World Market Leaders* (New York, NY: Springer, 2009).

hidden champions fall under the quality leadership approach. For broadly defined markets, they pursue a focus strategy. See Chapter 1 for more information.) Due to their strong focus on specific customer requirements, the sales volume potential of hidden champions is very limited. This is the primary reason why they avoid regional constraints and strive to conquer markets abroad. This helps them to not only increase revenues but also achieve cost-cutting economies of scale — in spite of their focused set of product offerings.

Hidden champions do not always have to leave their own country in order to achieve a high market share worldwide. The Carl Zeiss business in so-called EUV optics (EUV stands for extreme ultraviolet) is one such example. The business division is based in Oberkochen, a small town in southwestern Germany. The company develops components that bundle laser beams for computer chip manufacturing systems. Chip manufacturers such as Intel order this type of equipment for their worldwide production centers almost exclusively from ASML, a Dutch company that dominates the market for these production systems worldwide. ASML buys high-quality EUV optics for its systems only from Carl Zeiss due to their technological and operational excellence. Therefore, Carl Zeiss has become, by default, the global market leader in EUV optics. The company actually achieved this market position without having to fly salespeople around the world or set up production facilities outside of Germany.

This example is an exception because Carl Zeiss' business for EUV optics is dominated by a single customer. Under a more typical scenario, even the most focused suppliers have to address a number of customers and be internationally active on the ground. Hidden champions in industrial markets have a manageable number of customers, nonetheless. They have a narrowly defined range of products based on customer requirements. As a result, it is all the more important for hidden champions to identify relevant customers and address their needs. That is why these companies must choose the right focus.

In practice, finding that focus is not always easy. At the same time, hidden champions must achieve the right balance between maintenance and development. They must be picky about business opportunities that go beyond that defined focus. Because although those opportunities may seem attractive at first sight, companies run the risk of getting bogged down in details. In that case, a company loses the very focus that made it strong in the first place. On the other hand, companies should not maintain their existing market focus for too long if target markets shrink.

Hidden champions' customer segments are typically small. When customer demand declines, it can jeopardize the company's economic viability. Consequently, suppliers with a particularly strong focus need to be sensitive to changes in customer requirements and the competitive landscape. They must be open to strategic reorientation. To illustrate this topic, we now look at the example of the company EOS, mentioned above.

When Dr. Hans Langer founded EOS in 1989, it was a corporate pioneer in AM, or industrial 3-D printing (see Figure 2.2). The machines EOS developed were able to "print" different products such as turbine blades and dental prostheses by fusing layer upon layer of fine powder. One particular advantage of the 3-D process is that it provides a greater degree of freedom in product design. It also enables better and lighter construction while using fewer materials. Unlike milling, which renders objects by cutting away excess material from a larger block of material, 3-D printing creates products without generating any scrap.

The AM market was initially small, and it was limited to prototype production and special applications. EOS sold the machines for product manufacturing — including the required powder — to a select number of customers. In addition, EOS advised customers on how to produce product designs that were 3-D compliant and optimize production processes.

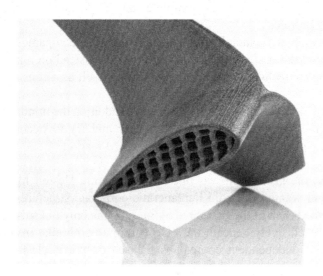

Figure 2.2: 3-D printing lightweight part produced by EOS.

Langer was convinced that industrial 3-D printing would soon grow out of its niche existence. He anticipated a multibillion-dollar market and expected that AM would soon be used to mass-produce manufactured goods — provided that manufacturers had already considered the opportunities and specific requirements of additive processes during product development. In an effort to rethink this concept on a broader level — and to accelerate the diffusion of AM technology — Langer licensed its patents to other companies. This included EOS customers and competitors.

Just as Langer had expected, starting in 2010, the use of 3-D technology grew rapidly. Industries began to use AM processes for more and more products. At the same time, EOS developed more specialized know-how. It focused on specific industrial and product applications as well as the technology and materials used by 3-D printing machines. As a result, it has become increasingly difficult for EOS to shape these developments, let alone lead them. In order to live up to its claim and reputation as a premium supplier, EOS had to shift its focus within the rapidly growing, industrial 3-D printing market. From a strategic perspective, Langer had to answer the following questions:

- Should EOS focus on specific areas of the 3-D product manufacturing process (e.g., machines only)?
- Should the company focus on a particular industry, such as dentures, thereby allowing it to deliver the complete value chain and potentially even the end product?
- Given the fact that financially robust manufacturing companies had already entered the AM market, should EOS focus instead on marketing its engineers' technical expertise and position itself as a consulting firm?
- Alternatively, should EOS actually consider abandoning the mindset of a premium medium-sized company altogether and try to become a large, broadly positioned company within the AM market?

For Langer, the last option was out of the question. He felt like an entrepreneur and wanted to avoid bureaucratic corporate structures. He eventually pursued each of the first three options, but he only did so selectively, and not exclusively beneath the EOS corporate umbrella. Instead, he launched new, independent companies focused on profitable niches within the AM market. To achieve that, he built up Scanlab, which marketed galvanometer scanner components — an important element in 3-D printing — across industries. By 2018, Scanlab was already the global market leader with more than 50,000 scanner heads sold. In addition, Langer's AM Ventures Holding invested in numerous start-ups focused on industry-specific AM applications such as printing human arm and leg prostheses and on producing certain materials such as high-quality aluminum alloys. He left mass markets such as 3-D footwear production to other firms. Even then, he still partially participated by pursuing the worldwide commercialization of his patents. Finally, within the EOS organization, he founded the consulting group Additive Minds, which specializes in AM applications.

Striving for the Technical Edge

We now return to ZPMC. The development of the double-container crane was decisive in driving the company's success in the worldwide container crane business: The crane could load and unload two containers simultaneously instead of just one. This technical innovation represented a competitive advantage over competitors' products. Technical product advantages of this kind are typical of industrial companies that operate in premium sectors.

This technological edge is typically accompanied by high levels of investment in a company's R&D activities. If Siemens, GE, or Mitsubishi develop a new type of gas turbine, it will cost them around a half billion euros. Airbus invested €10 billion for developing the wide-body aircraft A380. But it is worth noting that, in spite of such enormous R&D budgets, traditional industrial companies are no longer setting the records in R&D spending. The top positions have now been taken over by younger technology companies, particularly Amazon and Alphabet (Google), with $42.7 and $27.6 billion, respectively (see Figure 2.3).

Given their size, many hidden champions invest more in R&D than do large corporations. For example, Simon's study found that at 5.9 percent, hidden champions invested nearly one-third more of their revenue into R&D than the 1,000 companies with the world's largest R&D budgets. (This percentage is higher for software companies, primarily because of their industry's extremely low production costs.) With their strong focus on R&D, hidden champions get more for their money than large industrial companies. This is demonstrated by the number of patent

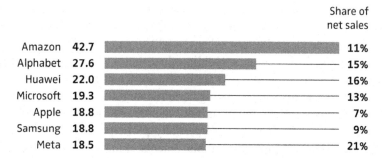

Figure 2.3:   Companies with the highest spending on R&D in 2020 (in USD billions).[3]

applications per employee, which is five times higher than for large corporations. Furthermore, hidden champions bring four times more applied
patents into business practice.[4]

These patents are used less to create the revolutionary innovative
products that modern management literature calls "disruptive innovations." Instead, they mostly serve to improve the technology of existing
product offerings (i.e., to make incremental innovations). The word
"incremental" should not detract from the significance of these developments. Continuous product development is an imperative for hidden
champions. It demonstrates an ongoing quest for technical improvements,
which is deeply rooted in many of their corporate cultures. It also means
never being truly satisfied with existing products. It challenges managers
to critically question things and look for further optimization opportunities. In the 1980s, this attitude was characterized by the Japanese term
kaizen. At the time, *kaizen* emphasized optimizing production rather than
product development. Yet, this approach still offers many interesting
insights for companies wanting to operate in premium markets.

High levels of R&D activity and numerous patent registrations are no
guarantee for market success; they only increase the chances of achieving

---

[3]A. Fleck, "The World's Biggest R&D Spenders," Statista, April 8, 2022. Retrieved from
https://www.statista.com/chart/27214/companies-that-spent-the-most-on-research-and-
development-in-2020/. (Accessed May 20, 2022).
[4]Quirin, interview with Hermann Simon: "Wer fokussiert ist, wird Weltklasse. Digitaler
Mittelstand" (2017). Retrieved from https://digitaler-mittelstand.de/koepfe/news/nur-mit-
fokus-wird-man-weltklasse-31907. (Accessed August 12, 2017).

a technological advantage. This advantage, of course, has to provide an actual customer benefit. It must overcompensate for a premium product's high price. Heraeus is a good example of this. The German family-owned company produces, among other things, silver pastes for photovoltaic panels. These silver pastes are used to convert sunlight into electrical energy. In the past, 82 percent of the produced solar energy was lost during the transformation process. The pastes were made of 90 percent pure silver; the remaining 10 percent consisted of a total of 30 elements. The mixing ratio was crucial for the paste's performance. In 2009, Heraeus developers produced a paste that could be applied more thinly, requiring less silver to coat the panels. With silver prices ranging from €1,000 to €1,500 per kilogram, this represented a huge cost savings. Secondly, the new paste's conducting properties were better than those of other products and lost less solar energy. Although this technical advantage only resulted in improvements in the per thousand range, it was enough to help a large solar park increase its energy production from 18 to 18.1 percent. This promised to produce millions of euros in financial benefits. As a result, Heraeus became the global market leader, in spite of its expensive paste prices.

Of course, companies must be able to reliably implement that technical advantage in the products they manufacture. Although many companies have tried in recent years to optimize their production costs through outsourcing (i.e., allocate value-added activities to third parties), many hidden champions insist on creating a high portion of the value chain on their own. They prefer to produce in-house to achieve greater control over the quality of their premium products. Because of product quality concerns, some companies have even reversed the trend toward relocating their production to countries with lower cost structures. For example, Stihl, a leading supplier of chainsaws, relocated its production from Brazil back to Germany in 2010.

Until very recently, other companies had had similar experiences with factories in emerging-markets that did not live up to high-quality, premium product standards. Today, that is the exception. Heraeus has largely relocated the production of its silver pastes to China and is very satisfied with the product quality. At the same time, Heraeus now produces its silver pastes in close cooperation with its customers. The manufacturers of panels for photovoltaic systems are primarily located in China. In general, broad-based studies confirm that it makes sense for premium suppliers to

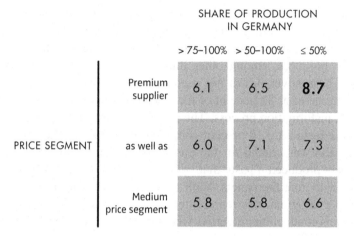

SHARE OF PRODUCTION
IN GERMANY

		> 75–100%	> 50–100%	≤ 50%
	Premium supplier	6.1	6.5	**8.7**
PRICE SEGMENT	as well as	6.0	7.1	7.3
	Medium price segment	5.8	5.8	6.6

Figure 2.4: Profitability in German mechanical engineering depends on the customer's willingness to pay and the degree to which added value is globalized.

organize production beyond their home markets. This includes a study published in 2014 by McKinsey and the VDMA on German mechanical engineering and plant manufacturing, and the impact of globalized production processes on profitability (see Figure 2.4).[5]

By building a technical advantage and producing quality products, companies have a good start in gaining a competitive advantage. The true art lies in maintaining that competitive advantage. This includes preventing competitors from copying product development efforts. Among the many forms of intellectual property rights, the patent system is particularly important for the technical field.

Patents can be very valuable. Patent infringement, on the other hand, can be very expensive for companies. It is worth noting that some legally clever companies actually acquire patents — often from companies that have fallen on hard economic times. They then accuse other companies of patent infringement in order to be paid for those patents. Defendants are sometimes unaware of the (often only alleged) infringements. They usually have to pay nonetheless. Many established technology companies are

[5] VDMA and McKinsey, *Zukunftsperspektive deutscher Maschinenbau* (2014). Retrieved from https://docplayer.org/1719599-Zukunftsperspektive-deutscher-maschinenbauerfol greich-in-einem-dynamischen-umfeld-agieren.html. (Accessed January 16, 2020).

even more concerned about suppliers who deliberately infringe patent rights. This is particularly true in developing countries, where companies do not face penalties under their own national legal systems. The colloquialism "pirates" is often used in this context to describe those who specialize in copying the profitable spare parts of established companies.

In the previous example of ZPMC, we know that the company entered the market before it became a supplier of innovative quality products using its own innovation. Keep in mind that European and American companies have ignored intellectual property rights in the past and gone unpunished in their home countries. Consider the well-known "Made in Germany" label. Now synonymous with high-quality technical products, the label was actually introduced in England in 1876 to warn domestic customers of the poor quality of cheap counterfeit products from Germany.

Given the challenges of using patent applications to protect successful technology innovations, a number of technology companies are avoiding this option altogether. They fear that patent office notifications actually draw the attention of unwanted counterfeiters, and that patent descriptions actually give would-be violators a product blueprint. That is why many companies only document innovative solutions internally or rely on the collective, institutional memory of their employees. Yet, this approach also carries risks. Firstly, the company's own product development can later be patented by others. Secondly, employees can leave the company. A particularly spectacular case example is the Chinese company Future Mobility. In 2016, the organization poached an entire group of BMW engineers who had been involved in developing the electric models i3 and i8.

Tesla, the manufacturer of battery-powered and software-dominated cars, has taken a very different approach toward dealing with patents. Since 2014, Tesla has made a large number of its patents available to anyone interested in them. Tesla is a prime example of another important trend among industrial companies: Products are increasingly defined by software as well as the development of technical product advantages. Software development cycles, however, are shorter than those of traditional industrial goods. The development of new car models takes years. Software versions are developed in one-month intervals. This fast pace causes errors. There is hardly any new software without so-called bugs. This issue poses a dilemma for premium companies that combine hardware and software. On the one hand, companies want their customers to always enjoy state-of-the-art software. On the other hand, they do not want their products to be flawed.

We now turn to Bosch for an example of this dilemma. Bosch is the world's largest supplier of high-quality products in the automotive sector, including engine injection pumps and windshield wipers. In order to radically rebuild its product portfolio, Bosch has been increasingly using modern information and communication technologies for several years through its "3S" program, which stands for sensors, software, and services. In 2017, managers displayed posters in the lobby of its corporate headquarters as part of a broader campaign to communicate the company's error culture to employees. Using the slogan "Just do it," employees were encouraged to respond quickly and not hesitate to act. At the same time, a quote from company founder Robert Bosch seemed to advocate other priorities: "Whatever is made in my name must be both first-class and faultless."

Rapid response is a necessary prerequisite for market success in the software industry. Companies that sell out-of-date products will not find acceptance in technologically dominated industrial markets, especially not as premium suppliers. Even if customers do not expect perfection in terms of software that is free of defects, they still want high reliability. Meeting this requirement is a prerequisite for being a premium supplier. It was against this backdrop in 2017 that, under the concept "zero outage," companies such as IBM, Hewlett-Packard, T-Systems, and Cisco introduced a zero-defect philosophy into the information technology (IT) industry's premium segments.

Striving for Gold Services

Business management services are services that have no materiality. It is the main criterion for distinguishing them from tangible goods. This is why a turbine is considered to be an industrial good, whereas its financing or operation training is a service. When we talk about services in an industrial context, we are most often referring to after-sales services, which primarily involve maintaining and repairing industrial goods. The spare parts business also falls into this category. Strictly speaking, spare parts are not services.

After-sales services are traditionally very important to many industrial companies, as they generate high profits. This is mainly because customers for high-quality industrial goods are often left with few alternatives but to have them maintained and repaired by the manufacturer. Ultimately, the manufacturer has the technical product knowledge and the right spare parts. Customers who consider giving maintenance and repair work to other service suppliers — including counterfeit spare parts — risk losing all product guarantees. As customers are in a dependent position, many suppliers are tempted to charge after-sales service prices that are far in excess of actual costs. At the same time, after-sales service quality is by no means always as excellent as its high price might suggest.

In the long term, these business practices are problematic for suppliers in B2B markets. Increased disclosure requirements, as well as modern information and communication media, reveal suppliers' high margins on services being offered to customers. Indeed, who likes to be dependent or enjoys being financially exploited in this situation? As a result, suppliers run the risk of creating angry and dissatisfied customers.

In the following section, we discuss how to impress customers with product-related premium services so that high prices appear justified in their eyes. After all, even five-star hotels, despite their prices, have satisfied customers who come back without being forced to do so.

Modern technology offers opportunities for improvements to be made in the quality of the product. This is particularly true for after-sales services, which are very important for industrial companies. A poignant example of a company that employs this strategy is Voith. This global technology company is one of the larger family-owned companies in Europe and the full-line supplier to the paper industry. In the past, Voith's maintenance staff traveled around the world to check the condition of customers' machines and perform repairs. Today, these same employees mainly work remotely. More than 1,000 sensors in Voith machines permanently record the condition of every important component. They also capture the products' manufacturing quality and the step sequences of manufacturing processes. By analyzing the data and evaluating it using algorithms, it is possible to find out where, when, and with what probability problems could arise on a machine. In this way, spare parts can be sent to the customer before a critical machine part becomes defective and fails. The customer's employees can then perform simple repairs thanks to OnCall.Video, an audio–visual connection with Voith specialists. With this offering, the customer gets the required support faster, and the full expert knowledge at Voith can be used. Furthermore, Voith and its customers save costs, as technicians only have to travel for complex repair jobs.

Once customers purchase a machine, Voith helps them adapt their production processes to meet their respective requirements. Wood, for example, is an important factor in paper and cardboard production. Yet, it varies in quality and price. Voith offers to analyze a large number of these factors and to constantly configure the production process in such a way that the machine's input and output remain optimally aligned. To achieve that, Voith creates a machine's virtual doppelgänger — a so-called digital twin. Technicians can then use the digital twin to simulate changes before applying them to the actual machine. Rather than making a machine's production processes as immutable as possible, Voith's service now ensures that customers can optimize their production processes for more flexible results (see Figure 2.5).

The many ways in which information services and communication technologies improve traditional services and deliver premium quality are currently being discussed using terms such as "remote control," "proactive maintenance," and "augmented reality." When new incoming data automatically improve a system's algorithms, it is also referred to as "artificial intelligence." When these technologies are successfully put into

Figure 2.5:   Voith device for the electronic support of after-sales service (© Voith).

practice, however, the amount and the quality of the data are often problematic. The reasons for this are complex. There can be difficulties in converting the data into a uniform data format. The ThyssenKrupp Elevator unit, for example, faced the challenge of translating elevator data into a unified database across more than one hundred countries — whereby many regions used different data formats and programming languages. Another difficulty may be that problems and product defects have not been sufficiently documented. This documentation is necessary to provide a robust database for the further development of algorithms.

Over time, businesses are likely to overcome these challenges, and automation in the service sector will continue to move forward. This does not currently include extensive and complicated repairs. As already mentioned above, specialists will continue to travel to the customer to perform this maintenance. This is because customers expect rapid turnaround times and a high degree of technical competence. Specialists must be flexible enough to adapt to the local corporate resources available as well as the culture of the company. There is still a tremendous opportunity for premium suppliers to build their reputations in industrial markets. Small and medium-sized enterprises often have good prospects, as the Swiss family business Rosen Group demonstrates in the following example.

In the 1980s, Rosen entered the pipeline inspection, maintenance, and repair business — a market with revenue of approximately €700 million worldwide. Customers include major oil companies that transport their products by pipeline. To inspect a pipeline, devices are used that move at high speed through the pipes (see Figure 2.6). When a vulnerability is discovered, it has to be resolved quickly and reliably. If oil transport is interrupted because of a pipeline problem, operators suffer significant revenue losses, not to mention major costs due to environmental damage. For this reason, customers gladly pay for inspection, maintenance, and repair work.

GE had been the market leader in this business, but Rosen was able to challenge that position. To achieve this, Rosen not only developed test equipment that met all of its customers' technical requirements but, first and foremost, also delivered faster and more flexible service offerings. In addition, the company owner, Hermann Rosen, was personally available to his customers at all hours of the day and night in the event of serious pipeline problems. He ensured that his most competent employees immediately tackled the problem. The company kept its promises and,

Figure 2.6:   Inspection tool for pipelines from Rosen (© Rosen Technology and Research GmbH).

over time, Rosen was able to solidify customer relationships built on his personal commitment.

Creating trusting relationships and guaranteeing this kind of service are not easy for large corporations. Complex decision rules and comprehensive process regulations stand in the way of highly flexible service offerings. In addition, long-time family entrepreneurs can build personal trust more easily than corporate managers, who frequently change their roles and responsibilities.

Premium service does not just involve the boss. It requires all staff to behave with a customer-oriented focus — just as we expect in a five-star hotel. Hidden champions achieve this broad customer-orientation base by bringing a significant portion of their employees in direct contact with customers. According to Simon's study, the number ranged between 25 and 50 percent. Large industrial companies are far from achieving these numbers.

In general terms, customer-orientation in B2B businesses has always been linked to physical proximity to the customer. To ensure this proximity, a company must, among other things, be prepared to adapt to the region as the geographic focus of the customer changes. One example is the previously mentioned Heraeus silver paste business. Due to the increasing dominance of Chinese customers, the division moved its headquarters to Shanghai, where managers hired Mandarin-speaking sales and R&D staff.

Of course, hidden champions are not the only examples of premium service suppliers. Service quality is also an important benchmark for many companies, for example, those in the pharmaceutical industry. It is imperative that hospitals receive medical supplies with the utmost reliability, just as doctors must quickly and flexibly handle emergency situations involving large numbers of seriously injured people. The aerospace and aviation industries offer numerous examples of high-quality service. In the meantime, the industries' service offerings have evolved well beyond maintenance and repair work. The most well-known example is the aircraft turbine manufacturer Rolls-Royce. With its "power by the hour" service, which it introduced in 1962, the company no longer sells aircraft turbines. Instead, it has a pure play service offering, which includes transport services. The turbines are owned by Rolls-Royce, and the company engages in numerous value-added activities previously performed by customers.

In the meantime, many industrial companies are seeking to establish themselves in their markets with similar business models. They are doing so because the data and analyses that can be gleaned from cross-customer product usage promise to deliver a whole range of advantages. In this way, these companies are transforming themselves into complex service solution suppliers, offering portfolios that go beyond industrial companies' traditional understanding of service. We discuss this topic in more detail in Chapter 4.

Striving for Brand Value

In previous sections, we discussed how companies with technical advantages and superior services can offer objectively better products than their competitors. We now look at how customers need to perceive this offer before it can be successful. Objective reality and subjective perception do not have to be aligned. Figure 2.7 shows an example of this phenomenon. The middle circles in both pictures are the same size. Nevertheless, most people find that the middle circle in the left diagram is smaller than the one on the right. This is due to the size of the surrounding circles and their relative position to one another.

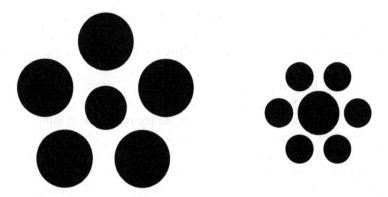

Figure 2.7:   Objective reality and subjective perception.

Premium companies, by analogy, must grapple with a series of related questions. What should its "middle circle" landscape look like in order to appear as big as possible? How can companies use branding to design a product landscape that presents customers with the most attractive image? This does not have anything to do with the offering's rational elements. Instead, it addresses the emotional positioning of the offering's value proposition. Successful brands ensure that the customer has made the "right purchase decision." Making the decision to purchase is validated by the customer's "good feeling."

Business literature deals with the topic of branding primarily within the context of markets for consumer goods. References to industrial markets are the exception. The major reason is that there is a relatively low level of public awareness about these products. Large corporations such as Airbus and Boeing have clearly managed to achieve name recognition worldwide. A closer look reveals a number of other industrial companies that are well known in their specific markets and whose brands are central to their business success. A prime example is Scania in Europe's truck market. The same applies to American company Oracle in the worldwide database market and Trumpf for laser machines.

A second reason why branding enjoys stepchild status in industrial markets is that customers themselves downplay — or even deny — the importance of non-rational aspects in purchase decisions. This is understandable. The individuals with the decision-making responsibilities have to justify their decisions. In a corporate environment, only business arguments are acceptable; personal and emotional reasons are taboo.

Although scientific studies have shown that non-rational aspects of purchase decisions play a role in industrial markets, most B2B premium suppliers do not like to talk about the marketing advantages of their brands because of the taboos concerning their customers: B2B customers do not want to believe that they have spent money on emotional value.

A brand's advantages are different in industrial markets than those for consumer goods. In B2C business, a brand's most important impact lies in achieving status for customers. When people drive a Porsche or wear a Rolex, they feel privileged and hope to gain social recognition when purchasing these products. In B2B markets, on the other hand, companies are less inclined to view the enhancing of their customers' status as a key brand benefit. Thorsten Borst — board member for marketing and sales for many years at EBM Papst, a medium-sized company producing electric motors and ventilators — is one of the rare exceptions. According to Borst, the presence of EBM Papst in Formula One racing is particularly relevant for Chinese customers. Purchasing the product makes them proud. Cases like this are the exception. In industrial markets, the more compelling argument is that a brand helps customers reduce levels of perceived uncertainty in making purchase decisions.

In fact, customers are unable to correctly analyze all of a product's costs and benefits before making a purchase decision. On the one hand, the process is too cumbersome. On the other hand, customers cannot verify all product elements. Consider this analogous service example from everyday life: How are patients supposed know the value of a particular dental treatment before they actually visit a dentist? Even when they do, they will not be able to assess all of the costs and benefits. How should they know whether or not the filling was properly performed or if the dental materials contain long-term carcinogens? Similarly, industrial customers cannot properly assess all of the transaction costs and benefits of a power plant or IT system before purchasing one. As a result, customers perceive uncertainty.

Trust compensates for perceived uncertainty. This is where a brand comes into play. It can influence customer expectations. When customers engage with a successful brand, for example, they assume that suppliers will keep their performance promises without neglecting care and reliability. In short, customers substitute their lack of control with trust in the brand. This not only increases their willingness to pay but also the speed with which they make purchase decisions.

The less that customers can directly verify product quality and compare competing offers, the more important trust becomes. That is why a well-established industrial market brand is particularly relevant when suppliers launch market innovations. It is precisely in situations like these that customers cannot rely on other people's referrals or experiences. This, in turn, makes customers particularly uncertain before making a purchase decision. This doubt is magnified when they have to justify a buying decision to others. As mentioned above, this is a common situation in industrial markets. A brand's ability to reduce uncertainty is well illustrated by the frequently quoted phrase: "Nobody ever got fired for choosing IBM."

As in the IBM example, a B2B brand communicates more about the suppliers than their products. If the products are assembled in small batches and subject to constant changes due to technical advances, building a product-related brand is not worthwhile. Though there are companies in industrial markets that are able to offer several brands under a single roof. Daimler Trucks is one example. The company addresses target groups across different regions of the world with the brands Freightliner, Western Star, Mercedes Benz, Fuso, and BharatBenz. These are not product brands in the strictest sense of the term, but rather a broad range of products positioned under a single brand. Rare examples of successful B2B product brands are the Boeing "747," the IBM "Watson" program, and the Siemens "SIMATIC," all of which are positioned beneath a strong corporate brand umbrella.

Customers are the primary target group for branding. In the age of the "war for talent", managers are increasingly using brands to recruit and retain employees. In addition, a successful brand has a positive impact on financial investors and other stakeholders. Customers of customers are another interesting target group in industrial markets. These customers are the result of downstream demand in B2B markets where, by definition, suppliers do not sell to end customers. Instead, they sell to customers who, in turn, serve their customers. When customers address customers, marketers refer to ingredient branding. The most frequently cited successful example is the slogan "intel inside". In the case of Intel, the supplier not only tries to market its products directly to customers (so-called push marketing) but also tries to generate demand among downstream customers (so-called pull marketing). Customers then put pressure on computer manufacturers to use Intel chips in their devices. At first glance, ingredient branding is tempting for suppliers, as it promises to give them independence from their direct customers. At second glance, suppliers actually run the risk of alienating these very same direct customers — and potentially even losing them. Direct customers will not be enthusiastic when suppliers sidestep them and speak directly to downstream customers — a move that would weaken the direct customers' own power position in the value chain (see Figure 2.8).

Regardless of which target group should be addressed, most companies ask themselves the following question: How do I build a premium brand?

At the very beginning of the brand-building process, marketers should be aware of the values or characteristics for which the brand stands. Brand identity definitions, however, can quickly lead to a multitude of positive attributes being ascribed to them — a common experience whenever humans pursue an ideal. Brands should appear modern and dynamic, convey tradition, stand for reliability, or look friendly and powerful, just to name a few of the most common examples. In fact, a brand's identity can be as diverse as that of a real person. Yet, brand managers must set priorities. This applies to external communication in particular. Joe Kaeser, the

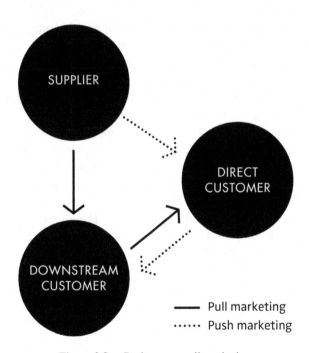

Figure 2.8:   Push versus pull marketing.

CEO of Siemens AG, limits himself to the three values of innovation, integrity, and sustainability when describing the corporate brand of Siemens in public.[6]

The premium company Trumpf is focusing on an even shorter brand message with its "Innovation promised" slogan. In addition to the focus on innovation, it is designed to underscore the brand's high reliability. These two words merely form the core of a broader set of values, which are divided into four categories: independent in attitude; open in dealings; convincing in performance; and strong in style. Incidentally, the Trumpf slogan is not used in its advertising. Rather, it is aimed primarily at employees to clarify the company's strategic direction.

Business literature and practice pay a great deal of attention to marketing communication actions in discussing brand management activities. Logos must be designed and placed according to fixed patterns. All advertising must follow a consistent visual and color language. The claim must capture the essence of the brand promise. In addition, a great deal of discussion is devoted to brand-consistent product design. For example, a brand that wants to convey modernity should express its products through contemporary design and the use of innovative technologies.

In industrial markets, reducing a premium brand identity to consistent communication policy and product design principles would be insufficient. B2C customers typically only experience a communication strategy's brand expression on its surface. In industrial markets, on the other hand, suppliers and customers have a closer relationship. They have a more diverse set of "touch points" to consider when trying to achieve a consistent market presence. If a brand is supposed to project reliability, service employees should not arrive too late for scheduled meetings. If the brand is supposed to be technically innovative, sales managers must master the use of modern communication. If the brand is supposed to stand for internationality, not all board members should come from one region. Employees are important brand ambassadors. The closer the relationship between supplier and customer, the more that the desired brand values need to be credibly rooted in the company. Credibility can only be achieved with authenticity.

In addition to consistency and authenticity, time is also required to successfully establish a brand. Customers only build long-term relationships with brands that they have frequently encountered. Their brand

---

[6]*manager magazin* (January 2018), p. 34.

experience has to be confirmed time and time again. That can take years. This is one important reason why the world's most famous brands are predominantly from industrialized countries. Companies in emerging-markets, on the other hand, prefer to buy traditional companies with strong brands. In doing so, they are able to avoid years of brand-building efforts.

Companies can extend their brand's value by using it for their other products. This is known as brand extension. The Nivea brand, for example, has successfully pursued this strategy in the consumer goods sector. In addition to the brand's original skin cream products, it now markets shampoos, deodorants, shaving cream, and much more. The more versatile the product range, the more difficult it is to live up to the brand promise. Due to the resulting high level of complexity, companies run the risk of raising customers' expectations and then disappointing them. In small industrial markets, where customers know each other and exchange views, this can have disastrous consequences. After all, brands make a quality promise just like humans do in relationships: It takes a lot to build trust, but it takes very little to destroy it.

As we have seen, there are three ways for a company to distinguish itself as a premium supplier in industrial markets. Each way is a valid path toward winning the "premium medal." Figure 2.9 summarizes the most important elements once again.

Growing with Advanced Premium Products

As we have demonstrated, hidden champions successfully offer advanced premium products. Although these companies have a relatively narrow industry or product focus, they strive for growth just like every other company. One of their options is to achieve growth with the help of international expansion; another option is to improve products and take market share from competitors.

In addition, these companies are continuously expanding their product range and can thus both generate additional sales with existing customers and penetrate new customer segments. In some cases, they venture into business areas outside of their current focus of expertise. Figure 2.10 shows three options for achieving growth through product development.

A good example for how to extend the core is provided by Kärcher, the global market leader for high-quality, high-pressure cleaners.

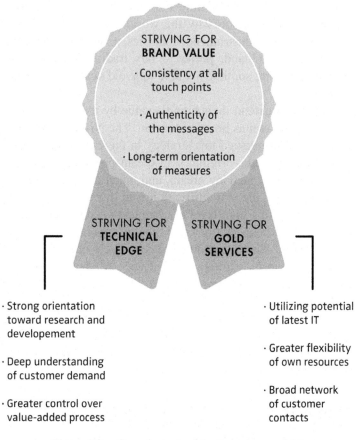

Figure 2.9:   Core elements of the "premium medal."

Improve the core	Extend the core	Explore the new

high ━━━━━━━━━━━━━━━━━━━━━━━━━━━━━ *low*

Usage of existing competencies (technology and/or market know-how)

Figure 2.10:   Growth options based on product development.

Kärcher's flexibility in production and digital processes enables the company to produce around 40,000 different variants of its products within 24 hours. Individual customer requirements can thus be met with high precision and on-time delivery.

Chargeurs, a successful publicly traded mid-market company based in France, brings together four business lines that manufacture high-quality products, all of which are market leaders, among which is Chargeurs Luxury Materials. In their production of luxury wool, the company has improved its offering and created a competitive advantage by using blockchain technology.

Blockchain means that transactions are built on earlier transactions, and each transaction confirms the previous one as correct — what we call "proof-of-work". It functions like a chain as transactions are added in chronological order. Each new block has a hash from the previous block so that all the information is saved there as well. This makes it impossible to manipulate or erase the existence or content of the earlier transactions without simultaneously changing all later transactions as well.

In the case of Chargeurs, this technology allows its customers to trace the luxury wool from the sheep and the farms to the final product that is sold in shops. Especially in the luxury segment, where Chargeurs operates, this proof of quality is vital.

Figure 2.11 shows how this works: All steps in the process across the value chain are stored in the blockchain, beginning with the greasy wool collected at a farm, to the combining mill that produces the wool top, the spinning mill where the wool yarn is produced, and lastly the weaving workshop where the wool is fabricated to create the final product. As a consequence, customers can easily trace the production process right up to the final product.

Many industrial companies are using digital technologies to improve their hardware-based product offerings and generate additional revenue. However, they are often dissatisfied with the commercial results of these new offerings, partly since their workforces lack the necessary know-how to market them successfully. We return to these problems and the ways to solve them in Chapter 5.

The classic way to extend the core means drawing upon existing competencies when developing new products. GRIMME Gruppe, the global market leader in machinery for the cultivation, care, harvesting, and storage of potatoes, was able to use its high level of expertise in potato technology to very successfully expand its portfolio to include machines for harvesting beetroots, carrots, and celery. Just like potatoes, celery, carrots, and beetroots are extremely sensitive vegetables and need machines that harvest them gently.

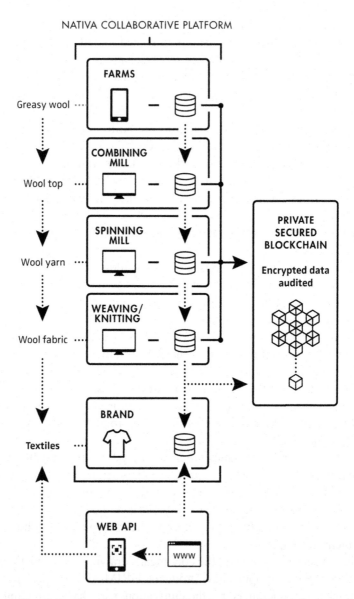

Figure 2.11: Improving the product offering by using blockchain technology at Chargeurs.

J. Wagner GmbH, a family-owned company, has extended its core by addressing new customer segments. Traditionally, this global market leader has offered innovative coating technologies for surface finishing, including powder and liquid coatings, paints, and other fluid materials. Their customers hail from industry, commerce, and home improvement. By now, the company has succeeded in using its expertise in a new industry, namely, the cosmetics industry.

The way into this new business was paved when WAGNER's executive, Valentin Langen, found that about 40 percent of sunburns were a result of patchy sunscreen application and could be avoided. He wondered if it were possible to develop a skin care product that could be applied seamlessly. Eventually, he came up with the idea of using the existing coating technology of Wagner Group to disrupt the cosmetics industry. With this mission in mind, WAGNER founded the corporate start-up IONIQ Skincare and invested a double-digit million amount in euros.

IONIQ ONE was launched in June 2021. The new device it created is a battery-powered (see Figure 2.12), handheld spray can that can be used to spray on sunscreen and other lotions much more precisely than any of the other spray cans on the market. The innovative device reliably steers the sunscreen particles away from clothing and hair and toward receding hairlines, the back of the body, and other areas that normally burn due to lack of protection in the sun. An app indicates how much sunscreen should be applied when as well as at what intensity in a current location and under the current weather conditions.

With 4,500 employees in more than 70 countries, BEUMER Group offers intralogistic solutions for conveying, loading, palletizing, packaging, sortation, and baggage handling. In 2017, the company extended its core by developing innovative solutions, among which was the travel technology start-up Airsiders. In collaboration with BEUMER, Airsiders developed a technology that connects airports, ground handlers, airlines, and distribution platforms to enable seamless virtual interlining, thus improving the passenger experience and at the same time creating a new stream of revenue for airports and airlines. This is a full-service solution that facilitates automated self-transfer baggage handling between non-interline flights, enabling airports to provide seamless connections even between non-cooperating airlines.

Viessmann has explored new business opportunities that are neither linked to their current markets nor related to their traditional competencies. Traditionally, the company has been a manufacturer of heating and

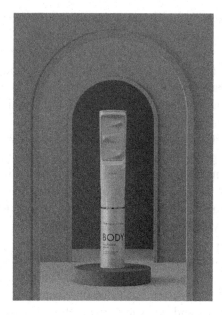

Figure 2.12:   IONIQ ONE, developed by IONIQ Skincare.

climate technologies and of energy systems for industry and commerce. In 2012, in order to enter new business areas, Viessmann established two venture capital funds, followed in 2016 by the subsidiary WATTx, an incubator offering a set of services tailored to challenging industrial innovations.

In 2018, WATTx initiated the incubation of a start-up called Hasty. Hasty created a tool that helps practitioners to build advanced, customized, and specialized vision artificial intelligence (AI) solutions supported by a community of machine-learning engineers, data scientists, and software developers. The idea was to use AI to speed up the process of data creation. Every annotation made is sent to Hasty's model builder, requiring the system to continuously learn and create tailor-made models. With the support of WATTx, Hasty was turned into a company named Hasty.ai in late 2019. It received additional seed investment from the renowned venture capital funds Shasta Ventures, coparion, and iRobot. By now, companies such as BSH Hausgeräte GmbH, Bayer AG, NVIDIA, and EnBW Energie Baden-Württemberg AG are among the customers of Hasty.

Other companies extend their core with the help of cooperations. Cooperations can serve to compensate for missing competencies and reduce financial risks, even if they limit a company's independence.

As one of the biggest automotive suppliers in the area of mechatronic components for vehicle doors, seats, and bodies, Brose has gone in this direction. In 2021, the company founded SITECH, a joint venture with Volkswagen, designed to develop and produce complete seat systems, seat structures, and components as well as connected interior solutions. Brose and Volkswagen each own 50 percent of SITECH. By partnering with an original equipment manufacturer such as Volkswagen, Brose is at the same time collaborating with one of its biggest clients, allowing both companies to shape rather than follow future seat developments. Both companies perceive seats as a key differentiator in interior car design, as they impact customer experience with respect to comfort and safety. Furthermore, both owners of SITECH expect that current trends such as e-mobility, autonomous driving, and cross-system connectivity will change the requirements for the interiors of tomorrow's cars toward personalized design. The joint venture is striving to expand its business with the entire Volkswagen Group, but at the same time, SITECH is expected to generate a significant share of sales with other vehicle manufacturers. However, the competencies and portfolios of Brose and SITECH complement each other well. As a leading supplier of seat systems and interior solutions, Brose has both system know-how and expertise in manual and power adjusters as well as comfort components, whereas SITECH has expertise in the development, assembly, and logistics of complete seats and metal structures.

Acquisitions are another strategic option for companies looking to grow in the area of advanced premium products without investing a lot of time, resources, and costs to upskill the existing workforce. Chargeurs, to name only one example, has carried out targeted acquisitions to strengthen its position and foster growth in all four niche markets in which it is operating. Between 2021 and 2025, these acquisitions are projected to contribute around €50 million to the company's operating profits and generate around €500 million in additional revenue.

The Dark Side of Uniqueness

Striving for high brand value, a technical edge, and great services, all three paths seek to achieve the most unique market position possible with the help of a compelling competitive advantage. Premium suppliers can, however, get on the wrong track. That can prove to be very expensive, indeed. The most important traps of unique product offerings are discussed as follows.

As already mentioned, technology companies in the premium sector are always working to further develop or improve their products. A new type of machine produces even more than the old one. A new truck is even more powerful than its predecessor. A new generation of computer chips is even faster than the previous one. That higher quality is usually associated with higher costs. Suppliers, in turn, want to sell their upgraded products at higher prices. There is a possibility that a majority of customers are not interested in product improvements. As a result, they may not be prepared to pay higher prices. The improvements do not add value in the eyes of these customers, even though the supplier's product development team may still be very proud of them. In cases like these, we speak of product over-engineering (see Figure 2.13). In this case, the supplier reduces the number of buyers to a few special customers, but the resulting revenues are too small to cover the total costs. Managers can counteract over-engineering risks by adopting a more market-oriented product development culture, cooperating closely with customers, and using specific market research tools.

A second type of unique situation can result from the peculiarities of B2B procurement processes. For many institutional clients, making purchase decisions from an economic perspective has become more important in recent decades. At the same time, purchasing departments have gained influence. Buyers are particularly interested in making side-by-side comparisons of product specifications, as well as bringing at least

Figure 2.13:   Example of over-engineering.

two suppliers into price competition with one another. Today, public institutions are sometimes not even permitted to conduct large-scale procurements without a call for tenders and obtaining several comparable, competitive bids. These rules do not apply, however, to vendors who have developed a unique product. Because other comparable competitive offers do not exist, other suppliers are disqualified by default.

For example, ThyssenKrupp Elevator experienced this dynamic when the company launched the "TWIN" innovation in 2002. The innovation involves deploying two elevator cabs inside a single shaft, which allows large skyscrapers to be designed for greater efficiency. Because passengers do not always want to ride from the lowest floor to the top, elevators often alternate between the floors, particularly when a high-rise building contains office complexes. This insight allowed the ThyssenKrupp engineers to optimize elevator use. Under this concept, two elevators operate simultaneously in the same shaft. Passengers choose the floor they want by pressing a corresponding button before they actually enter the cab. As a result, a skyscraper that normally requires 16 elevator shafts can manage traffic with six single-cab shafts and six twin-cab shafts (see Figure 2.14). This eliminates four elevator shafts, allowing engineers to repurpose the extra space somewhere else in the skyscraper. Given modern skyscrapers' numerous floors, this can unlock enormous financial potential.

Although the TWIN technology was tested and proven to be safe, ThyssenKrupp Elevator was unable to sell the concept on a large scale. The reason was the procurement process. Elevator contracts in high-rise

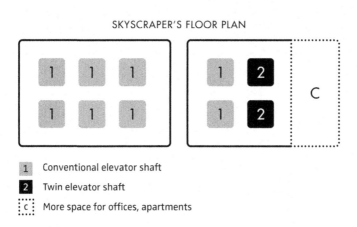

Figure 2.14: TWIN versus conventional elevator system.

buildings are usually awarded through a tendering process. In order to obtain comparable offers from several competitors, one bidding announcement specification called for elevator shafts that could accommodate single cabs. In the above example, a contract for 16 elevator shafts was announced instead of 12. Due to this bidding specification, ThyssenKrupp Elevator was unable to exploit the advantages of its unique TWIN product from the start.

This example would not be complete without discussing what ThyssenKrupp Elevator had learned from this experience. The company's recent innovation, "MULTI," is a cable-free elevator system. It allows elevator cabs to move vertically and horizontally in skyscrapers. The company is currently exploring opportunities to market licensing agreements with competitors. During a tendering process, customers could then pursue price-based competition between suppliers with similar product offerings.

A third mistake comes into play when a supplier's market success or its profits are too large. This attracts the attention of regulators. Government officials intervene in cases where a supplier has a so-called dominant or superdominant market position. IBM experienced this in 2011, for example, thanks to its dominant position in the mainframe market. It made high profits in its after-sales business, which is standard for many industrial companies. The European Union authorities forced IBM to provide its parts to competitors so that they, too, could perform maintenance and repairs on IBM mainframes. Currently, data-driven companies such as Google are the target of competition authorities. This may be due to the company's size as well as public pressure. Experience shows that antitrust authorities are less likely to intervene in smaller industrial markets.

Chapter 3

No-frills Products: Achieving Profitability in Low-price Segments

Abstract

In this chapter, we discuss how companies can successfully deal with the global increase in demand for low-priced industrial products. We describe ways of how to adjust a company's technologies and costs for this demand and which obstacles need to be surmounted during this process. In this context, we show different approaches to both product development and the design of business models. We analyze the pros and cons of whether to promote these products under a company's umbrella brand or separately, and we demonstrate the impact that low-priced industrial products have on a company's sales channels. Finally, we discuss the influence of no-frills or low-priced products on a company's organizational structure.

No-frills for Industrial Products

Airbus and Boeing have enjoyed an almost utopian era. Thanks to an increase in air travel, the demand for passenger aircraft has grown in recent decades. In the past, airline customers only had two aircraft options in the attractive 150-seat passenger jet segment: the Airbus A320 and the Boeing 737. With a unit price of around $100 million, both manufacturers have made high profits with their aircraft. Customers had to wait up to five years for delivery. But those times may soon be over. In addition to

81

the technical problems of Boeing's new model 737 MAX in 2019 and a drop in demand due to COVID-19 in 2020, both suppliers will have to deal with a new competitor from China. On May 5, 2017, the Chinese aircraft manufacturer COMAC started the first flight of its C919 model. The C919 has a similar seating capacity as the Boeing 737 and the Airbus A320, and it is scheduled to be available in 2022. The price per plane is around $50 million — half of what Boeing and Airbus charge.

In August 2018, COMAC already had more than 1,000 orders and purchase options for the C919 (see Figure 3.1). Yet, as attractive as the price of this aircraft is, it does not distinguish itself for its above-average quality and technical innovation. It is not an advanced premium product. Industry experts mock the C919, because it is equipped with last-generation engines. However, this does not bother COMAC's price-sensitive target customers in China and Africa in the least. They consider the C919 to be "good enough."

This trend in the passenger aircraft market has also been apparent in several other industries in recent decades. The changes have been particularly prevalent in mechanical engineering, but they are also occurring in sectors handling trucks, fire protection devices, intraocular lenses, and combine harvesters. Under these changing scenarios, new competitors have challenged premium product manufacturers by launching significantly less expensive offerings on the market. This has been driven by the economic

Figure 3.1:   The C919 during takeoff in Shanghai.

rise of numerous emerging and developing countries, as well as the increased demand for inexpensive products. Focusing on consumer goods, economist C. K. Prahalad started a discussion at the beginning of this century about these new business growth opportunities, as well as the differences in product requirements, using the term "Bottom of the Pyramid".[1]

To date, a majority of new, price-aggressive competitors have prevailed in environments with the greatest development needs. These competitors come from emerging and developing countries, and they target customers in their respective home markets. Most of these low-price suppliers cannot sustain themselves over the long term. Some of them, however, have been successful. Thanks to their regional focus, low-price suppliers in China and India have even evolved to become top-selling suppliers worldwide. Among these players are the truck manufacturers Dongfeng and Tata Motors.

Once new competitors succeed in exporting their inexpensive products to other emerging and developing countries, they reach the next growth stage. The most ambitious among them, however, are pursuing another strategy: They want to penetrate premium market segments. In Chapter 2, we presented ZPMC, the Shanghai-based company that entered the container crane market in 1992. Initially, ZPMC simply copied the spare parts of established manufacturers such as Liebherr and Terex. It then used the cost advantages that existed in China at the time. ZPMC reinvested its profits into research and development until it could build complete cranes and enter the market with its own innovations. One of these new products was the "double-container crane," and it was very successful. The innovation allowed port operators, for the first time, to move two containers simultaneously with only one crane. With this product, ZPMC has found a permanent position in the largest ports of Europe and North America.

Western industrial companies have often faced rising Asian competitors with a mixture of arrogance and helplessness. At first, companies mocked Asian products for their supposedly inferior quality. Later, however, these same critics accepted the new competitors' above-average growth as inevitable. It is hard to find anyone who shares this mindset

---

[1]C. K. Prahalad and S. Hart, "The Fortune at the Bottom of the Pyramid," *Strategy & Business* 26 (2002); it should be noted that the economist Schumacher had already initiated similar considerations in 1973, see E. F. Schumacher (1973), *Small Is Beautiful: A Study of Economics As If People Really Mattered* (London: Blond Briggs, 1973).

today. Now, many established industrial companies are standing up to their new rivals from a position of competitive strength. In other words, these companies have developed needs-based products for markets in emerging and developing countries, where they can enjoy both location and cost advantages.[2]

Since 2009, for example, Siemens has sold inexpensive fire alarms under the name "Siemens Cerberus ECO" in the building services engineering market. Siemens originally sold these devices for around €22 in China under the premium brand "Siemens Sinteso". Yet, customers in China's rapidly growing cities were only willing to pay a third of this price. Regional suppliers filled the demand for low-price fire detectors until Siemens entered this customer segment. Siemens had already embraced a companywide vision of entering low-price markets by the turn of the millennium and began this journey by conducting a cross-market study, which segmented customers worldwide according to their willingness to pay. Segments with a very high willingness to pay were designated "M1". Those with a very low willingness to pay were designated "M4". By examining the markets and Siemens' position in them, it became clear that the company only had a presence in the M1 and M2 segments. This was in spite of the fact that the greater share of worldwide growth was happening in the M3 and M4 segments (see Figure 3.2).

Today, Siemens Cerberus ECO is just one of more than 200 products that the company uses to target M3 customer segments.[3] Siemens' competitor GE has similarly expanded its offering. The portable electrocardiograph MAC 400 became particularly well known in this context. The price was one-third of GE's premium equipment and was particularly attractive to rural doctors in India.

Now, medium-sized companies from Europe and North America are also targeting price-sensitive customers in emerging and developing countries with affordable products. One example is the company Trumpf, which is mentioned in Chapter 2. This premium manufacturer of machine

---

[2]In addition to the examples mentioned below, there are others with reference to B2B markets that can be found in M. Zeschky, B. Widenmayer, and O. Gassmann, "Innovation in Emerging Markets," *Research-Technology Management* 54, no. 4 (2011): 38–45, published online December 2015.

[3]Siemens deliberately did not address the M4 customer segment, among other things because managers were concerned that the economic framework conditions for procurement, production, and sales would not always be compatible with group-wide compliance rules.

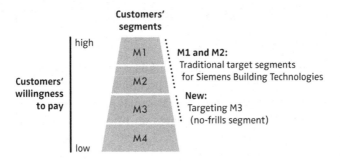

Figure 3.2:   Siemens' market segmentation based on customers' willingness to pay.

tools is the global market leader in high-quality laser-cutting machines. In order to benefit from the growth in its industry's no-frills segments, the company acquired Chinese machine manufacturer JFY in 2013. With Trumpf's help, JFY is not only active in China today but also in markets outside of China. The same applies to Kion, the world's second-largest manufacturer of forklifts after Toyota. Kion acquired Chinese forklift supplier Baoli in 2010 and Indian manufacturer Voltas a year later. These forklifts belong to the same weight class as Kion's premium brands Linde and Still. Yet, they cost only half as much.

Unlike Trumpf and Kion, which entered no-frills product markets by acquiring companies in emerging and developing countries, Körber has leveraged its own resources to achieve growth in this area. Körber is the global market leader in machines for cigarette production. To expand its portfolio, the group initially bought Fabio Perini, an Italian premium manufacturer of paper- and tissue-processing machines, in 1993. Fabio Perini had a strong market position. New competitors had emerged there, however, to address the Chinese market's growing demand for tissue. Among these competitors were Baosuo, DCY, and OK Machinery Manufacturing in Guangzhou. They focused on offering tissue-manufacturing machines that were less sophisticated but much more affordable. Körber also founded the company Sheer in China in 2017. Sheer not only started a price war with its products in no-frills customer segments but it also located its production facilities in the immediate vicinity of OK in Guangzhou. Furthermore, it did not hesitate to entice employees away from its Chinese competitors.

We have applied the classification "no-frills products" to Sheer machines, Siemens fire alarms, GE electrocardiographs, JFY machines, and Voltas and Baoli forklifts. We define the term in the following way:

- No-frills products reliably meet fundamental customer needs. They provide all the essential advanced premium product functionality, but they do so without including non-essential product features.
- No-frills products offer customers a price advantage of at least 50 percent.

Established industrial companies usually pursue the strategy of no-frills products for four reasons:

1. Pursuing sales growth.
2. Achieving profits.
3. Creating market barriers to entry for competitors.
4. Creating sales and cost synergies.

For many top managers of industrial companies, sales growth is the most important goal. Strong global growth in low-price segments makes these markets very attractive. Managers can use this strategy to develop completely new customer groups. Consider GE and its electrocardiograph in the previous example. This product made it possible for doctors in poorer parts of India to buy these types of devices for the first time.

Sales growth opportunities are particularly attractive when no-frills products are marketed globally. Mettler Toledo, a manufacturer of precision laboratory balances and scales, is a good example of this. The company initially developed no-frills products for the Chinese market. Now, it offers them worldwide as an inexpensive alternative to its premium products in industrialized countries. The literature refers to this phenomenon as "reverse glocalization."[4] The potential demand for no-frills products is enormous. Yet, there are hardly any examples of established industrial companies that generate more sales with them than with their premium products. In spite of successful market launches and good growth rates across numerous countries, for example, Siemens earns less than a quarter of its total sales with no-frills products. This includes the

---

[4]In addition to the examples mentioned below, there are others with reference to B2B markets in M. Zeschky *et al.*, "Innovation" (see note 2).

Siemens Cerberus ECO fire alarm, which is part of its Building Technologies segment.

Making profits is just as important as achieving sales growth. Established industrial companies therefore find managing no-frills products to be more difficult than the companies that have built their businesses with this strategy. A well-known example of this comes from commercial aviation. For many years, Ryanair's low-price flights within Europe were more profitable than those of more expensive airlines such as Lufthansa and British Airways. Although these carriers launched their own no-frills airline brands, including Germanwings and Go, they could not achieve the same profitability as Ryanair. As a result, Lufthansa decided to phase out Germanwings. In the meantime, British Airways sold Go to no-frills competitor EasyJet. These two case examples also illustrate why strategic realignments should not be frustrated by short-term failures. Indeed, even premium companies can adjust to price-sensitive customer segments over time. Both British Airways and Lufthansa, for example, have learned from their experience. They are now successfully offering cheap flights within their group, albeit no longer under their previous no-frills brands. At the same time, the annual results of both groups have improved between 2010 and 2019. By contrast, Ryanair's profitability has declined during the same period.

Even if profits and sales growth do not increase significantly over the long term, premium companies may have other good reasons to offer no-frills products. It was this very insight that guided Siemens' Building Technology CEO, Johannes Milde. He led the market launch of the low-price fire detector Siemens Cerberus ECO in 2007. On the one hand, Milde saw that new Chinese competitors were succeeding in the very inexpensive, rapidly growing M3 customer segments that Siemens had not yet addressed. On the other hand, he found that a number of these new competitors made high profits in spite of low prices. As in our previous case example of ZPMC, Milde assumed that some of these competitors would also use profits to improve their innovation capabilities and product quality. Sooner or later, Milde feared that they would be in a position to move into those premium segments that were earning Siemens reasonably adequate profits. As a result, Siemens entered the price-sensitive M3 segments with Cerberus ECO and exerted price pressure on its Chinese competitors. Consequently, they were forced to lower their prices, could no longer make high profits, and had fewer funds to invest in research and development.

Milde summarized the strategic logic as follows: "I would rather make life difficult for the new competitors in their M3 market segments before they make life difficult for me in our M1 segments." Milde strategically used the market launch of no-frills products to make it more difficult for new competitors with lower-quality products to access premium market segments. From his perspective, profit and sales growth played a less significant role. Because no-frills products earned relatively low profit margins, high sales turnover would not have helped the overall profitability of this business segment. Other established building technology companies, such as Schneider, United Technology, and Honeywell, have operated in a similar way. To date, none of the new competitors' products from emerging and developing countries have managed to take a leading position in the global market for building technology.

For established industrial companies, entry into no-frills products also offers the opportunity to achieve synergy effects that new competitors cannot achieve; for example, they can gain price advantages by purchasing larger quantities. This, in turn, has a positive impact on the budgets of no-frills products as well as higher-quality products. In addition, established players can leverage existing business relationships with those customers who need both premium and no-frills products. This is particularly true when companies use the same corporate brand name for both premium and no-frills segments, just as Siemens is doing with Cerberus ECO and GE with their electrocardiograph device MAC 400. These synergy advantages are nonetheless offset by risks. We take a closer look at this dynamic in Chapter 5.

Defining the Offer

The decision on whether or not to pursue a no-frills product strategy — and if so, how — begins with a needs analysis. Potential customers' price sensitivity must be weighed against product benefits, as well as the customer segment's regional distribution. The combined analysis of a region's competitive, legal, and social landscape can help managers determine whether or not market entry is worthwhile. No-frills strategies typically focus on fast-growth markets in emerging and developing countries. Yet, the example of low-price airlines demonstrates that there is also a corresponding need in industrialized countries. Both aspects should be included in the needs analysis.

Furthermore, premium providers should avoid contacting existing customers as part of the analysis. This is standard practice in the market research activities of many industrial companies. Consider this example: When GE wanted to address high-growth, no-frills customer segments for electrocardiographs in the Indian market, it would have made little sense to speak to representatives of India's major metropolitan hospitals. These organizations were already working with GE. It was much more important to engage rural doctors and heads of small rural medical centers — the very people who are responsible for supplying the majority of the population. This segment's needs are driven by a special set of essential requirements. Healthcare delivery logistics is a prime example. In India, many patients lack a means of transport and cannot travel to the doctor. As a result, physicians typically travel to patients. This, in turn, impacts training standards, hygienic conditions, and financing options.

Another common difference between premium and no-frills customer segments is the standard by which customers evaluate their investments. Premium customers frequently judge industrial products by their total costs of ownership (TCO). This leads supplying companies such as Siemens or Daimler Truck to aim for low TCO when designing new offerings, and to emphasize TCO in their marketing communications. For no-frills customer segments, however, the initial price often plays a more important role than TCO. This is partly driven by budgetary constraints, which force customers to limit their initial investments. Additionally, no-frills segments often follow less professionalized purchasing processes and do not systematically juxtapose initial investments against lifetime costs, for example, through net present value calculations.

Once industrial companies have understood the needs of no-frills customer segments, they can proceed to the technical design of no-frills products. Two distinct conceptual approaches are available. The first option is to use an existing product platform. Alternatively, new products can be developed from scratch. The first option can also be broken down into further variations. A no-frills product, for example, could be built on "mature technology" by leveraging the product platforms of previous generations. Another option is to simply remove specific features from an existing premium product (i.e., "defeatured premiums"). In many cases, however, the more promising route today is to actually develop innovative products that specifically address the needs of price-sensitive customers. For these scenarios, the term "frugal innovations" is used, which can include new products. Alternatively, companies can also achieve price and

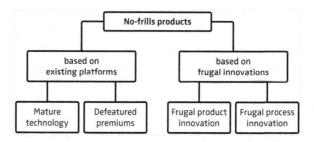

Figure 3.3:   No-frills product development approaches.

cost advantages with process innovation. Today, the use of digital technologies is particularly important in this area. Figure 3.3 shows the different approaches for developing a no-frills product range.

Businesses can pursue a "mature technology" strategy in two ways. On the one hand, they can relaunch production. Alternatively, existing products can be remarketed. The latter involves selling used products — a sector that is rarely featured in media reports or scientific studies. This market has nonetheless grown in relevance because of the numerous new production companies in Asia's growth markets. In the mechanical engineering sector alone, global sales volumes for second- or third-hand equipment are estimated to be more than €100 billion annually. Trade fairs such as USETEC, Fitmac, the International Fair for Used Machinery, and the Used Machinery Expo are very popular. In addition, internet-based trading platforms are also increasingly popular. *Machineseeker*, for example, offers customers a selection of more than 200,000 different machines. Dealers are not the only players who are responding to the high demand for inexpensive, used machines; manufacturers have also become increasingly active in this market. This is why DMG Mori, a premium manufacturer of CNC lathes, also describes itself as the world's largest supplier of used machines in this product category.

Another way to meet the demand for no-frills products with mature technology is to relaunch the production of older, less technologically complex products. A good example in the heavy vehicle sector is the legendary Mercedes short-nose truck. It is still considered to be the epitome of toughness in truck design. Introduced in Western Europe in the 1950s, these trucks were subsequently taken off the market there in the 1970s. While new models were being launched in Western markets, modified versions of the truck continued to be produced in developing and emerging countries

Figure 3.4: The Mercedes short-nose truck.

until the end of the last century. This classic truck, with its robust technical design, still turns up occasionally in these regions (see Figure 3.4).

Like other sectors, older truck models are often manufactured in cooperation with a partner company in a related target market. As early as the beginning of the 1960s, Tata was already manufacturing Mercedes trucks in India. The company later marketed only slightly modified versions of these models under its own name. In this type of collaboration, the premium product supplier provides pre-manufactured CKD (completely knocked down) components as parts sets for subsequent assembly. In some cases, the partner company is also granted a license to manufacture the parts. MAN — one of Mercedes' competitors in the truck market — granted licenses for several hundred million euros to leading Chinese heavy goods vehicle manufacturers to build cabins, motors, and axles.

Another approach is to deliberately opt out of keeping pace with technological progress altogether in terms of product design. In 2010, Ron Adner and Daniel Snow published an article about this "bold retreat strategy."[5] They offered the poignant example of clock and watch manufacturers who, at the beginning of the 1970s, decided not to embrace the advanced technology of quartz and digital models. Instead, they

---

[5]R. Adner and D. Snow, "Bold Retreat: A New Strategy for Old Technologies," *Harvard Business Review* 88, no. 2 (2010): 76–81.

continued to produce mechanical timepieces. For some of them, such as A. Lange & Söhne and Piaget, this product positioning has proven to be extremely profitable to this day. There is, however, no known example of a "bold retreat" among Western quality leaders in technology-oriented B2B markets. This approach would conflict with these companies' self-image. Companies such as Siemens or GE would also have little to gain from launching steam locomotives in today's railroad marketplace. One important reason is that customers are not emotionally invested in the decision-making process for these goods in the way that they are for B2C products.

Defeatured premiums are another way for established industrial companies to address the demand for no-frills products. At first glance, this approach seems obvious. Quality leaders reduce the amount of performance features available for existing products and then sell pared-down versions at a lower price. The B2C watchmaker Cartier, for example, is just one of a number of companies that brings new models onto the market each year. Cartier makes watch casings out of solid gold. For customers who cannot afford such a timepiece, however, Cartier also offers models that are gold-plated or made of steel. These cost up to 60 percent less. Many B2B customers who buy technical products in emerging countries also expect different price levels. Applying a defeatured premiums concept to B2B products is, however, more complex than simply deciding whether to gold-plate a watch or not.

The price reduction process is fairly straightforward when the related parts do not define a product's technical core. That is the reason why manufacturers of high-quality railway trains, such as Alstom, are able to fit lower-grade seats and floor coverings into passenger car interiors. Certain performance features can also be pared back in the after-sales sector. Indeed, it has been standard practice for some time now for technology companies to offer differing levels of service. That is the case with XIAMETER, a low-price silicone product from the US chemical company Dow Chemical. The company had been in this market for decades, producing and delivering silicones to fit customer-specific requirements. Dow Chemical's industry-specific specialists also provided consulting, even for small orders. When new competitors significantly increased price pressure in the silicone market, the company responded by launching XIAMETER. In this case, consulting was eliminated. Customers could also only buy large quantities over the internet, and Dow Chemical set the delivery times. The company achieved market success with this offering.

However, the price advantages derived from the reduction in services only amounted to 15 percent. Under our definition, this does not constitute a no-frills product.

Siemens has had similar experiences with defeaturing premiums in the healthcare sector. In China, the company developed magnetic resonance imaging (MRI) devices for its ESSENZA product range, which was mainly based on premium product technology (see Figure 3.5). The Chinese machines look similar at first glance, but they have a more limited spectrum. They offer a smaller range of options for diagnostic examinations, for example. At the same time, the related price and costs are lower than those for the premium products. In order to stay within the narrow cost parameters, the company's China strategy focuses on achieving savings with external features such as plastic machine housings and other core technical elements. The long, fixed spine arrays required for spinal examinations, for example, have been shortened and fixed to the machine to save space. In addition, the number of separate computing units that are typically fitted to a superconducting MRI was reduced from three to two. Engineers had to integrate some of the third unit's specific functions into the remaining two. This required a new design. Even though the machines' features are more limited, Siemens had to further develop core technical elements to guarantee their functionality. This — and the related approval processes — took almost four years. As a result, premium product costs were significantly reduced in this case, but not by more than 50 percent.

The Alstom, Dow Chemical, and Siemens case examples mentioned above suggest that it is difficult for industrial companies to achieve a cost advantage of more than 50 percent through defeatured premiums. There is also the risk that the defeatured products will not meet no-frills customers' specific needs, and that more innovative solutions will be required. This brings us back to GE's MAC 400 electrocardiograph for the Indian market. It was an innovation, if only due to the fact that it was a portable device. This gave the MAC 400 new utilization characteristics, making it not only less expensive but also better than existing premium products within the target group. In this context, we speak of frugal innovation. In the business literature, it often appears under the term "more for less".[6] Unlike some analysts, we do not believe that sustainability is a definition

---

[6]See, for example, N. Radjou and J. Prabhu, *Frugal Innovation: How to Do More with Less* (London: The Economist, 2015).

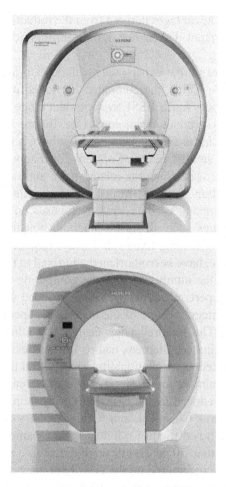

Figure 3.5: A premium magnetic resonance imaging (MRI) device from Siemens (top), ESSENZA MRT from Siemens Healthineers (bottom) (© Siemens).

criterion for this category. Frugal innovations may nonetheless achieve environmental goals by consuming less energy and fewer materials.

Products in the consumer goods sector were initially referred to as "frugal." The word derives from the Latin *frugalis*, meaning usable, modest, or economical. An often-cited example is the work of OneDollarGlasses. Local individuals can execute the organization's eyewear design concept in the poorest countries of the world without expensive equipment and materials. Similarly, anyone can assemble and operate India's small clay refrigerator, MittiCool, without electricity. These examples demonstrate how frugal innovation frequently refers to small suppliers — often private individuals — who create new solutions that require very modest means and skills for people in developing countries. The ingenuity of these innovations lies in their simplicity. The economist Ernst Friedrich Schumacher's famous aphorism, which is often attributed to Albert Einstein, perfectly captures this idea: "Any fool can make things bigger, more complex, and more violent. It takes a touch of genius — and a lot of courage — to move in the opposite direction."[7]

Nevertheless, the rich variety of frugal innovations should not be limited to emerging and developing countries. According to our definition, it also includes SpaceX, the space company owned by the American billionaire Elon Musk. Thanks to an innovative product concept that focuses on the Falcon 9 launchers, SpaceX has managed to cut the price for space transport by more than half. Costs have been reduced even more, as Space X achieves high profit margins per order. This example shows how difficult it is for established companies to develop no-frills products. For decades, the US National Aeronautics and Space Administration and the European Space Agency have been unsuccessful in developing cost-effective space mission offerings. Although they had more resources and more experience, they were unable to outmatch SpaceX's innovative product concept.

A different way of offering frugal innovations in established markets is through "naked solutions with options", a phrase coined by James C. Anderson, Nirmalya Kuma, and James A. Narus in their book *Value Merchants*.[8] A naked solution is the bare minimum that all customers in a segment value. Companies can market these naked solutions as standalone offerings to customers who want the minimum at the lowest possible price. For other customers, the naked solution is enhanced through options that customers value and for which they are willing to compensate the company.

This model is already widely established in the software industry. Companies frequently offer a basic "no-frills" version of a software product at a low price, or even for free. Customers can then upgrade to more advanced versions of the software. A good example is salesforce.com's

---

[7] See Schumacher, *Small Is Beautiful* (see note 1).
[8] J. C. Anderson, N. Kumar, and J. A. Narus, *Value Merchants* (Boston: Harvard Business Review Press, 2007).

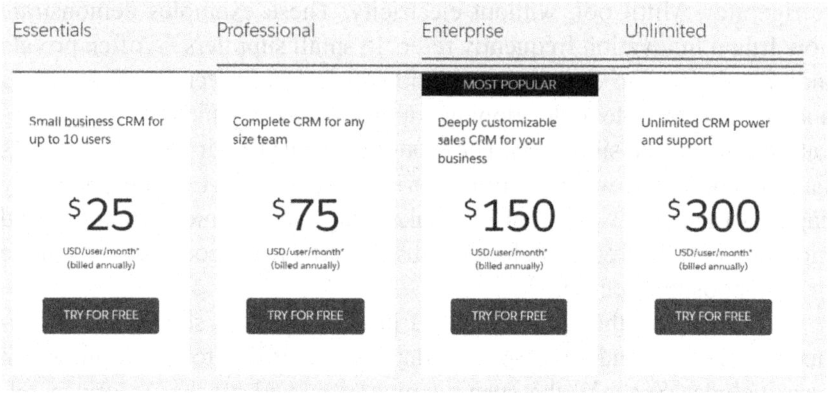

Essentials	Professional	Enterprise	Unlimited
		MOST POPULAR	
Small business CRM for up to 10 users	Complete CRM for any size team	Deeply customizable sales CRM for your business	Unlimited CRM power and support
$25	$75	$150	$300
USD/user/month* (billed annually)	USD/user/month* (billed annually)	USD/user/month* (billed annually)	USD/user/month* (billed annually)
TRY FOR FREE	TRY FOR FREE	TRY FOR FREE	TRY FOR FREE

Figure 3.6:   salesforce.com's Sales Cloud editions.[9]

Sales Cloud, the most widely used CRM system worldwide. As of July 2021, for the "most popular" bundle of options, salesforce.com charged a license fee of $150 per user per month. In comparison, the most advanced bundle was priced at $300, and thus at 200 percent the price of the most popular bundle. Notably, basic versions of Sales Cloud were available at 50 percent (US$75) and 17 percent (US$25) discounts, rendering these versions no-frills products by our definition (see Figure 3.6).

Unlike one-dollar eyeglasses, clay refrigerators, SpaceX, or software, frugal innovations do not always have to focus on the product. These innovations can also address underlying manufacturing processes. Therefore, it is important to differentiate between frugal products and frugal process innovations. India offers an interesting example of the latter. A low-price washing machine manufacturer set out to investigate why sales suddenly began to grow in an Indian province. The company discovered that the region's street vendors were using its machines to make Lassi, a popular Indian yogurt drink. In doing so, they were able to significantly reduce their production costs.

Today, a number of industrial companies are also using modern communication and information technologies to significantly reduce production process costs. Philips, for example, does this with its "Mobile Obstetrics Monitoring" telemedicine product for pregnant women in Africa. After examining patients with an ultrasound device, experts can

---

[9]Salesforce, "Sales Cloud Pricing." Retrieved from https://www.salesforce.com/ca/editions-pricing/sales-cloud/. (Accessed May 2022).

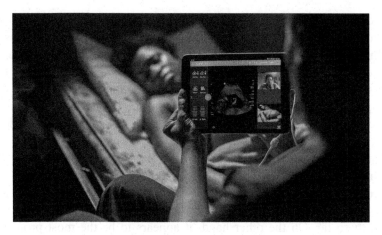

Figure 3.7: Diagnosis with Philips telemedicine.

transmit the data to a remote facility. From there, doctors can later diagnose the potential risks of the pregnancy. Only one person is required on site to operate the ultrasound device. Thanks to handling instructions, the system can even support interactive examinations. Since doctors do not need to diagnose the potential risks of a pregnancy at the patient's site, healthcare providers can achieve significant cost savings using telemedicine (see Figure 3.7). Given the small number of doctors per capita in Africa, this advantage cannot be underestimated. Since the system was introduced in 2013, it has helped millions of pregnant women there. In addition to a web portal that documents patient data and helps midwives organize their work, Philips has also developed an app that helps answer pregnant women's postnatal questions. Using digital technologies, the company has developed a comprehensive solution package that incorporates an interesting combination of both no-frills products and complex service solutions. These are discussed in Chapter 4.

This example once again illustrates that the demand for cost-effective solutions is not just limited to emerging and developing countries. Other industrialized countries are also interested in making their healthcare systems more efficient through the use of digital technologies. Philips, for example, has established a teleradiology group in the United States. Using advanced technology, images are captured on location and electronically transmitted to remote diagnostic centers. Philips not only markets the necessary technology but also provides the healthcare professionals. In the

United States alone, the company currently employs more than 100 radiologists to generate test results. Customers usually receive their results within 15 minutes after being X-rayed. In urgent cases, results can even be produced in 8 minutes — turnaround times that are rarely achieved in hospitals. This Philips offering made medical imaging processes more efficient, and the company has since expanded its traditional range of imaging device products. In doing so, it has transformed its own business model.

Compared to the first two alternatives of mature technology and defeatured premiums, frugal innovations appear to be the option that requires the greatest investment. In addition, it is the most likely to lead to tensions within the company as a whole. This may be the reason why several Western technology companies have shied away from this particular path so far. On the other hand, it appears to be the most promising strategy to properly address the needs of new growth markets that have a low willingness to pay and harbor considerable potential for synergy. Therefore, the following sections of this chapter focus on this option.

Designing the Business Model

The business models for frugal innovations and premium products are very different. Each requires its own revenue logic and its own way of organizing value creation processes. In Chapter 2, we discussed how advanced premium products generate the highest profits with after-sales services. Elevators, lathes, and trucks earn the manufacturers low profit margins. The maintenance and repair services that come later, however, generate high profits. Suppliers try to create more or less monopolistic market structures for after-sales services. This strategy gives customers little choice but to use the provider or an authorized, licensed third party for maintenance and repairs. These companies achieve customer loyalty, for example, by voiding product warranties if a customer buys spare parts elsewhere. Some suppliers apply the same logic by replacing a product's mechanical parts with electronic components that can only be serviced with special equipment. Software provides another opportunity to achieve high profitability in after-sales. By ensuring that the software's usability and compatibility expire over time, suppliers can force customers to switch to newer versions for a lot of money. This opens the door to competitors who want to disrupt this monopolistic customer–supplier relationship with inexpensive maintenance and repair offerings. Established manufacturers often refer to these rivals as "pirates".

Figure 3.8:   Reusable cotton towel dispenser.

In the case of no-frills products, revenue models geared toward after-sales services are unlikely to succeed. To begin with, the model ignores customer needs. No-frills customers do not want to depend on a provider for maintenance and repair work. Instead, they want to be able to have their machines repaired either by their own employees or by low-price pirates. In return, customers accept the lack of a product guarantee. Thus, no-frills products rarely make sense for these types of suppliers. Once they take away the customer's ability to choose who performs product maintenance and repairs, it is the suppliers themselves who must deliver these services. A commercial vehicle manufacturer who wants to sell trucks in Mongolia, for example, would also have to operate a repair station network there. That would be a high cost factor. Hence, it is more advantageous for drivers to repair their own vehicles when they break down.

One company that has had a painful experience with a misfit between its premium business model and a no-frills market is CWS-boco, a subsidiary of Haniel Group.[10] CWS-boco offers solutions under two brands: CWS and boco. CWS supplies solutions for out-of-home washrooms.

---

[10] See J. Habel and Z. Han, "Andreas Keller in China," *ESMT Case Study* (Berlin: ESMT Berlin, 2018). Retrieved from https://store.hbr.org/product/andreas-keller-in-china/ ES1791.

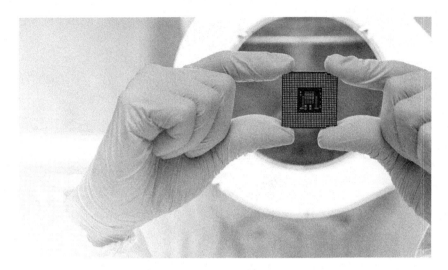

Figure 3.9:   Cleanroom workwear.

The brand is best known for its hand-drying dispensers of reusable cotton towels, which CWS-boco washes in its own laundries, as well as hand-drying dispensers of one-use paper towels (see Figure 3.8).

Under the boco brand — acquired in 1998 — CWS-boco designs, produces, rents out, washes, and maintains workwear for corporate customers. Beyond rather simple workwear (e.g., for the hospitality industry), boco offers solutions for cleanroom workwear (see Figure 3.9) (e.g., for the pharmaceutical and high-tech industries). Such workwear requires special expertise regarding production and laundering.

Despite their different markets, CWS and boco have three common denominators, which are the reasons why both brands are united under one roof. First, both CWS and boco solutions require expertise in logistics, as CWS-boco's service contracts consist of regularly collecting towels and workwear, washing them, and redelivering them to customer firms. Second, solutions under both brands largely rest on CWS-boco's resources and expertise in laundering. Third, the success of both brands rested on CWS-boco's direct sales capabilities.

In 2007, CWS-boco founded an office in China following the internationalization of two of its big European customers. By 2015, CWS-boco China had 105 employees, two laundries, and offered the same product lines as in Europe. Financially, however, CWS-boco China was deep in the red, because the business model on which their success was built hardly worked in the Chinese market.

In the washroom business line, CWS-boco rarely succeeded in selling service contracts to its customers. If anything, customers would purchase towel dispensers and then source low-cost paper towels from other suppliers. Similarly, the workwear business line rarely succeeded in renting out workwear. Instead, they mainly sold workwear without a contract for laundering, because customers preferred to use local low-cost laundries. Thus, CWS-boco only generated revenue with existing customers if these customers hired new employees or the workwear of an employee was irreparable and had to be replaced.

The only business line in which CWS-boco's rental-based business model worked just as it did in Europe was cleanroom workwear. The reason that customers — mainly Chinese subsidiaries of international pharmaceutical companies — purchased these solutions was that they had to adhere to international cleanroom standards. This gave CWS-boco a competitive advantage, because they were the only supplier in China that provided laundering in line with these standards. However, cleanroom workwear only accounted for about 20 percent of revenue in China. In 2016, CWS-boco surrendered and decided to sell its Chinese operations.

In contrast to CWS-boco, Siemens did not try to replicate its Western business model in a no-frills market but designed a new one. Siemens decided not to assume maintenance responsibilities when it introduced its series of inexpensive Siemens Cerberus ECO fire alarms. It chose this business model in spite of the fact that after-sales services generated nearly half of its revenues of premium products. On the one hand, no-frills products require less maintenance than the complex fire protection systems, which are embedded in premium products. On the other hand, Siemens operates its own branches in China's major cities, but not in medium-sized cities, although that is where Siemens expects the greatest growth potential. For this reason, Siemens looked for trading partners in these locations who could work with customers before and after purchase. This, in turn, freed Siemens up to focus on product development and manufacturing.

For this reason, Siemens not only redesigned its no-frills product revenue model but also its entire value creation process. In addition to working with new customers, the company engaged new suppliers, distributors, and cooperation partners. Each played different roles than those required for premium products. In short, Siemens built a completely new value creation ecosystem. For the numerous industrial companies that have focused exclusively on premium products in the past, this approach is likely to make sense. If this approach is pursued, one of the key strategic questions is whether suppliers should enter no-frills markets through acquisitions, as Siemens did in the case of Cerberus ECO. Alternatively, companies can pursue no-frills opportunities through those organic growth or strategic partnerships that leverage core value creation processes.

The latter option is best suited for industrial companies with little no-frills market experience. This scenario allows them to leverage the expertise and relationships of a local partner without investing too much. By contrast, company acquisitions are much more expensive. They pose a bad investment risk if the acquired company's strengths and weaknesses were misjudged prior to purchase. However, when acquiring a company, the buyer can act more independently — an advantage that also exists with the organic growth option. One disadvantage of growing organically, however, is that it takes more time. There is also a greater risk of making incorrect operational decisions due to the premium company's lack of relevant expertise.

The success of the three options — organic growth, strategic partnership, and corporate acquisition — depends on too many individual regulations and variables to draw any general recommendations. The following matrix (see Figure 3.10), however, gives a rough overview of the main advantages and disadvantages.

Under a strategic partnership scenario, several established industrial companies choose to partner with a company that is already active in no-frills markets. They work closely with this strategic partner on essential value creation processes and share the economic rewards. The participants pursue this cooperative relationship, in part, as a formally established joint venture. Initial hopes, however, are often followed by a phase of disillusionment. Conflicts frequently emerge because of regional and cultural differences. After all, the partnership consists of a company from an industrialized country and an emerging developing country. Problems can also arise because of cultural differences between businesses, ownership structure, or premium and no-frills products. Even a family-run delicatessen and a supermarket chain can have deep cultural differences, in spite of the fact that they are located in the same city.

	Corporate acquisition	Strategic partnership	Building own resources
Time required	low	low	high
Investment required	high	low	high
Exercise individual influence	medium	low	high

Figure 3.10: Matrix illustrating the important advantages and disadvantages of no-frills market-entry options.

Truck manufacturer MAN faced cultural-driven problems with the owner-managed company Force Motors in India. The two companies entered into a joint venture in 2006, and MAN intended to produce a new vehicle in India together with this new partner. For the established truck maker, the cooperation was designed to be a successful first step in entering the no-frills truck market. Force Motors agreed to assume sales responsibilities in India; MAN played this role in other emerging and developing countries. Disagreements between the partners emerged fairly quickly, particularly because of disappointing earnings. In addition, MAN feared damage to its own reputation across markets because of the vehicles' unexpected quality issues. To reduce its dependency on Force Motors, MAN took over this business area in 2011. The parties agreed, however, to continue working in parallel with some local Force Motors ecosystem partners. In the period that followed, it resulted in conflicts with these partners, especially if they had a close relationship with the Force Motors owner. When the anticipated business success still did not materialize, MAN ended this business in India in 2018 and sold the Pithampur-based production plant to Force Motors.

As mentioned above, MAN was more successful in China. Following the mature technology approach, MAN had already been selling its engines, driver's cabins, and axles over there for decades. In 2009, MAN then acquired a 25 percent stake in the truck company Sinotruck. At the time, it was still unique for a Western and a Chinese company to have this type of relationship. Subsequently, the two companies agreed to cooperate on smaller joint projects. The scope of these projects was expanded over time. In 2018, MAN reinforced the move toward cooperation when it announced a joint venture. The Volkswagen Group, which took over MAN in 2011, has pursued this approach with partner companies. In 2016, for example, MAN acquired almost 17 percent of the US truck manufacturer Navistar, in which MAN's leadership is currently interested in taking a majority stake. This would allow the truck maker to overcome one of the partnership model's weaknesses, namely, the reduced ability to exercise individual influence.

For this reason, a number of premium suppliers are beginning to enter no-frills markets by acquiring companies that are already active there. The laser machine manufacturer Trumpf, and Kion, the forklift supplier mentioned earlier, are both examples of this trend. Even when the acquiring firm and the business units it has purchased continue to mutually cooperate, problems can emerge because of cultural differences.

To avoid these problems, some established industrial companies accept the disadvantages of organic development. They decide to pursue frugal innovation in no-frills markets without key partners or company acquisitions. This is the strategy Siemens followed with Cerberus ECO. In this case, companies first have to make a set of critical, strategic decisions. They must determine, for example, customer requirements and targets, as well as the product concept and business model. Finally, vital operational questions need to be answered. Who should develop the frugal innovations, and where? What has to be done to achieve the necessary low manufacturing costs?

Developing and Producing Frugal Innovations

In general, it makes sense to have a product developed by people who are familiar with target customers' requirements. When a company enters no-frills markets in emerging and developing countries with a regional customer focus, it makes sense to involve employees who are familiar with local customs. This is also one of the reasons why many Western industrial companies have developed human resources in those countries in recent years. Because Siemens initially targeted the Chinese market, for example, it created a team of Chinese development engineers to build Cerberus ECO. GE deployed a group of local engineers to develop its portable electrocardiograph in India. Making this kind of location decision entails cost advantages. Even if development engineer salaries in China and India have increased rapidly in recent years, they are still lower than those in industrialized countries.

Yet, managers should not overestimate the cost advantages of lower, location-specific wages. In many industrial companies, personnel expenses only make up 10–15 percent of total production costs. Bosch provides an interesting example in this area. In order to develop a no-frills ABS braking system for cars, the company commissioned an engineering team in Japan, a high-wage country where inexpensive motorcycle braking systems had already been developed. Engineering competence, as well as an existing ecosystem, offered Bosch an ideal environment for developing an inexpensive product for the automobile market. After all, product design has a far greater influence on costs than the location of the development team. Design determines material requirements and purchase volumes. It also determines the amount of investment and employee training that will be required for production.

In developing needs-based no-frills products, engineers can draw upon a number of methods and approaches that have been widely used in recent years, particularly for digital products and services. Design thinking, which is presented in Chapter 4, is one example. When launching IT-based no-frills products, for example, managers can pursue open innovation opportunities. In this case, external partners are invited to contribute to the development process, for which they usually receive little or no financial compensation. The logical extension of this approach is the creation of a so-called hyper-collaboration, in which a large number of external partners collaborate in a flexible way to impact even the production process.

It does not always take a team of engineers, however, to develop inexpensive, creative solutions. The countless no-frills inventions that have been launched by individuals with modest means support this idea. The innovation community in India uses the word "Jugaad" in this context (as an example see Figure 3.11). It describes a frugal innovation development process that is based on creativity and improvisation.

In the meantime, this term has also become firmly established in the specialist literature.[11] Some industrial companies are trying to integrate this

---

[11]N. Radjou, J. Prabhu, and S. Ahuja, *Jugaad Innovation* (Oxford: John Wiley & Sons, 2012).

Figure 3.11:   Jugaad vehicle in India.

underlying mindset into their own development processes. Philips, for example, has been operating an innovation center in Bangalore since 1996. The center's former director, Wido Menhardt, offers these insights: "There is sometimes a tendency for Western companies to over-engineer products — to make them perfect, account for all possible use cases, and make them last forever. (...) Jugaad thinking helps us focus on the essence, the real requirements, and often leads to taking the mental leap that is required for a disruptive new design or product."[12] Today, the Philips innovation center employs more than 2,000 development engineers.

Siemens Healthineers has almost as many employees in Bangalore. In fact, more than 400,000 employees work in this city in the development centers of foreign companies. According to *The Economist*, Bangalore ranks number one among cities that offer companies the best conditions for digital innovation development, ahead of San Francisco.[13]

---

[12]Interview by Ian Wylie (December 2012), see https://www.thinkwithgoogle.com/future-of-marketing/management-and-culture/jugaad-innovation/.

[13]See   https://www.eiu.com/public/topical_report.aspx?campaignid=Liveability17   or Telstra, "Connecting Commerce - Business Confidence in the Digital Environment" (September 1, 2017). Retrieved from https://www.telstra.com.au/business-enterprise/news-research/articles/connecting-commerce.

Although new product ideas based on creativity and improvisation do not always translate well into an industrial company's mass production strategy, they nonetheless emphasize one of the key characteristics of no-frills products: They must be simple. Simplicity keeps material consumption levels low and achieves economies of scale through production standardization. This often contradicts industrial premium product strategies, in which suppliers address customers' individual preferences with a high degree of product customization. More customization, however, generates high complexity costs. In the mechanical engineering sector, this can account for up to a quarter of the costs of a product. Managers must avoid this when they deal with no-frills products. At the very least, suppliers in this area should be able to charge special prices to compensate for customizing their standard products.

The Indian hospital chain Aravind Eye Hospitals is an impressive example of how standardization enhances efficiency, in addition to India's location-driven cost advantages. The first clinic was founded in 1976 by the ophthalmologist Dr. G. Venkataswamy. His goal was to make cataract surgery affordable for poorer segments of the population. He achieved his goal. In industrialized countries, patients pay $1,500 to $3,000 for cataract surgery; in conventional Indian hospitals, it is still $300. At Aravind clinics, the average price is $50. Depending on their incomes, patients may pay up to $300, but according to the clinic, 60 percent of patients are treated free of charge.

Despite this, Aravind Eye Hospitals are profitable: The cost per operation has been reduced to $25; the operating time was reduced from around 30 minutes to 10 (see Figure 3.12). The driving force behind these efficiency improvements is consistent process standardization. Unlike other clinics, Aravind involves a larger number of employees for each procedure. By taking over all other non-medical, operation-related tasks, these employees relieve doctors — the most expensive personnel resource. This, in turn, allows physicians to focus on a procedure's core activities. At other hospitals, doctors perform about 400 operations of this type each year. At Aravind clinics, the number is 2,600. Thanks to the higher number of operations, Aravind doctors can also gain more experience, which has a positive impact on procedure quality. Aravind Eye Hospitals are now the largest and most recognized clinics of their kind in the world. Today, the Indian chain consists of 14 clinics. By establishing a clinic in Nigeria in 2018, Aravind has taken its first step toward expanding abroad.

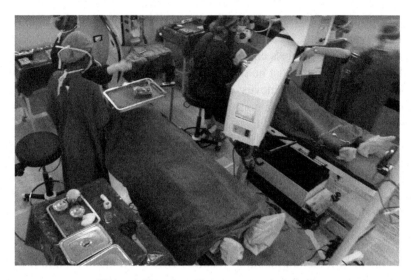

Figure 3.12: Operations at an Aravind clinic.

Aravind Eye Hospitals' frugal process innovation has also had an impact on other products in this market. The normally expensive intraocular lenses were manufactured by the Aravind subsidiary Aurolab. Instead of acrylic, the company uses plexiglass — a material that is less flexible and requires a larger tissue incision. The cost advantages, however, significantly outweigh potential drawbacks. Established lens manufacturers — among them Alcon in the United States and Zeiss in Germany — still work with the more expensive acrylic. At the same time, they have expanded their product range to include plexiglass lens material, some of which still costs a tenth of the premium products. Those suppliers can now successfully target the customers who are willing to pay with offers that fluctuate between Aurolab lens prices and those of premium products. China is currently the most important market for these products.

In addition to product simplicity and the standardization of manufacturing processes, supplier selection has a strong influence on manufacturing costs. In order to keep costs low, no-frills suppliers should work with partners who, in turn, operate in the lower price segments and still meet quality standard requirements. With no-frills products, external suppliers can generally take a larger share of added value than they can for technically sophisticated premium products, because confidentiality requirements play a smaller role. The higher a manufacturer's own production costs are, the more advantageous outsourcing is. Given the risks associated with defective or missing deliveries, industrial companies should be able to realistically assess their suppliers' performance and reliability. This is often difficult for medium-sized Western companies, which are not familiar with supplier networks in emerging and developing markets.

The cost targets for no-frills products are ambitious. The approach for achieving them can be operationalized and enhanced with a number of additional tactics. Managers should pay particular attention to overhead costs. Although ethical rules such as job security are just as important as those governing premium products, expensive office equipment and complex administrative processes do not fit the no-frills strategy. A no-frills product approach also means no frills when it comes to internal structures.

Choosing a Brand

Industrial companies have to decide whether to manage no-frills products under separate brands (second brand) or integrate them into a premium product brand family (brand stretch) or hybrid structure (see Figure 3.13). The term "Siemens Cerberus ECO" is an example of the latter. In this case, the "Siemens" brand was combined with the new "Cerberus" brand.

Inside established industrial companies, the very idea of using an existing premium brand for no-frills products frequently becomes a topic of heated debate. Emotions run particularly high when the established brand is closely connected to the company's history. Opponents' main argument is that integrating no-frills products threatens to damage the premium brand name. Behind this rationale is the fear that a no-frills engagement would damage a brand image that is already associated with

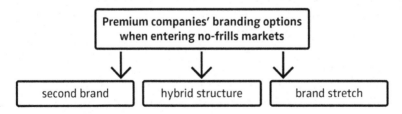

Figure 3.13: Branding opportunities for premium companies when introducing no-frills products.

high performance, technological innovation, durability, aesthetics, and similar positive values. In general, brand stretch has the potential to destroy market goodwill. Naturally, this becomes even more true if no-frills products fail to live up to their quality specifications.

These fears particularly come into play when the company decides to use frugal engineering. The risk of damage to the brand's reputation is considered to be lower if the company offers mature technology or defeatured premiums instead. The reasons for these divergent opinions are obvious. Old or pared-down products are still very much part of the company's tradition. They have direct links with the latest premium products. By contrast, new frugal products conflict with the company's traditional self-image. They do not settle well with premium-sector advocates. Psychological dynamics play a role here, too. Although there has been little research in this area to date, the dynamics are undoubtedly centered on terms such as pride and dignity. The selection of a remote location to develop and manufacture no-frills products also fuels intense debate. Ultimately, this relates back to the fear of losing fundamental power structures that have become part of the company's core paradigm.

For this reason, many Western industrial companies decide to sell no-frills products under a second brand. This is particularly the case if they have acquired a company from an emerging or developing country that is active and successful within its home market. The acquired company's product brand is typically used to market the less expensive product lines. This is an obvious solution as long as the brand is only sold in the region of the acquired company. Once marketing activities extend beyond these borders, however, new challenges emerge. In this case, managers must invest in the second brand to generate awareness in other countries. There may also be additional difficulties if the secondary brand name does not fit within the diverse cultural contexts of the other countries. This is where the advantages of being integrated into an internationally established premium brand become clear. Strong brand recognition and reputation make it easier to acquire new customer segments for their no-frills products beyond local borders.

Sub-brands are a hybrid approach for differentiating between premium and no-frills products. This is in spite of the fact that they share a common master brand name. Volkswagen is an excellent illustration of this strategy. Throughout the world, the carmaker sells both large SUVs, such as the Touareg, and inexpensive small cars, such as the Volkswagen up! Yet, the shared use of the Volkswagen brand does not damage the image of the carmaker's higher-quality cars. The sub-brands are so well positioned that customers see a clear relationship between their needs, product performance, and price. In order to further refine the brand-driven customer perception, Volkswagen has introduced an additional layer of branding. This includes performance sub-brands such as GTI that emphasize a vehicle's sportiness.

Incidentally, Volkswagen offers an interesting example as to cannibalization. In 1994, the group acquired the Czech car manufacturer Škoda. The carmaker produces cars similar in size to Volkswagen but sells them at a lower price. Volkswagen decided to continue using the Škoda brand and to gradually improve the quality of the cars. Volkswagen brand proponents were critical of this acquisition. They feared that Škoda could poach Volkswagen's customers and put margin pressure on Volkswagen vehicles. When the Volkswagen Group's then-CEO and co-owner, Ferdinand Piëch, was asked about it, he justified his decision with simple logic. He said he preferred to cannibalize Volkswagen with the company's own products rather than leave it up to competitors. This is a compelling argument. If a competitor such as Toyota or Ford had taken over the Czech carmaker, Volkswagen would have lost customers to them. Under this scenario, of course, the Volkswagen Group would not have benefited from the profits.

Managers should not lose sight of the ultimate goal of branding, particularly during intense discussions on the proper use of an existing parent brand. Historically, businesses have created brands in the consumer goods sector. This is because for certain products (e.g., beer) quality differs. Customers would not be able to recognize these differences before making a purchase. Brands help make performance promises. Despite a lack of product knowledge, customers could rely on the fact that when they buy a certain branded product, they will get exactly the quality they expected — regardless of place or time. Particularly in the consumer goods industry, companies engage in an intense effort to manage customer attitudes. Communications tactics can even prompt customers to perceive something in a brand that does not actually exist. For example, supermarket chains feature certain products that consumers believe are inexpensive. Extensive competitive analyses, however, do not confirm this assumption. In cases like this, suppliers use their brand to take advantage of non-transparent markets and a lack of product competence on the part of the customer.

In the B2B area, however, most markets are more transparent than those for consumer goods. There are fewer suppliers, and customers are more familiar with competing products; they have specialist knowledge and product competence. In fact, customer business managers sometimes have the same training and industry experience as those of supplier companies. Therefore, if the products do not have a high degree of complexity or customization, customers can make a good product assessment. Brands then play a less important role. This does not mean that brand choice is irrelevant for no-frills products, but rather that brands do not outweigh more decisive factors.

Bringing No-frills Products to Market

Industrial companies typically go to premium markets by using a direct sales force. They often complement the sales force with additional channels, such as technical sales, inside sales, and online channels. This multichannel structure reflects the premium positioning of these companies, allowing customers to purchase in multiple ways and according to their needs.[14]

When it comes to organizing no-frills product distribution, however, a key goal is achieving low overheads. Let us take a second look at the Siemens Cerberus ECO example to understand why. China was the largest growth market for these fire protection products. This growth was strongest in the medium-sized cities outside of major cities such as Beijing and Shanghai. Siemens had already employed thousands of sales employees across the Group in China to sell its premium products. Most of these people, however, worked in major cities. In a large country such as China, it would have been very expensive for the fire protection products division to create its very own international sales network. It also would have taken a lot of time.

Furthermore, sales staff from the major cities would have resisted being relocated to high-growth regions. This move would not have been cost effective, either. Salaries in Beijing and Shanghai were higher than

---

[14]P. Thaichon, J. Surachartkumtonkun, S. Quach, S. Weaven, and R. W. Palmatier, "Hybrid Sales Structures in the Age of E-commerce," *Journal of Personal Selling & Sales Management* 38, no. 3 (2018): 277–302; J. Habel, S. Alavi, and K. Linsenmayer, "From Personal to Online Selling: How Relational Selling Shapes Salespeople's Promotion of E-commerce Channels," *Journal of Business Research* 132 (2021): 373–382.

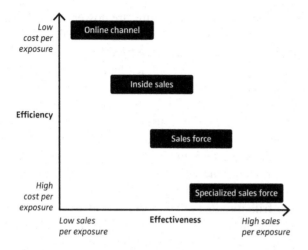

Figure 3.14: Efficiency and effectiveness of sales channels.[15]

those in cities outside of major metropolitan areas. In addition, these employees' relatively high salaries were based on their high qualification levels — a critical ingredient for marketing Siemens premium products. The sales staff had excellent technical knowledge. They were often engineers and able to present customized product variants to customers. This type of qualification, however, was not necessary to sell Siemens Cerberus ECO. As previously mentioned, no-frills products must be simple and largely standardized. The resulting products require fewer explanations. Customers, in turn, avoid having to conduct an in-depth requirements analysis, which would lead to expensive product customization.

For these reasons, industrial companies typically aim to use less expensive sales channels to reach no-frills customer segments. However, they thereby need to manage a trade-off between efficiency (cost per exposure) and effectiveness (sales per exposure), as illustrated in Figure 3.14. Sales forces tend to be effective but inefficient: Because they can closely engage with, consult, and influence customers, sales forces generate the highest sales per exposure. However, building up and maintaining a sales force is expensive, with average costs per sales call of more than $300. In contrast, online channels tend to be efficient but less effective: Customers serve themselves, which renders costs per exposure

---

[15]Based on A. A. Zoltners, P. Sinha, and S. E. Lorimer, *Sales Force Design for Strategic Advantage* (New York, NY: Palgrave Macmillan, 2004), p. 108.

marginal; however, sales per exposure are lower as well. Inside sales reside in the middle, with average costs per sales call of about $50.[16]

Accordingly, some companies have tried to save distribution costs by selling no-frills products through online channels. However, in emerging and developing markets, online channels are unlikely to generate the desired performance. First, they are inbound channels and thus rely on prospects approaching the seller. Ensuring that prospects know about the seller's online channel would require substantial investments into marketing communications. Second, in many emerging-markets, buyers regard personal contact with sellers as paramount, rendering online channels particularly ineffective. This brings us back to our earlier notion that the pursuit of a no-frills product strategy starts with a needs analysis — not just regarding the question of *what* customers want to purchase but also regarding the question of *how* customers want to purchase.

As a result, industrial companies typically conclude that selling no-frills products in emerging and developing markets *does* require an in-person sales force. However, in contrast to advanced premium products, the lower level of complexity of no-frills products allows sales staff to focus more on sales and less on customer consulting. According to the very simple marketing typology of Jagdish Sheth from Goizueta Business School, salespeople are either hunters or farmers. Sales-oriented hunters are more suited for no-frills products, whereas farmers and their relationship-building skills are more appropriate for managing premium product marketing. The sales employee compensation schemes should reflect these differences. Consequently, no-frills products have a higher variable salary component. Final compensation is based on actual total sales results.

The "hunting" sales approach was atypical for Siemens. It was one of the reasons why the company chose external sales partners to market Siemens Cerberus ECO. Managers sought "hunters" to sell within the target regions. An external sales force was tasked with building relationships with new, price-sensitive target customers to whom Siemens lacked access. Sales representatives were embedded into an existing functioning distribution system. Using their local expertise, these employees were better able to assess customer requirements, purchasing criteria, and

---

[16]See A. J. Frost, "60 Key Sales Statistics That'll Help You Sell Smarter in 2021," *Hubspot*, January 8, 2021. Retrieved from https://blog.hubspot.com/sales/sales-statistics. (Accessed July 2021).

creditworthiness of customers than Siemens. At least in the short term, choosing this indirect sales approach was more cost effective for Siemens than building up its own sales resources. It also shortened the time-to-market entry.

To achieve lower costs, faster market access, and closer customer proximity, most Western industrial companies eventually decide to use external sales partners to market no-frills products in emerging and developing countries. There is also another good but rarely mentioned argument for this strategy. Customer interaction, particularly with no-frills products, often falls into a gray area when it comes to Western compliance regulations. It is better therefore to manage sales with independent distributors. In this way, the manufacturers avoid legal problems and reputation damage, even though this approach can be criticized from an ethics perspective.

For no-frills product manufacturers, the main disadvantage of indirect selling is that it provides little control over external partners' activities. Their lack of control weighs particularly heavily, because sales staff in emerging and developing markets tend to carry out selling tasks less "professionally" than is preferred by Western managers. In fact, a recent study by Selma Kadić-Maglajlić, Nawar N. Chaker, and Maja Arslanagić-Kalajdžić concluded that "sales in emerging-markets are not professionalized and that, for the most part, salespeople do not receive specific training regarding the steps in the sales process (rare exceptions are the few salespeople who work for large multinational corporations)."[17] The authors noted the following differences in selling:

- To identify new prospects, salespeople in emerging and developing markets tend to heavily rely on publicly and internally available databases. Because these tend to be unreliable, salespeople also identify prospects through informal channels — sometimes illegally.
- Before approaching new prospects, salespeople in these markets tend to spend almost no time preparing. Relatedly, there are hardly any systematic processes in place to help salespeople prepare for meetings with prospects.

---

[17] S. Kadić-Maglajlić, N. N. Chaker, and M. Arslanagić-Kalajdžić, "The Same Only Different: Seven Steps of Selling in Emerging Markets," *A Research Agenda for Sales*, ed. F. Jaramillo and J. P. Mulki (Cheltenham: Edward Elgar Publishing, 2021), pp. 109–134.

- Once they have established contact with a prospect, salespeople in these markets tend to spend significantly more time building the relationship. They schedule several dedicated meetings to get to know the prospect before discussing business-related issues.
- Salespeople in these markets tend to spend less time identifying customer needs, and they are less likely to use a systematic process or questioning technique. They also tend to use standardized presentations rather than customizing their presentations to individual prospects.
- When it comes to overcoming objections, negotiating, and closing, salespeople in these markets typically have no dedicated training — and once again, no systematic processes in place.
- In after-sales, salespeople spend significant time taking care of accounts receivable. This is because customers in emerging and developing markets often do not respect payment deadlines. The authors quote one sales manager who states that "selling does not end when we sell the product, but when the invoice is paid."

Obviously, these insights cannot be generalized to all emerging and developing markets or to all salespeople within these markets. However, they point to the fact that Western managers' expectations are often challenged in no-frills markets, with little control in case managers decided to go to market through an indirect sales channel.

Industrial companies also fear the effects of cannibalization if external sales partners try to sell lower-priced products to premium customers. This threat, however, is not so much a matter of incorrect sales structures as it is a lack of product differentiation. If no-frills and premium products clearly target different needs, only one of the two offers will meet customer requirements. Once there is sufficient differentiation, the two offers will not compete against one another. For some customers, on the other hand, the two product categories may actually complement one another.

With this dynamic in mind, Körber uses the same sales representatives to sell its tissue-processing machines in India, its premium products from Fabio Perini, and its inexpensive machines from Sheer. The product that customers ultimately choose depends on their needs and willingness to pay. We explain the synergy opportunities between no-frills products and premium products, as well as their related risks, in more detail in Chapter 5.

Organizational Setting

It is possible that brand and go-to-market considerations take up too much time during the no-frills market-entry planning phase. As a result, companies can pay too little attention to profit targets and group-related overhead costs. "Group-related overhead" refers to cost allocations for the head office. They include board member salaries, central advertising budgets, additional training activities, and even basic research. In most industrial companies, these costs are added to manufacturing costs as a percentage. Accordingly, they are included in no-frills product calculations, as well as in the responsible business unit's profit and loss figures. At the earliest sign that a no-frills business segment will miss profit targets, managers begin to question whether or not this business should carry the same overhead costs as an established premium product business with many years of market presence. Managers with no-frills product responsibility typically argue that the levels of competition and cost pressures are particularly high. Compared to competitors from emerging and developing countries, they claim high group overhead costs put the no-frills business at a considerable cost disadvantage.

From the perspective of the overall organization, how to deal with this argument has to be considered. Some companies have changed group-wide overhead cost allocation rules altogether. They have lowered the corresponding surcharge rates for no-frills business segments. Under this scenario, no-frills entities are only charged for the services that headquarters specifically provides for that business segment. This might include the right to use the company's premium brands, for example. Market rates could then be used as a reference price. In terms of cost accounting, no-frills entities would be treated as an external institution. This applies even if they belong entirely to the premium supplier.

Central controlling departments, however, are not keen to allow sector-specific exceptions to the traditional cost structures. Usually, they pave the way for other business segments to request further exceptions. In this respect, making exceptions in the cost rules for no-frills entities can create disunity within a company. It can also make the accounting process more complex. Rather than exposing the organization to these challenges, companies would be better advised to set alternative profitability targets to assess no-frills business success. Industrial companies such as Siemens and GE, which operate in numerous business segments, typically establish profit targets that are tied to specific industries. This allows managers to set different profit targets without major complications — even if both no-frills products and premium products are sold within the same industry.

The topic of goal-setting, however, raises some vital questions. Who defines business goals for a no-frills product segment in the first place? Where should this segment be positioned within the corporate group? These distinctions are especially important for established industrial companies with successful premium product business units. It should be carefully considered whether new no-frills product units should be placed under their control. There is a risk that premium-segment managers will not give the no-frills business enough freedom to develop successfully. The premium managers' emotional resentment toward no-frills products was mentioned in the previous section. Even if premium product managers are acting in good faith, they will often find it difficult to free themselves from their resentment. This can lead to frustration and the loss of good employees in the no-frills segment. This is particularly true when the no-frills entity has been incorporated into the premium company through acquisitions. Trumpf applied this rationale when it acquired the Chinese no-frills provider JFY for its laser machine business unit in 2013. Consequently, the head of JFY reported directly to Trumpf's top management and co-owners.

Separating these two segments within the organization, however, makes little sense if senior management forces them to collaborate. One reason to do this would be to realize potential synergies that benefit no-frills and premium segments alike.[18] Both segments should cooperate when there is growing market demand for products positioned between no-frills and premium products. Kion faced this market trend. As previously mentioned, Kion began selling no-frills forklifts when it acquired Baoli in China in 2010. At the same time, it sold forklifts in the premium segment under the established brand Linde. In the 2010s, however, Chinese demand grew for a forklift solution in the medium-quality and medium-price range. Linde's attempts to meet this need by "defeaturing" were not compelling. Neither were Baoli's efforts to upgrade its forklift trucks. In both cases, the companies failed to achieve the necessary balance between quality and cost requirements. Kion responded by moving

---

[18]See the discussion on synergy potential in Chapter 5.

in a new direction in 2019. The company asked the engineers of both subsidiaries to jointly develop a new forklift that would address the market requirements for an "intermediate product."

Similarly, Trumpf aims to step up cooperation between its premium division and JFY, because managers increasingly see a very clear synergy potential. In order to ensure cross-segment coordination and foster tighter operational collaboration, in 2019 Trumpf decided to no longer have JFY lead the companies' top management and co-owners, but rather to use managers who are one hierarchy level lower and closer to the operative business.

In addition to these types of organizational changes, a common cultural understanding among the team members of both groups is even more important for achieving successful collaboration. A longer integration process may also be necessary, particularly if the no-frills area has worked independently for a long time or under another corporate umbrella. In this respect, integrating a no-frills business unit within an organization is also a matter of time. Although the units should be allowed to operate separately during the initial phase, integration should be a priority after that. The same applies in the reverse scenario, in which no-frills suppliers launch or acquire premium product business units. Managing these types of integrated segments requires managers who are familiar with both businesses.

Opening Up for a No-frills Product Strategy

The promise of additional sales growth, profits, competitive entry barriers, and new sources of synergies should entice Western industrial companies to eagerly bring no-frills products to market. Some experts even go so far as to label this an imperative. For example, the discoverer of hidden champions, Hermann Simon, recently stated that hidden champions "must not ignore the ultra-low-price segment."[19]

More often than not, however, top managers of industrial companies do not implement true no-frills product strategies. We observe three reasons for this. The first reason is managers' wrong assumption that they are already offering no-frills products, when in fact they are not. Although

---

[19]H. Simon, *Hidden Champions — Aufbruch nach Globalia: Die Erfolgsstrategien unbekannter Weltmarktführer* (New York, NY: Campus Frankfurt, 2012), p. 257.

many industrial companies have lower-priced offerings for emerging and developing markets, these offerings are frequently still premium by local standards. An example is BharatBenz, Daimler Truck's brand for the Indian market. BharatBenz might qualify as a low-cost/low-priced offering compared to Daimler Truck's other brands, such as Mercedes-Benz Trucks or Western Star. Compared to local competitors in the Indian truck market, though, BharatBenz is a premium brand, "[e]ngineered with globally proven technology, the best-in-class safety, unmatched reliability and the lowest total cost of ownership."[20]

The second reason for managers to refrain from implementing a no-frills product strategy is the considerable risk such a strategy involves. As we explained, bringing no-frills products to market requires companies to take vastly different approaches, including the design of different business models, different development and production processes, different sales channels and approaches, and the development of different organizational setups. Given the scope of these changes, managers fear a high probability of failing and thus shy away from no-frills product strategies.

Third, as we pointed out earlier, a more covert reason might be at play: pride and dignity. Western industrial companies' identities often revolve around their premium quality and premium prices. Managers who advance this premium positioning receive respect and admiration from their customers, peers, shareholders, and the general public. Managers who do not, do not. This may contribute to managers' previously discussed resentment toward no-frills products. It may also lead them to focus on implementing novel premium strategies rather than no-frills strategies. One premium strategy that leads to particular gains in pride and dignity is the move from goods to solutions. We discuss this strategy in the next chapter.

---

[20] See BharatBenz homepage: https://www.bharatbenz.com/. (Accessed July 2021).

Chapter 4

Complex Service Solutions: Bringing Digital Offerings to Industrial Markets

Abstract

In this chapter, we discuss how industrial companies can exploit digital technologies to develop complex service solutions. For this purpose, we first analyze the discrepancies between the high expectations and the sobering results inherent to this strategic option. We then show which targets are realistic for industrial companies and how to successfully develop complex service solutions. We discuss which communication policy to use when marketing them and analyze the financial logic of innovative business models — in particular, the risks and opportunities of usage-based or performance-based pricing. Additional emphasis is put on the need to reorganize a company's sales system when introducing complex service solutions. We examine the qualifications that salespeople must have and the organizational structure that industrial companies need to create in order to successfully market complex service solutions worldwide. We also discuss the challenges that industrial companies face when bringing digital services to market — a common first step on their way toward complex service solutions.

The Siemens Soarian Case

In 2001, Siemens AG launched Soarian in the healthcare business sector. It was a revolutionary offering. By using an IT-based solution platform that collected and evaluated data, hospital processes could be improved for all types of patients and treatments, as well as for departments and products. The system allowed hospitals to follow the progress of individual work steps and automatically identified anomalies and weak points, in addition to proactively alerting hospital staff.

Siemens initially focused on the North American market. The company was soon able to gain a number of customers, including the renowned Massachusetts General Hospital in Boston. Nevertheless, the new business area's profitability numbers remained below the set targets for many years. As a result, management decided to sell the business in 2014 and sold Soarian that very year to Cerner — a well-known IT and consulting company in the industry — for $1.3 billion.

Why were profits unsatisfactory in spite of successful customer acquisition? When it launched Soarian, Siemens AG had already been in the healthcare sector for more than 100 years. The company focused on developing, producing, and marketing imaging devices based on X-rays, ultrasound, computer tomography, and magnetic resonance imaging (see Figure 4.1). Yet, new competitors — many of whom were concentrated in emerging and developing countries — were increasingly approaching the market with their devices. Among them was Mindray Medical International Limited, a global medical instrumentation developer, manufacturer, and marketer founded in Shenzhen, China, in 1991. Some of these competitors were able to achieve a high level of device quality in a short time. At the same time, competitors were not always in compliance with intellectual property protection regulations. Their low prices put pressure on established suppliers' profit margins. For this reason — and because healthcare cost-cutting had become an increasingly important issue in many countries — Siemens wanted to offer hospitals innovative service solutions to help customers achieve more effective and efficient processes.

The complexity of this new offering went far beyond Siemens' traditional businesses, which focused on medical devices, and the related maintenance and repair services. To launch the new solution offering, Siemens AG bought a software company that was active in the healthcare sector. At the same time, the company created a new business area within Siemens Healthcare. As many as 1,400 software engineers started developing the comprehensive solutions platform. Siemens gave hospitals a choice when they made their purchase decision. They could buy the software license, software adaptation, system implementation, maintenance, and consulting services at fixed prices. Alternatively, they could base compensation on future efficiency improvements.

Figure 4.1:   A Siemens Soarian advertisement.

In order to adapt the solutions to a hospital's specific needs, specialists from Siemens first needed to analyze a hospital's related work processes. They then identified areas for potential improvement. Subsequently, they configured and implemented the IT system. All the necessary process changes could be implemented in a way that suited employees.

In 2016, we interviewed Tom Miller, then head of Soarian and member of the board of Siemens Healthcare from 2005 to 2013. We asked him about the key lessons he had learned from the Soarian business failure. He identified five:

- "We lost too much time and money developing software that fulfilled our vision for the customer's functional requirements, and we lost sight of the true prioritized needs and costs of the actual customer."
- "We overestimated our knowledge and capabilities of the entire healthcare enterprise, as well as the necessity to integrate the installed base of competitors' products in our complex service."
- "We overestimated our knowledge and ability to change processes and culture when going from the business for high-tech machines to the business of complex service solutions. Our extremely successful processes for medical device capital equipment development and sales were actually a liability in the solutions business."
- "We underestimated how different our people's skills portfolio requirements would be. The people from the traditional business did not even have the right skills to interview the necessary candidates."
- "We miscalculated the financial logic of these kinds of businesses regarding time, cash requirements, and flows, as well as risk projections and mitigation."

These statements contradict the preconception that managers do not admit their mistakes. At least that is not the case with Miller. In addition, his responses reveal the problems and causes that are equally relevant for other industrial companies as they enter the complex service solutions market.

What Are Complex Service Solutions?

To answer this question, we turn once again to Soarian. To what extent did Soarian projects differ from the traditional Siemens imaging devices business? Three criteria were decisive:

1. The new projects were highly complex.
2. They included a high proportion of customized services.
3. They had a strong business impact on customers.

We refer to transactions with these characteristics as complex service solutions. In the following discussion, we focus on solutions that place a high priority on the use of digital technologies.

A high level of complexity means that the solution's functionality is influenced by many variables. Some of these functions are interdependent, making the exact results unpredictable. Soarian had an impact on so many employees, devices, and diverse processes in a hospital that it was impossible to predict detailed results. Transactions with a high degree of complexity have always existed, of course. Just think about plant construction, in which power plants, drilling rigs, or entire production factories are sold on a turnkey basis. Digital technologies allow more industrial companies to increase the complexity of their offerings and enable them to take over larger parts of their customers' added value.

Digital technologies, of course, are not new. They have been in use since 1959, when IBM introduced its legendary transistor computer "1401" to improve operational process efficiency. Back in 1973, Joseph Harrington introduced his "computer-integrated manufacturing" (CIM), a forerunner to the networking concept known today as "Industry 4.0." CIM, however, has never been implemented on a broad basis. The company-wide use of digital technologies has only recently become more widespread with the explosion in potential uses. This, in turn, is based on more powerful hardware and software for generating, storing, and processing data.

An often-cited example of this development that we introduced in Chapters 1 and 2 is the "power by the hour" offering from the Rolls-Royce aircraft turbines division. The company introduced this business model as early as 1962, but its industry-wide breakthrough only came with increasing digitization. Today, an aircraft turbine includes thousands of sensors. The related data are then transmitted to IT-based systems for analysis and evaluation. The turbine's technical condition can be monitored at any time, and both maintenance and utilization can be improved. The more turbine data, the greater the impact. In the meantime, Rolls-Royce no longer sells the majority of the aircraft turbines it manufactures. Instead, the manufacturer operates them as part of its power by the hour offering. In doing so, the company is able to collect more data than the airlines and can maintain the turbines more efficiently. Yet, Rolls-Royce's two major competitors — Pratt & Whitney and GE — introduced this type of complex service solution as well. GE is now even the market leader, and it sums up the digital core of its offerings with the slogan "Collect, Connect, Detect, Direct".

Using these concepts, manufacturers no longer sell physical products to customers. Instead, they offer a service. In the case example above, it is a transport service for aircraft. These services are considered to be intangible and are viewed as being different from tangible goods. Research has revealed further criteria by which goods and services differ.[1] It should be noted that, in order to deliver these services, suppliers and customers must cooperate and thereby "co-create" the service. Even with a relatively simple service such as a haircut, the supplier and customer need to co-create. Hairdressers, for instance, can only provide their services if customers express what they want and keep their heads still during the service.

For complex projects, co-creation begins with an initial situation analysis, in which the customer gives the supplier essential information. If a hospital provides incorrect data about the number of patients or treatments performed, for example, processes cannot be optimized with Soarian. Even after implementing a solution, customer behavior is critical to success. If hospital staff operate the new software incorrectly, the hoped-for improvements will not be achieved.

---

[1]V. A. Zeithaml, A. Parasuraman, and L. L. Berry, "Problems and Strategies in Service Marketing," *Journal of Marketing* 49, no. 4 (1985): 33–46.

Although the added value of complex service solutions is service driven, goods can help complete the overall solution.[2] The many variables that affect the success of complex service solutions are different for each customer. That is why they must be customer-specific solutions to the greatest extent possible, even if the offering includes standardized hardware and software products in addition to services. Accordingly, we discuss solutions instead of products.

In addition, complex service solutions only refer to solutions that strongly impact the customer's value creation processes and the related costs and revenues. This means that successful implementation can deliver significant advantages to the customer. Failure, on the other hand, can cause significant damage. With Soarian, for example, hospitals realized substantial savings. But a system crash during a surgery would be a catastrophe. That is why customers attach great importance to the purchase of complex service solutions. They are aware of the tremendous risk involved with the purchase decision.

Given this business impact for their customers, suppliers of complex service solutions hope their customers are willing to pay more in order to receive high sales returns. They also hope to achieve smooth revenue streams to counteract the industrial product business cycle. In the latter approach, they expect upside revenue potential for their traditional business. If Soarian gave Siemens insight into a hospital's entire set of processes, it would recognize customer demand for new imaging devices before competitors did. In addition, complex service solutions promise to provide industrial companies with market entry barriers for new competitors. This is because the skills required to provide complex service solutions are difficult to copy.

As a result, many established industrial companies from industrialized countries view complex service solutions as a new strategic opportunity for the future of their businesses. In the past, most of these businesses were satisfied with the development and sale of advanced, continuously improved premium products such as imaging devices, elevators, and gas turbines. But the number of competitors has increased, with many of the new entrants coming from emerging countries. This trend has been

---

[2]Ulaga and Reinartz also refer to hybrid offerings in this context. The focus is only on goods and services, however. They are less geared toward software or digital solutions. See W. Ulaga and W. J. Reinartz, "Hybrid Offerings: How Manufacturing Firms Combine Goods and Services Successfully," *Journal of Marketing* 75, no. 6 (2011): 5–23.

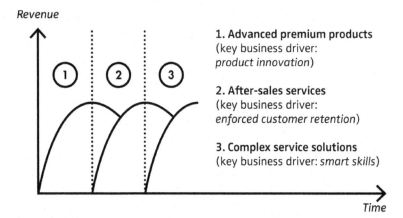

Figure 4.2: Three phases of business model development of established industrial companies.

accompanied by price pressure. As a result, established suppliers have changed their business models in order to focus their profit generation from product-selling to after-sales services. But here, too, competitive and margin pressures have increased in recent years because of copied spare parts, regulatory interventions, declining customer loyalty, and reduced profits. Complex service solutions are an alternative in this scenario. The scope of the offering gets broader while the development of the new offering is based on previous business. Figure 4.2 illustrates the three phases of business model development.

In order to take advantage of market entry barriers with complex service solutions, industrial companies must first overcome their own barriers. We explore the "smart skills" mentioned in Figure 4.2 later. Even without a more detailed analysis, there are clearly enormous challenges associated with complexity, digital technologies, and customer-specific requirements. In addition, the level of customer pressure on suppliers is particularly high because of the business impact of complex service solutions. Suppliers also face the pressure of performance-based compensation (e.g., power by the hour models).

Setting the Goals

Before suppliers define sales and earnings goals for complex service solutions, they should first be clear about their strategic market relevance.

Industrial companies that are successful with advanced premium products must ask themselves the following questions:

- How will our market position develop if we do *not* pursue this strategic option?
- To what extent will we continue to maintain our quality leadership in traditional markets through constant innovation?
- Can our products be copied?
- Are our high profits in after-sales services guaranteed in the future?
- To what extent will the new digital technologies change our customers' needs, industry value chains, and market position?

An example from the automotive industry illustrates this issue concerning strategic market relevance: The residents of large cities increasingly want to rent cars on short notice instead of buying them. Carsharing is a digital platform-based business model that addresses this need. An automobile manufacturer such as Daimler has to pose a critical question: What happens if a company such as Google achieves a dominant market position in the carsharing business? Daimler could still sell cars. Instead of selling to private customers as before, it would primarily sell to Google. Given the purchasing power of a market leader such as Google, Daimler could hardly expect high margins in this scenario. This is what prompted Daimler to pursue carsharing in its own right.

In addition to such defensive measures, suppliers are trying to generate new sales and achieve profit growth with new strategies. The Soarian example demonstrates why this is not always possible when introducing complex service solutions. In fact, the company did not meet set earnings targets for 12 years. Similarly, profits for Rolls-Royce's power by the hour model have not been particularly strong in recent years. In some cases, there have been losses. In both cases, the results fell short of expectations for management, employees, and shareholders. What were the underlying causes?

Erroneous actions or unrealistic expectations are the reasons behind disappointing results. At Soarian, the implementation was clearly wrong. But Tom Miller's mentioning of a different "financial logic" points to false expectations. It is important to realize that complex service solutions follow different cost and revenue stream patterns than the advanced premium products that helped Siemens succeed. These patterns are shown in a simplified form in Figure 4.3.

FINANCIAL PATTERN OF THE TRADITIONAL GOODS BUSINESS

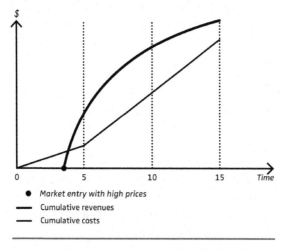

● *Market entry with high prices*
— Cumulative revenues
— Cumulative costs

FINANCIAL PATTERN OF SOARIAN BUSINESS

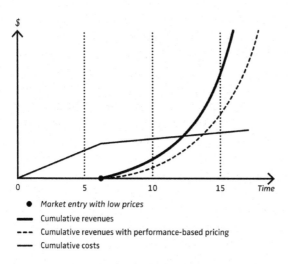

● *Market entry with low prices*
— Cumulative revenues
--- Cumulative revenues with performance-based pricing
— Cumulative costs

Figure 4.3: Development of cost and revenue streams for the advanced premium products of Siemens Healthcare (top) and Soarian (bottom).

Imaging equipment manufacturers initially invest in innovative product development. In addition to personnel costs, companies typically incur expenses for production facility equipment, raw material purchases, and parts. Because new product models are more powerful than their predecessors, the companies can command higher prices. If the new devices become technically obsolete over time, the price level drops and the sales curve tips downward. The cost and revenue flow patterns were different at Soarian. The company incurred initial development costs. Yet, no expensive production facilities had to be set up. There was only the need for employees to be hired and trained.

An even bigger difference between traditional product business and complex service solutions is the revenue curve. On top of that, the basis for creating value with data-based solutions must be understood. The more data that are evaluated, the more valuable the analytical results. It generates more valid predictions and actionable recommendations. By engaging with a larger number of customers over a longer period of time, suppliers can build a better knowledge base. Because of constantly improving data analysis, software errors can be eliminated over time with the help of version updates. As a result, an offering such as the one from Soarian provides customers with more benefits over time than during market launch. Customers are aware of this, and it impacts their willingness to pay. The benefits start out small and gradually increase. This results in the concave sales curve shown in Figure 4.3. If suppliers link earnings to customer-driven performance improvements (i.e., "performance-based pricing"), revenues are delayed once again. This is because performance improvements will only appear over time. This phenomenon is illustrated in Figure 4.3 with a dashed line.

In spite of this diagram's simplified approach, it makes one point very clear: The level of profitability of complex service solutions is lower in the early years when compared to a traditional product business. Over the following years, profitability can improve significantly. In the case of Soarian, it may very well be that the time periods shown above actually reflect reality. This is because Cerner, which bought Soarian from Siemens in 2014, is "very satisfied" with Soarian's results.

As with complex service solutions, revenue curves of this shape can be observed in other categories of offerings. One example is telephony. The telephone's core customer benefit only exists if other customers have a connection. The more customers there are, the more calls can be made, and the greater the value of the telephone for the customer.

Obviously, the Siemens Central Executive Board and healthcare sector colleagues set overly optimistic financial goals for Soarian. The financial logic and the risks of complex service solutions were misjudged. How can this happen to such experienced managers? Research by Kahneman and Lovallo provides surprising and insightful answers in this regard.[3] The two scholars (Kahneman became well known as the winner of the Nobel Prize in Economic Sciences in 2002) examined human risk behavior. They found that people are fundamentally risk averse. When people are presented with the same probabilities and quantitative effects, they will rate the impact of a potential loss higher than a potential profit. Given the business risks that managers take, the researchers wondered whether managers are less risk averse than other people. They found that this was not the case. Instead, they observed that managers either did not perceive risks or they overestimated their ability to handle them.

If managers' decisions have led to business success and personal advancement, this can lead to high levels of self-confidence. Such self-confidence can, in turn, lead managers to infrequently seek out other opinions or brush off critical feedback about their own plans. As a result, they may think they are able to master any challenges that arise. Even when the board of directors' culture allows for an open exchange of views, misjudgments can persist if all involved parties evaluate business matters from a similar perspective. This can lead to the confirmation of wrong opinions. In order to remedy this, Kahneman and Lovallo suggest involving external, independent participants when evaluating ideas or strategic plans.

In addition to the risk of overoptimistic projections, there is the problem of inappropriate target criteria. This often happens when an industrial company deals with complex service solutions for the first time. The new business requires different target criteria than the traditional business. This, at least, is the result of studies by O'Reilly and Tushman, which differentiate between "exploitation" and "exploration" in business.[4] With exploitation, the focus is on improving the efficiency of existing businesses, including incremental innovations. Exploration, on the other hand, focuses on building new businesses based on extensive innovations. O'Reilly and Tushman demonstrate that each approach requires its own

---

[3]D. Kahneman and D. Lovallo, "Timid Choices and Bold Forecasts: A Cognitive Perspective on Risk Taking," *Management Science* 39, no. 1 (1993): 17–31.
[4]C. A. O'Reilly and M. L. Tushman, "The Ambidextrous Organization," *Harvard Business Review* 82, no. 4 (2004): 74–81.

processes, culture, and leadership. The same applies to the target criteria. In traditional business, it is appropriate to set profit margin targets. In new business, it makes more sense to base targets on process goals, including successfully performing certain activities. This is because the information for reliable sales and cost planning does not yet exist. Without these important distinctions, the introduction of complex service solutions quickly generates unrealistic projections. This, in turn, leads to irritation and disappointment down the road.

Designing the Offering

The initiative to develop complex service solutions should come from the supplier, not the customer. This statement is supported by the results of an academic study from 2020. Researchers examined 299 European industrial companies that had introduced complex service solutions.[5] Managers rated the financial results of internal corporate initiatives significantly higher than the ones initiated by the customers.

How can we explain these results? The second group's decision to start development may have been linked to deadlines or even price commitments. As shown above, these can quickly turn out to be too optimistic. If the commitments are part of a contract, suppliers may earn limited profits. In addition, suppliers can be overwhelmed by inaccurate forecasts. This, in turn, can put so much pressure on employees that their performance suffers. The Yerkes–Dodson law,[6] which was introduced in 1908, provides a psychological explanation. According to this research, individual performance levels grow when the level of activation increases. If the level of activation continuously increases, performance levels decline. Figure 4.4 illustrates this phenomenon.

In order to avoid the risk of over-activation, it is better for suppliers to start the development process for complex service solutions before they make firm customer commitments. This process should be customer-oriented. Accordingly, suppliers must first analyze the customer's value creation processes and related ecosystems, as this provides the foundation

---

[5] J. Dannenbaum, L. M. Edinger-Schons, M. Rese, O. Plötner, and J. Wieseke, "What Does It Take to Successfully Implement a Hybrid Offering Strategy? A Contingency Perspective," *Journal of Management Research* 4, nos. 2–3 (2020): 100–120.

[6] R. M. Yerkes and J. D. Dodson, "The Relation of Strength of Stimulus to Rapidity of Habit-formation," *Journal of Comparative Neurology and Psychology* 18 (1908): 459–482.

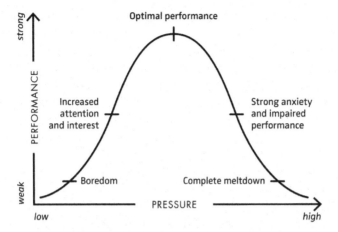

Figure 4.4: Relationship between individual activation and performance.
Source: Yerkes and Dodson (1908).

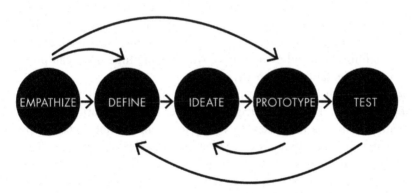

Figure 4.5: The five process stages of design thinking.

for pursuing potential efficiency improvements. They can also use "design thinking" methodology — a structured procedure for creating ideas. Design thinking helps to shed light on complex user problems and to find underlying — that is, not obvious — root causes. Customers do not actually need to be aware of a specific need. In this respect, this methodology is a particularly suitable option for industrial companies that are pursuing complex service solutions.

The design thinking methodology usually comprises five phases, which are shown in Figure 4.5. Innovators do not necessarily have to follow them in consecutive order but can iterate them.

When analyzing the customer's value creation process, innovators often use a so-called persona. It is a fictitious character that represents a typical customer type, including specific traits and usage patterns. Innovators usually build personas from customer interviews. This analysis helps them to closely align new offerings with actual customer needs and keeps the development process from getting out of hand. Otherwise, innovators may try to please every customer and lose focus. For Soarian, for example, Siemens could have analyzed a hypothetical university clinic in a Western country. The persona specification could have been as precise as possible without being unique. In this way, suppliers can later apply at least some of the analytical findings to other customers in the corresponding market segment.

For a further examination of design thinking, please refer to the comprehensive literature available.[7] We emphasize one aspect here, as it is atypical of the development processes of industrial companies. When using design thinking, suppliers should build diverse teams with members from different disciplines. We discussed this recommendation in the previous section as part of the Kahneman and Lovallo research results. By ensuring diverse experiences and views among those involved, managers can minimize risk and avoid errors. At the same time, they can promote customer-orientation and creativity.

Anyone who uses the design thinking method will develop a whole range of ideas. These then need to be assessed and prioritized. The key question concerns the extent to which the implementation can improve efficiency in the customer's value creation process and how it can achieve benefits. This customer benefit should be quantified more precisely over the course of the process. A clear case for customer profits will make a subsequent market launch much easier.

In addition, managers must keep an idea's feasibility and business benefits in mind. Suppliers should prioritize accumulated ideas by focusing first on the "lowest-hanging fruit" — applications that give customers as many advantages as possible, and that suppliers can deliver relatively quickly, cheaply, and reliably. When expanding the scope of an offering, industrial companies that have previously marketed advanced premium products should avoid taking on activities with weak added value or those

---

[7]T. Brown, "Design Thinking," *Harvard Business Review* 86, no. 6 (2008): 84–92. M. Kupp, J. Anderson, and J. Reckhenrich, "Why Design Thinking in Business Needs a Rethink," *MIT Sloan Management Review* 59, no. 1 (2017): 41–44.

which require employee qualifications that are seldom available in-house. The mechanical engineering company Voith gained this insight when it assumed system maintenance responsibilities for its newly launched Industrial Services division. This involved taking on numerous employees who performed simple cleaning jobs and other unskilled activities. The employees benefited greatly from Voith's high level of social benefits. Yet, the high related labor costs made it difficult for the company to become cost competitive. The loss-making division was sold again in 2016.

The Siemens Building Technology division had a similar experience in the 1990s. Instead of simply selling its hardware products to airports, Siemens wanted to start to partially operate the facilities. As it turns out, Siemens found managing personnel-intensive security services to be overwhelming because of the company's employee culture. The division quickly incurred costs that were significantly higher than those of its competitors. After a short time, the Building Technology division gave up on operating airports. It did not, however, stop pursuing the strategic option of complex service solutions. Managers had learned that complex service solutions should be designed in such a way that modern technology — rather than employees — could assume simple, repetitive tasks. Accordingly, the division developed digital applications under the name "Navigator." These solutions made it possible to comprehensively analyze and proactively optimize the energy consumption of buildings. Most of the work is done by sensors and intelligent software programs, which are controlled by a handful of highly qualified employees. Based on that, Siemens Building Technology successfully took over the building management of 1,000 office buildings of the Credit Suisse Group AG. Incidentally, Siemens Building Technology's primary form of compensation is based on its customers' energy savings.

When developing software, industrial companies should not adopt the processes and quality standards of their traditional product areas. This is another lesson from the Siemens Soarian case, in which the company developed software to the same high standards that it did with its imaging devices. Yet, it is impossible to design software that is completely free of errors. Even if it were possible, it would cost so much time and so many resources that business parameters would be unmanageable. That is why the famous Mark Zuckerberg rule "Done is better than perfect" still applies to companies such as Amazon, Google, and Facebook. In the case of software-based innovations, advocates of design thinking even advise testing market acceptance with a version that has been reduced to its essentials — a so-called minimum viable product or prototype. The perfection trap is all the more daunting when a supplier's market approach includes satisfying every single customer requirement. When suppliers ask customers what they want, it creates customer expectations that are not worthwhile or cannot be realistically pursued. The balance between customer-orientation and cost-orientation would be lost. At the time, Soarian addressed its customers' diverse requirements by creating one of the most extensive software products available on the market (measured in lines of code). Yet, it was not completed on time. From a technical perspective, it was almost impossible to manage.

Customer collaboration is nonetheless a key success factor for complex service solutions. As we pointed out above, service-driven offerings require a greater degree of customer co-creation. This means that customers must become an integral part of the actual service provision process. In doing so, they become a production factor.[8] For this reason, it is vital to plan customer collaboration and to align it with the supplier's own processes.

A helpful approach to visualization is "service blueprinting", introduced by Lynn Shostack in the 1980s. It was later developed most notably by Kleinaltenkamp and Fliess.[9] A service is presented in the form of a chronological flow chart that illustrates work processes from the customer's perspective. The activities are assigned to specific action levels. These are then further subdivided according to the following criteria: A customer interaction is required (interaction line), the interaction is visible to the customer (visibility line), and the processes require internal coordination with the supplier (internal interaction line). Figure 4.6 illustrates this approach.

This type of structure helps suppliers develop structured methodologies and workflows, which prevent having to start new projects from scratch.

---

[8] Since the publication of Vargo and Lusch in 2004, a new theoretical paradigm has even developed in management science under the keyword "service-dominant logic." See S. L. Vargo and R. F. Lusch, "Evolving to a New Dominant Logic for Marketing," *Journal of Marketing* 68, no. 1 (2004): 1–17.

[9] G. L. Shostack, "Designing Services That Deliver," *Harvard Business Review* 62, no. 1 (1984): 133–139. M. Kleinaltenkamp and S. Fliess, "Blueprinting the Service Company: Managing Service Processes Efficiently," *Journal of Business Research* 57, no. 4 (2004): 392–404.

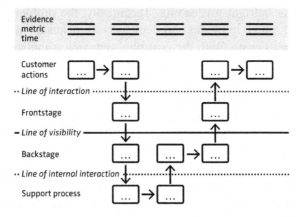

Figure 4.6: Service blueprint.

Complex service solutions are difficult to scale, as they are highly complex and customer specific. We see this as one of their greatest challenges. Yet, that is precisely why suppliers should design individual service elements and processes — so that they can be used in other projects. This provides an important opportunity to generate acceptable profits by keeping costs under control. In summary, the following axiom applies to developing complex service solutions: "As much customization as necessary. As much standardization as possible."

Setting the Price

For a traditional industrial company, the development of complex service solutions is associated with radical changes in business models. Companies must redefine the ownership of assets and data. They must assign value creation processes to market partners. Finally, they must rethink how to redistribute value-added profits among market partners. The structure of the price, terms, and conditions, then, is critically important for these processes.

In many industrial companies, price is still determined on the basis of "cost plus". Businesses start by calculating direct product costs. A surcharge is then added to cover overhead costs based on a calculated rate. Finally, a profit margin is added. This pricing method, even for advanced premium products, is not a preferable approach. For digital-based offerings, it is outright misleading. Technically, the problem lies in the software's marginal, individual product costs. It makes no sense to apply related overhead costs. With the cost plus approach, suppliers risk either setting prices too high above the market level, or missing out on profit opportunities due to low prices.

In principle, prices should reflect the value that a service provides for the customer. Hermann Simon, one of the most renowned experts in this field, likes to refer to the Latin word *pretium*, which stands for both the price and the value of a service. The problem is that it is difficult to determine the value of a service to a customer. In B2B markets, for example, several people are often involved in a purchase decision on the customer side. People make different individual assessments, which may be subject to change. We can pour a glass of water at home from the water faucet. We can also reach for that same glass of water in a half-dehydrated state in the middle of the desert. The relative value of these two glasses of water is very different. Therefore, the value of a service is not a stable quantity. It is instead a question of subjective perception at a specific point in time.

Even outside the range of complex service solutions, the problem for many industrial companies is that customers do not recognize the value of a service offering. The amount they are willing to pay is lower than the target price of the supplier. Managers of mechanical engineering companies, for example, report that Asian customers, in particular, are fixated on the purchase price. They do not adjust their willingness to pay according to a machine's value in terms of long-term consumption savings, even when presented with lifecycle cost analyses. This is true even when long-term consumption costs greatly exceed the purchase price.[10] As discussed in Chapter 3, washroom and workwear supplier CWS-boco faced similar challenges and failed to succeed with complex service solutions on the Chinese market.

In addition to the fundamental difficulty in anticipating the long-term value of a service, customer skepticism plays a role — both in terms of the analyses and promises that suppliers make. This is particularly

---

[10]Twenty years ago, Wise and Baumgartner analyzed the difference between a product's value at purchase and its value throughout the lifecycle for a variety of industrial assets. They found that the costs for working with locomotives are 21 times higher than their purchase price. R. Wise and P. Baumgartner, "Go Downstream. The New Profit Imperative in Manufacturing," *Harvard Business Review* 77, no. 5 (1999): 133–141.

important if the customer faces high upfront risks and costs, but the actual benefits of the service only become apparent over time.

This aspect plays a major role in complex service solutions. As mentioned above, the value of an imaging device decreases over time, whereas the value of data-based services, such as those of Soarian, increases over time. One reason for this is rising volumes of data. Complex service solutions make it difficult to compare offers from different competitors due to their high levels of complexity and individualization. For many customers, the technologies are new and therefore difficult to assess, particularly in terms of their long-term value-in-use. All of this heightens the customers' perception of risk in making a purchase decision. They fear that the long-term benefits may not be worth the cost. These perceptions of risk reduce customers' willingness to pay for complex services and also lead them to demand deeper discounts.[11]

How can suppliers manage this? According to the theory developed by Raymond A. Bauer, the perception of risk is based on two factors: the potential consequences of a loss event, and the uncertainty surrounding if and when a loss event could happen.[12] To perceive a high risk, both factors must be significant. If only one of the two is reduced, the overall risk is perceived as being smaller. Accordingly, as shown in Figure 4.7, there are two ways that suppliers can influence a customer's perception of risk.

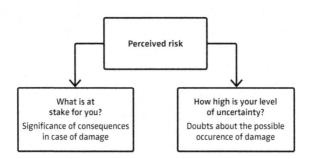

Figure 4.7:   The elements of perceived risk.

[11] S. Alavi, J. Habel, M. Schwenke, and C. Schmitz, "Price Negotiating for Services: Elucidating the Ambivalent Effects on Customers' Negotiation Aspirations," *Journal of the Academy of Marketing Science* 48, no. 2 (2020): 165–185.
[12] R. A. Bauer, "Consumer Behavior As Risk Taking," in *Dynamic Marketing in a Changing World*, ed. R. S. Hancock (Chicago, IL: Proceedings of the 43rd Conference of the American Marketing Association, 1960), pp. 389–398.

On the one hand, suppliers can reduce the chances of negative consequences resulting from breaking a promise or a loss event. Above all, this affects price, terms, and conditions policies. On the other hand, suppliers can try to convince customers that there are no such negative consequences. To achieve this, they will use marketing communication.

One of the first ways to reduce customers' perceived risk about pricing policy terms is to not charge any money for the service offering at all. In marketing, one speaks of "freemiums" or "freebies" (i.e., free product samples). The terms are predominantly used in the consumer goods sector. For example, everyone is familiar with the strips of perfume samples that are stapled in magazines, or with smartphone apps that can be used for free in a basic version. Customers can familiarize themselves with a product's quality by testing it first and without having to pay for it.

If an industrial company wants to adopt a gradual approach to offering complex service solutions, free samples can be applied in a similar fashion. By giving customers digital or consulting services free of charge, for example, they can get to know and appreciate the service supplier. After this experience, customers may be ready to pay. This would reduce the level of skepticism about the supplier's promises. As a result, customers may be willing to buy more comprehensive offers. In this context, salespeople speak of "land and expand".

Reciprocity can have an additional positive effect. Cialdini investigated this phenomenon in the 1980s. His research demonstrated that people want to give something back to those who have given them something.[13] However, this cannot easily be transferred to business practice. In the consumer goods sector, for example, it was not worthwhile for television electronics retailers to offer free advice before customers made a purchase. Customers were happy to take advantage of this service, but they subsequently bought their television sets at the supermarket or on the internet at a lower price.

A similar trend occurred in B2B markets for telephone switching systems in the telecommunications sector. In terms of suppliers, this market was dominated by companies such as Lucent, Siemens, Alcatel, and Nortel in the late 1990s. On the customer side, large-network operators such as AT&T and Deutsche Telekom led the industry. These operators usually acted as monopolists in their respective countries. With the

---

[13]R. B. Cialdini, *Influence: The Psychology of Persuasion* (New York, NY: William Morrow and Company, 1984).

deregulation of telecommunications markets at the end of the last century, however, they faced new competitors. Yet, the new competitors still lacked the knowledge to design the architecture of a telecommunications network. The established switching system suppliers supported their customers in this regard by providing them with a complex set of consulting services to help them create the architecture design for a nationwide network. The established suppliers did so in spite of the work and enormous effort involved, assuming that the costs would be offset by future switching system sales. In the end, these orders were often awarded to a new network equipment supplier from China: Huawei. At the time, this company could not — and did not want to — provide comprehensive consulting to customers. As a result, it saved the related costs. Instead, Huawei manufactured inexpensive switching systems. They were often bought by customers who had previously received free advice from an established supplier. Today, Huawei is the global leader in switching systems in the telecommunications industry, and the abovementioned suppliers from North America and Western Europe have largely been pushed out of the market.

That is why it is important to find the right time to switch to sales mode when giving away services. If a supplier is adding value with a growing proportion of new services, long-term business results will deteriorate — even if these services are provided free of charge. This is true for traditional industrial companies that want to develop a complex service solution offering. At least that is the case when service costs are not offset by higher revenues from other offerings. The longer that suppliers give away their service, the more likely customers will become irritated when the strategy shifts to sales mode.

The situation is similar in markets for products in which it is necessary to have a certain number of customers before the products create value. The market for telephones in the last century is an example. The value a customer ascribes to a telephone is low as long as no one else has one. Therefore, the price for those kinds of products is low when they are introduced to the market. The higher the number of customers with the product, the higher the value for the customers, so suppliers might increase the price over time. But customers are less likely to accept significantly higher prices during repeat purchases. It is difficult to make the argument to an annoyed customer that the product's value has increased due to better usage opportunities. Instead, customers suspect that the supplier is exploiting the situation for their own financial gain. To prevent this, the supplier should make pricing policies transparent, announce price increases early, and whenever possible justify them through increased costs to gain customer acceptance.[14]

In summary, it should be noted that freebies are not a suitable price concept in all scenarios. They can, however, be helpful during the market entry phase, although it is far from certain that offering a small gift will result in large sales later. This is particularly true for B2B segments. That is why companies must carefully manage the transition from free services to a profitable marketing mode.

Another pricing policy option is the subscription. Subscriptions make it less expensive to acquire customers, and they reduce the customers' perception of risk before purchase. We speak of subscription-based pricing in this context. Similar to leasing, the customer pays relatively small sums at regular intervals instead of a high one-time purchase price. In addition, customers are sometimes granted the right to cancel the subscription. This pricing model is often used in traditional industrial goods businesses, including large truck manufacturers.

Although low prices are an advantage for customers, they are a disadvantage for the suppliers' cash management. Under this pricing model, suppliers typically continue to own the numerous components of their complex service solutions. As a result, they must show these assets on their balance sheets. This, in turn, requires capital and the related interest costs for the supplier. On the other hand, revenue flows remain constant — something that the financial markets like to see for industrial companies. What makes this pricing model truly interesting for suppliers that launch complex service solutions is the access to customer usage data, which present a valuable information base for the continued development of innovative products and business models.

There is another subscription-based pricing development that lowers the customer's purchasing risk even further. It does this by linking compensation to a customer's usage time, production results, or market success. This is what is known as "performance-based pricing." Especially with IT companies such as Microsoft and Tencent, it has become common to sell "software as a service." Under this model, customers only pay for the time they actually use the software. At €80 billion, this price model currently accounts for around a third of global software sales, and it will

---

[14] J. E. Urbany, T. J. Madden, and P. R. Dickson, "All's Not Fair in Pricing: An Initial Look at the Dual Entitlement Principle," *Marketing Letters* 1, no. 1 (1989): 17–25.

continue to grow in the future.[15] Rolls-Royce's power by the hour pricing model presented above is another example of performance-based pricing. It allows customers to transform fixed costs into variable costs and helps them to avoid the risk of wasting more expensive resources.

Customers reduce the amount of risk even further when they pay based on production output rather than usage time. This is the case if a supplier of beverage filling systems is compensated by the number of bottles filled, or if a copy machine manufacturer is paid by the number of pages printed. An extreme type of performance-based pricing takes place when payment is directly linked to customers' market success — and only indirectly related to the supplier's solution performance. The consulting firm Bain & Company took this path. By offering clients a rate based on their stock market performance rather than the usual per diem rates, the company was able to gain significant market share from its competitors McKinsey and the Boston Consulting Group. Behind this pricing strategy is the increased popularity of a customer-centric mindset. It has also played a visible role in the rise of so-called customer success managers, whom suppliers have been hiring in recent years.[16]

The idea of variable pricing models is nothing new, of course. There are stories — albeit without historical evidence — that a Chinese emperor's personal doctor was paid by the number of days that the ruler enjoyed good health. James Watt and Matthew Boulton are further examples. They were only successful with their famous steam engines in 1776 when, instead of selling them, they leased them to mine owners for a third of what it cost them to feed their horses. Rolls-Royce's power by the hour concept is also decades old. The company trademarked it in 1962, but it only began using it much later with the rise of data management technology.

Supporters of performance-based pricing see it as the ultimate way to overcome the zero-sum game between buyer and supplier. Instead of one party only being able to win something if the other one loses, both now

---

[15]Gartner Group, cited from *manager magazin* (July 2019), 96.

[16]See B. Hochstein, D. Rangarajan, N. Mehta, and D. Kocher, "An Industry/Academic Perspective on Customer Success Management," *Journal of Service Research* 23, no. 1 (2020): 3–7; or A. A. Zoltners, P. K. Sinha, and S. E. Lorimer, "What Is a Customer Success Manager?" *Harvard Business Review* (November 18, 2019). Retrieved from https://hbr.org/2019/11/what-is-a-customer-success-manager. (Accessed December 20, 2019).

have a common interest. Rolls-Royce has just as much interest in keeping aircraft in the air as the airlines themselves. The airlines no longer have to fear paying too much for spare parts, and they can manage their costs better with the new business model. They also no longer need to pay fixed salaries for maintenance staff. In light of these customer benefits, it is easy to lose sight of the fact that this model entails higher levels of risk for Rolls-Royce than the traditional pricing model. Aircraft may have to be grounded for reasons other than engine problems. Pilots and crew, for example, may go on strike, which can lead to a loss in earnings for suppliers. Something that was once not a risk at all is now something beyond their control.

Whenever suppliers choose to share their customer's market risks through performance-based pricing, they should know these risks well. Before Rolls-Royce signs a contract with an airline, the company must be able to accurately assess the future strike risk of a customer, just to name one example. The risk probably varies between individual airlines, and even between the number of years a specific company has been in business. Rolls-Royce also needs to know how the customer's flight routes will expand over time. More desert region destinations, for example, mean that the engines require more maintenance because of sand content in the air. In summary, it is no longer enough for Rolls-Royce to ensure that customers have sufficient resources to buy an engine. Now, the engine maker must assess how the airline will utilize the engine across its lifespan.

In the case of performance-based pricing, suppliers who want to avoid nasty and expensive surprises need to know more about the market situation and customer trends than they did before. In this context, we refer to a supplier's need for a *deep* customer understanding. It is a prerequisite area of expertise for sales managers, and we visit this topic later in this chapter.

Figure 4.8 summarizes the pricing approaches. It illustrates how risk transfers and payment structures work in the customer's favor.

Notwithstanding the difficulties explained above, performance-based pricing gives suppliers a clear set of advantages. The most important are as follows:

1. Increased purchase likelihood (because customers perceive less risk).
2. Access to usage data (which customers would otherwise prefer to keep to themselves).
3. Market entry barriers for competitors (especially for lower-quality solution suppliers with whom customers cannot achieve any performance improvements).

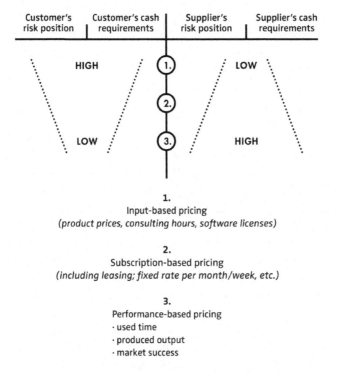

Figure 4.8: Various approaches to the pricing of complex service solutions.

4. Exceptional revenue opportunities (if the customer achieves exceptional increases in performance).

To illustrate the fourth point, Rolls-Royce's profits increased in the years following its introduction of the power by the hour pricing model to the Royal Navy. The model raised the aircraft's operational readiness from 70 to 80 percent.[17] When a supplier realizes extraordinarily high profits, there is always a question of how long customers will tolerate them. As soon as there are sufficient competitors, customers will pursue more favorable terms once their initial contract has expired. They will take efficiency improvements for granted, and they will only want to allow suppliers to participate in further improvements. This shows that performance-based pricing by no means reconciles the natural conflict between

---

[17]D. J. Smith, "Power-by-the-hour: The Role of Technology in Re-shaping Business Strategy," *Technology Analysis and Strategic Management* 25, no. 8 (2013): 987–1007.

supplier and customer. Both parties will have a common interest in optimizing the shared value creation process. Yet, negotiations on sharing the related achieved efficiency gains will be just as conflict ridden as price negotiations in traditional sales processes.

That customers pursue their own interests is a given. Several Soarian projects at Siemens offer some helpful insights. At Soarian, customers could choose to pay for software licenses and consultancy hours at fixed prices or pay based on achieved efficiency improvements. Siemens made several observations. Hospitals that were convinced from the outset that they would achieve the desired efficiency improvements favored fixed-price offers. Customers who experienced internal difficulties in implementing efficiency improvements opted for performance-based pricing. In economics, these phenomena have been analyzed as "moral hazards". They reflect the customer's viewpoint that suppliers are acting opportunistically. The Soarian case example reversed this risk. This forced Siemens to strengthen the sales managers' understanding of their customers. They had to adjust customer assessment and selection processes accordingly.

Yet, even deeper customer insights cannot completely rule out the problem of moral hazard. This also applies to the other supplier risks mentioned above, in which payment is linked to future customer behavior. As long as suppliers are convinced that the opportunities offered by the revenue model outweigh the risks, they will prefer input-oriented pricing approaches. This is in line with the goal of solid growth (i.e., customers pay according to products delivered, hours of consulting, and software licenses sold). In these scenarios, however, it is important to convince customers that the impact of the services business is worth the price. In the context of the perception of risk, suppliers must then reduce the customer's level of uncertainty and create trust through communication activities.

Guiding Marketing Communication

In order to reduce the customer's level of uncertainty, suppliers must offer targeted information in their marketing communication.[18] What content should these communication measures target?

---

[18] In the marketing theory context, or new institutional economics to be more precise, one refers to signaling. See also M. Spence, "Job Market Signaling," *Quarterly Journal of Economics* 87, no. 3 (1973): 355–374.

Whenever companies offer advanced premium products, a large portion of their communication activities are related to their actual products. Marketing focuses on the creation of "fact sheets" that list the performance data of machine tools, trucks, and gas turbines, showcasing the data at trade fairs. This builds the starting point for subsequent sales discussions, in which salespeople are accustomed to explaining product data in detail. Complex service solutions, on the other hand, only have a few visible product elements that can be put on public display. The solution is created after the purchase decision is made. Even after a supplier has delivered the solution, it cannot be displayed easily in a brochure, on the internet, or at trade fairs. As a result, marketing communication for complex service solutions requires a different frame of reference.

The field of new institutional economics has developed an approach that illustrates the available options. It begins with the assumption that customers seek to reduce the level of uncertainty they perceive during transactions by gathering information about the offering. The approach distinguishes between product performance features that can be verified before and after the purchase decision. In some cases, the extraordinary amount of work involved in verifying each and every performance feature would not make sense. This framework is captured in the matrix structure shown in Figure 4.9.[19]

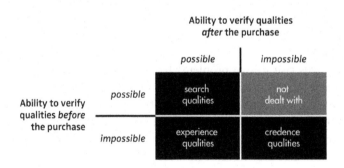

Figure 4.9:   Ability to verify product qualities.

[19]P. Nelson, "Information and Consumer Behavior," *Journal of Political Economy* 78, no. 2 (1970): 311–329; M. Darby and E. Karni, "Free Competition and the Optimal Amount of Fraud," *Journal of Law and Economics* 16, no. 1 (1973): 67–88.

Search qualities can be verified before the purchase. When customers buy a second-hand car from a dealer, they consider specific factors such as the model, trunk size, and color, among other things. However, customers can only test experience qualities after they have completed their purchase. It is at this point that the buyer finds out how repair-prone the car is and how much gas it consumes. Test options like these are not available for a product's credence qualities. One such example is a car's airbag system. When customers sell their cars after a number of years, they typically do not check to see if the system still works. In other words, they buy on trust. In the same way, customers simply have to trust that Soarian will optimize the hospital's workflow processes. They cannot check whether a different process structure would have achieved even better results.

These three product quality categories — search qualities, experience qualities, and credence qualities — create a good foundation for establishing the core marketing communication activities of a supplier. It is important to note first that complex service solutions have a small share of search qualities, as they are only provided once customers have made a purchase decision. There are, however, a few components that can be presented before the purchase decision, such as the solution's standardized, integrated hardware products. Although these items can be communicated to the customer in advance, it may not be enough to significantly reduce the level of uncertainty. Complex service solutions do, however, possess experience qualities. Overall, experience qualities are best communicated through references. Instead of focusing on a solution's specific functionality, communication activities focus on the actual experiences of customers who use, or have used, similar solutions in the past.

This gives rise to two problems for complex service solutions. First, individual projects are difficult to compare because of their high level of customization. This makes it hard for potential customers to draw conclusions about their own projects based on the statements of reference customers. In addition, some customers do not want other market participants to even know that they have been involved in a complex service solution project. They also do not want to reveal the identity of their supplier. This is particularly true when projects have a direct impact on a customer's competitiveness.

Because of the limited communication opportunities for search and experience qualities, credence qualities take on a special role in marketing complex service solutions. In this case, customers do not have access to any related, solution-specific information. Instead, customers have to

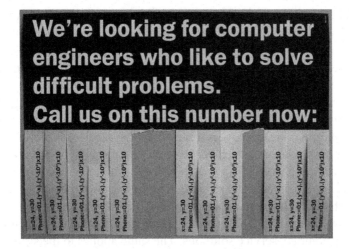

Figure 4.10: McKinsey advertisement.

look at a supplier's credentials and compare the company's reputation with its product offerings. In this case, a complex service solution supplier might want to communicate the company's international locations, its long and venerable history, or its financial strength. Above all, marketing communication should focus on the people who will manage the projects. Strategy consultancies such as McKinsey and the Boston Consulting Group — whose offerings contain a high share of credence qualities — have succeeded in portraying their employees as experts. Their communications strategy is devoted to reinforcing this message. They like to let others know that their recruitment requirements are very tough (see Figure 4.10).

Experienced consultants are also encouraged to build specialist knowledge in specific areas so that they can be positioned effectively in the press. At the same time, the company invests in webcasts and customer conferences to position its employees as professional customer partners among relevant target groups. Another employee-focused communications tactic that consulting firms leverage is to send potential customers the CVs of the consultants who would be working on their projects. These CVs often feature the names of renowned universities and outstanding examination results.

All of this information is designed to provide customers with a sense of security, even if the information has no direct bearing on the specific consulting project. To put it another way, because customers cannot check the complex service solution before making a purchase decision, they rely on information about the supplier instead. They use this as a basis of trust to compensate for the lack of information. This reduces the level of uncertainty before making a purchase.

A complex service solution supplier must use communication that does justice to this logic. Customer trust can relate both to the company as a whole and to its employees in detail. Corporate trust is closely related to brand management, which we covered in Chapter 2 on advanced premium products. Consistency, authenticity, and longevity are the key aspects here. The image and reputation of well-known technology companies such as IBM, Siemens, and GE provide excellent opportunities for employing brand-stretching tactics. They help leverage the company's brand for complex service solutions. The same applies to the strong reputations of hidden champions in their respective market niches.

Nonetheless, it is ultimately the level of trust between the employees of the customer and the supplier that drives the purchase decision. Given the limited scope for control, customers must be convinced of the commitment and integrity of project participants. Customers must also be confident that the implementation leadership for complex service solutions will remain committed to project success at all times. They expect the supplier to stick to the agreed course of action — even when the customer's employees or others put them under pressure. In addition, customers must be confident that the supplier's employees will treat internal information confidentially. This confidence must even extend to potential projects that involve a customer's competitors, clients, or suppliers.

The customer's expectations of trust toward a specific person are primarily centered on the behavior of a specific individual who has been assigned a project. In doing so, the customer assumes that the trusted individual will not damage these bonds of trust in specific situations. Numerous studies have been conducted to investigate how those involved in a customer–supplier relationship can build trust.[20] Consider the following three key aspects:

1. Cultural similarities among the involved parties are an important factor in building trust. This does not mean that the supplier's employees have to adopt the values and attitudes of the customer for a given

---

[20] O. Plötner, *Das Vertrauen des Kunden — Relevanz, Aufbau und Steuerung auf industriellen Märkten* (Wiesbaden: Springer Fachmedien, 1995).

project at the expense of their own authenticity. However, cultural similarities can play a role during the selection of staff for complex service solutions. For example, suppliers with an international customer base should hire employees with diverse backgrounds and take cultural similarities into account when setting up project teams.

2. Reciprocity engenders trust. In other words, one party is more likely to trust the other party when it also feels trusted. Experiments in game theory in particular have shown that people who extend trust receive trust in return. By contrast, general mistrust is a surefire recipe for generating an impasse.

3. Like corporate brands, behavioral consistency plays a key role in building trust. Consistency is used to predict how a supplier will act in the future. In other words, the more often people prove their trustworthiness, the more consistent their image will be. As a result, customers will be more likely to trust that such behavior will be consistent and used during future projects. Such experiences usually develop over the course of long-term business relationships. The fulfillment or breaking of promises takes on enormous significance. This aspect plays a prominent role in the acquisition process, in which rash promises are made, sometimes just to win a contract. Trust is fragile. A single breach of trust can quickly destroy a relationship that has been built up over a lengthy period.

It is important to maintain trusted relationships with customers, even after they have made a purchase decision. This is particularly important with complex service solutions. First, the relationship is necessary to answer open questions and manage conflicts that will arise in the subsequent phases of collaboration. A trusted supplier relationship increases future customer sales opportunities. Finally, this kind of relationship can be used as a reference to acquire additional customers.

Levels of trust rise when promises are kept. Customers must be able to see, however, that this is the case. When introducing a complex service solution and delivering the work, customers' employees are often so focused on their own contributions that they lose sight of the solution's value for the company and the supplier's services. Suppliers need to counteract this by initiating communication processes with the customer on their "value-in-use".[21] By doing so, suppliers can improve customer satisfaction.

---

[21] It was Adam Smith who actually introduced the concept of "value-in-use". Smith distinguishes between the "value-in-exchange", which is based on the comparison of buying

At the same time, suppliers can increase the customer's awareness of their performance contributions. While problems and disappointments are likely to be addressed, research has shown that addressing customer dissatisfaction can have a positive impact on the supplier.[22] Customers feel that they are being taken seriously. At the same time, suppliers can analyze a complaint — even if the issue does not fall within their area of responsibility. On this basis, they can clear up misunderstandings, address customers' disappointments, and initiate improvement processes in their own company. Each element works together to strengthen a customer relationship that is built on trust.

Shaping the Sales Process

The role of trust in purchase decisions for complex service solutions and the need to co-create with customers impact the way businesses organize the sales function. The first fundamental question is as follows: Who should drive the sales? A company's own employees or external trading partners? Careful consideration should be given if it is the latter. From the outset, it is unlikely that external partners can develop the necessary competencies to market complex service solutions. Given the necessary investment requirements, these partners may not even want to do so. In addition, complex service solution suppliers are not keen on seeing a mediator positioned between themselves and an industrial customer. This is not just about reducing the manufacturer's margin or increasing the price to the customer. More importantly, communication for complex service solutions is highly complex, even in the acquisition phase. Intermediaries can quickly create misunderstandings, especially if they do not have the necessary skills. In addition, customer relationships created through close collaboration are one of the reasons that many industrial companies offer complex service solutions in the first place. They pose higher barriers to

---

alternatives, and the "value-in-use", which is the customer's resulting value creation. The latter is also increasingly used in current marketing science, in particular by matching the expected value-in-use and the experienced value-in-use. See A. Eggert, M. Kleinaltenkamp, and V. Kashyab, "Mapping Value in Business Markets: An Integrative Framework", *Industrial Marketing Management* 79 (2019): 13–20.

[22] J. Ferguson and W. Johnston, "Customer Response to Dissatisfaction: A Synthesis of Literature and Conceptual Framework", *Industrial Marketing Management* 40, no. 1 (2011): 118–127.

entry for competitors. This fact alone is why industrial companies only reluctantly share customer relationships with dealers, particularly if they do not guarantee exclusivity.

In this respect, direct sales are suitable for the suppliers of complex service solutions. But how do suppliers manage such sales in a global context?

Even before submitting an offer, suppliers must know their customers, processes, and resources well. Suppliers can achieve this more quickly if they are close to the customer and belong to the same culture. Because of the high level of investment associated with building up their own on-site sales resources, complex service solution suppliers should also focus on the most promising countries. Once there, they should identify and proactively target the most promising customers. Suppliers should avoid acquisition efforts for customers who do not fit the target profile. This is because demand analyses for complex service solutions are personnel-intensive during the acquisition phase. Only a few employees have the necessary expertise. Staff shortages may exist because employees have to perform analyses of customer needs and create quotes. They must also realize the project once it has been awarded.

This recommended approach addresses the potential friction during the analysis of customer needs, acquisition-phase promises, and the subsequent implementation. The second and more important reason is the customer's level of uncertainty before purchasing a complex service solution. As discussed above, the supplier's employees should counteract this by gaining the customer's trust through their competence and actions. If this succeeds, customers will feel that they are in good hands.

About Heroes and Orchestrators

We observe two competing schools of thought on how to organize the sales force for complex service solution sales. We label the first one the "hero" approach and the second one the "orchestrator" approach.

Proponents of the former contend that salespeople need to accept end-to-end responsibility for entire complex service solution projects, including the sale, implementation, and servicing. Strategy consultancies such as McKinsey and the Boston Consulting Group are following this approach. Both companies have branches and partners in all relevant countries, and they maintain strong contacts with potential local customers.

These relationships come into play when their corporate management needs advice. The partners who acquire the customer are usually also responsible for the project's subsequent implementation. Although they are supported by other employees with comparable consulting experience, it is the partners who remain the customer's central point of contact at all project stages. Sales and production are thus rolled into one. This organizational approach is recommended for the distribution of complex service solutions, but it is unusual for traditional industrial companies.

Traditional industrial companies have always been organized into sales and production. Truck salespeople, for example, may not even know where their product's parts are manufactured, where the body and engine are assembled, or how the vehicle paint is applied. Similarly, managers of development and production divisions may know nothing about target customers, prices, and business models. Unlike consulting firms, there are "silo boundaries" between the individual functional areas: Managers of one area often show little interest in other colleagues' tasks. In addition, senior managers in development and production sometimes enjoy a higher status than their sales colleagues. Being promoted to partner at a consulting firm, though, includes the responsibility for sales.

The hero's competence profiles are demanding. In addition to in-depth knowledge of customers and their markets, they require technical expertise — particularly in the field of modern information and communication technologies. Instead of having an in-depth mastery of specific technology elements, it is more important for these employees to have a sound overview of a technology's strengths and weaknesses among various settings. This requires "all-rounders", which is a challenge, given the high degree of specialization among engineers. In addition, solid business knowledge is necessary. This is because the customer's top management team is involved in the purchase of complex service solutions. These individuals are typically more interested in key business indicators than in technical contexts. If managers follow our recommendation and combine the sales and implementation tasks into a single role, then those team members will also need the required knowledge concerning project and cost management. Fortunately, employees can develop competencies in these areas largely through training activities. There are only a few hard-to-understand elements that are based on practical knowledge. Among them is so-called tacit knowledge, a skill which cannot be taught.[23]

---

[23] Scientists refer to the concept of tacit knowledge. See Y. Soliman and H. Vanharanta, "A Model for Capturing Tacit Knowledge in Enterprises", in *Advances in Human Factors,*

Acquiring extensive specialist skills does not guarantee that employees will use them with customers. This requires social skills, or so-called soft skills. Because complex service solutions are tailored to customers' specific needs, cognitive empathy is particularly important. Unlike emotional empathy, which enables a person to feel what others feel, cognitive empathy enables a person to know how others feel. It helps sales and project managers to identify problem areas within a customer's business that are not obvious. However, managers should exercise cognitive empathy with a certain amount of social distance. This will help them to objectively evaluate the customer information they have received. They can then draw conclusions that are independent of personal sympathy or antipathy.

The social competence to understand another person's mindset and interests goes hand in hand with communication. The sales process of traditional industrial companies focuses on making compelling product presentations. Yet, when it comes to complex service solutions, managers need to be able to ask the right questions. This is the only way to determine specific customer requirements. Training courses on "consultative selling" help to develop these skills. Another communication element is the ability to use a didactic approach in conveying knowledge that customers need for the co-creation process. At the very least, the same should apply to project managers toward their colleagues. After all, not all project team members will have the necessary knowledge from the outset. This, in turn, is a strong indication that project managers must have leadership skills when dealing with their own employees as well as their customers. These skills can then be combined with critical core values, among them integrity, authenticity, and intercultural openness. Figure 4.11 illustrates the wide range of complex service solution requirements that sales and project managers have to meet.[24]

In order to meet this wide range of requirements, managers can build multi-disciplinary teams. The individual members' abilities will not address all areas. Instead, they will complement one another. In order to be able to lead these types of teams successfully, managers themselves should possess as many of these skills as possible. This will ensure that all

---

Business Management and Leadership, ed. T. Ahram and W. Karwowski, International Conference on Applied Human Factors and Ergonomics (Cham: Springer, 2019), pp. 141–148.

[24]In the second section of this chapter, we also spoke of "smart skills". This is a key success factor for this strategy option.

Figure 4.11:　Requirement profile for heroes.

skill sets are available across individual areas. It is difficult for industrial companies to find such employees on the job market. That is why it is all the more important for complex service solution suppliers to ensure that such employees are on board, feel comfortable, and do not switch to competitors. This touches on cross-company issues that go beyond the sales and project management perspectives.

It becomes apparent that the "hero" approach hits a wall when service solutions become very complex. Consider Soarian, which we introduced at the beginning of this chapter. To assume end-to-end responsibility, a hero would have required deep expertise in healthcare, pharmaceuticals, hospital management, process management, software engineering, risk management, and business administration. On top of that, the hero would have had to be an excellent salesperson with outstanding social skills. Heroes with such a skills profile are difficult, if not impossible to recruit. Consider Tom Miller's previously cited insight that "people from the traditional business did not even have the right skills to interview the necessary candidates".

Accordingly, the second school of thought aims to reduce the burden on salespeople by dividing the sales process into highly specialized roles — with the salesperson acting as the orchestrator between them.[25] We thus label this the "orchestrator" approach.

Salesforce is working in this way. The company sells the world's most frequently used customer relationship management (CRM) system, which allows firms to systematically manage their sales leads, opportunities, and existing customers. Although not an industrial service, a CRM system like the one at Salesforce ticks the boxes of being a complex service solution:

1. A CRM system is complex, comprising elaborate automation and analytics solutions.
2. Implementing a CRM system includes a high proportion of customized services, for example, redesigning sales processes, mapping them into the system, configuring process automation rules, migrating existing data, establishing interfaces with other IT systems, and training employees.
3. A CRM system has a strong business impact on customers, as it requires a customer company's sales personnel to substantially change their practices. In return, it offers substantial performance increases.[26]

If Salesforce followed the hero approach, it would assign one sales role the responsibility for finding prospective customers, understanding its needs in detail, closing deals, redesigning sales processes with customers, implementing the CRM system accordingly, and ensuring that customers enjoy high value-in-use from the CRM system. But the company takes a different approach. Rather than assigning responsibility to one hero, Salesforce divides the sales, implementation, and servicing process into various parts and assigns responsibilities for individual parts to functional experts.

---

[25] See B. Hochstein, N. N. Chaker, D. Rangarajan, D. Nagel, and N. N. Hartmann, "Proactive Value Co-Creation via Structural Ambidexterity: Customer Success Management and the Modularization of Frontline Roles", *Journal of Service Research* 24, no. 4 (2021): 601–621.

[26] Many research studies have established the business impact of CRM systems. A recent example is S. Chatterjee, N. P. Rana, K. Tamilmani, and A. Sharma, "The Effect of AI-based CRM on Organization Performance and Competitive Advantage: An Empirical Analysis in the B2B Context", *Industrial Marketing Management* 97 (2021): 205–219.

First, so-called business development associates are in charge of finding and researching prospective customers. Second, sales development representatives (SDRs) and business development representatives (BDRs) call these prospects and aim to qualify them — that is, evaluate whether these prospects might be interested in purchasing a CRM system and have the authority and budget to do so. Whereas SDRs contact "warm" prospects that have reached out to Salesforce, BDRs contact "cold" prospects that may not even have heard about Salesforce. They then pass qualified prospects over to account executives, who consult prospects and close deals — supported by technical experts if needed.

Account executives "own" customers, and from here on out act as orchestrators of the customer relationship. For example, once a prospect has made the purchase, technical specialists implement Salesforce's CRM system in the customer's organization while keeping account executives in the loop. After the implementation, customer success managers take responsibility to ensure that customers achieve high value-in-use. To that end, they educate and engage customers to use all the functionalities that are possibly helpful to them. They also identify cross-selling and up-selling potentials for Salesforce's account executives to pursue.

Figure 4.12 juxtaposes the hero and orchestrator approaches and summarizes their advantages and disadvantages. A first advantage of the hero approach is that it reduces customers' perceived risk. Customers can find comfort in knowing that one key person is taking charge for the ultimate success of the project and cannot push off responsibility. This is different in the orchestrator approach. For that reason, orchestrators need to take different approaches to reduce customers' perceived risk. For example, they should stay in close contact with customers throughout the project and give them confidence in the abilities of any new contributors to the project.

Second, the orchestrator approach complicates coordination. An orchestrator needs to manage multiple interfaces inside the supplier organization to ensure a smooth sale, the implementation, and the servicing of the complex service solution, often without formal authority over coworkers. Conversely, a hero takes charge of the sale, the implementation, and the servicing, and has formal authority over other contributors. Consider once more the partner on a management consulting project, to whom all other project members typically report via solid or dotted lines. In that model, coordination is also easier for the customer, who can regard the hero as their main point of contact.

Approach	Hero	Orchestrator
Nature of the sales process	Sales, implementation, and service as a one-stop shop	Fragmentation of sales, implementation, and service
Responsibility of the salesperson	End-to-end responsibility for the entire complex service solution project	Responsibility for orchestrating the various responsible contributors to complex service solution projects
Required expertise of the salesperson	· Deep customer industry and firm understanding · Generalist with high expertise in all areas of the complex service solution (e.g., technical, managerial) · Very high sales expertise · Very high social skills	· Customer relationship management · Process orchestration · High sales expertise, including team selling · High social skills
Typical other contributors	· Project stream managers · Subject matter experts	· Business/sales development representatives · Technical sales specialists · Implementation specialists · Customer success managers
Influence of the salesperson on other contributors	Formal authority (solid or dotted lines)	Influencing without formal authority
Examples	· Management consulting firms, such as McKinsey and BCG	· Salesforce
	Evaluation	
Perceived security	+	−
Ease of coordination	+	−
Hiring of talent	−	+
Scalability	−	+

Figure 4.12: Schools of thought on how to bring complex service solution projects to market.

Third, however, the hero is at a disadvantage when it comes to hiring talent. As mentioned earlier, their broad skill requirements make heroes difficult to find, particularly as service solutions gain in complexity. Hiring talent for the orchestrator approach is substantially easier, because the skills required for any of the divided sales roles are more readily available in the labor market and also easier to train. Fourth, related to the previous point, the orchestrator approach allows suppliers to scale the complex service solution business more easily.

Evolving Step by Step

The high-capability requirements of the suppliers of complex service solutions run the risk of overwhelming traditional industrial companies. Consider the Soarian example. Siemens started by optimizing the very complex processes of one of the best-known hospitals in the United States. The better approach might have been to gradually introduce the strategic option. This corresponds to the philosophy of "solid growth" and implies a gradual increase in the use of digital technologies. Figure 4.13 offers an example from the agricultural industry of this step-by-step approach.

Claas, a leading global manufacturer of agricultural machinery, used digital functionality as early as the 1980s to regulate the speed of its combine harvesters. Over time, Claas expanded its digital offering well beyond combine applications. The company developed digital yield mapping, for example, to help farmers identify harvest yields on individual field parcels. This type of information, however, only provides significant customer benefits if it is networked with other information and processes. By using yield mapping, for example, farmers can improve the next fertilizer application. To this end, Claas founded the subsidiary 365FarmNet in 2013. It offers farmers a digital platform to drive comprehensive process optimization across their entire agriculture operations. Farmers receive harvest day recommendations based on data analysis of the weather, crop growth, and price developments. They also get information on where to obtain specific resources.

Farmers can purchase access to this information separately from other Claas products. In the meantime, Claas is offering a growing number of complex service solutions. These include machine and software product solutions for process optimization, as well as consulting services (i.e., complex service solutions).

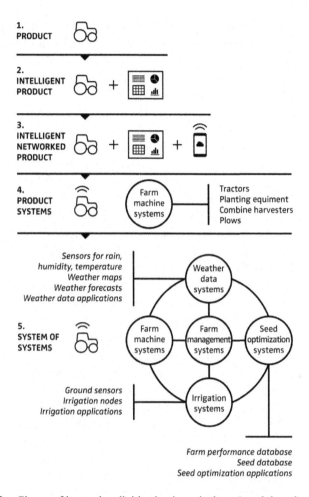

Figure 4.13: Phases of increasing digitization in agriculture (graph based on Porter and Heppelmann[27]).

The same scenario applies to MAN, a European truck manufacturer. The company has developed a digital service with the RIO logistics platform for more efficient vehicle utilization. With RIO, freight forwarders can optimize route management. This allows customers to monitor their usage profile and their truck's technical condition at any time. MAN

---

[27]M. E. Porter and J. E. Heppelmann, "How Smart, Connected Products Are Transforming Competition," *Harvard Business Review* 92, no. 11 (2014): 64–88.

expanded this functionality to support truck drivers in meeting their safety reporting requirements. Drivers must typically complete lengthy, legally mandated safety reports on the condition of their vehicle lights, wheel nuts, and trailer couplings. With the RIO solution, drivers receive all of the necessary information on their smartphones. At the same time, all information can be viewed at headquarters and archived in the cloud. Similar to 365FarmNet, customers can purchase RIO without having to purchase a MAN vehicle. However, RIO only unlocks the solution's full functionality when customers buy individual digital services together with a complete solution package or complex service solution. This goes hand in hand with business model transformation. In this case, the customer no longer buys vehicles from MAN but leases them. It is the manufacturer who continues to own the actual trucks.

Of course, an industrial company can develop digital services that are completely unrelated to previous products or customers, although this type of diversification is rare. From a competition perspective, it is not very promising. In scenarios like this, industrial companies typically forego their knowledge advantage in "domain know-how." When a supplier's knowledge and skills offer a critical competitive advantage in a given market, existing product and market expertise can provide the necessary edge for success. This is particularly true when compared to the situation of new competitors from the start-up scene or IT companies.

This does not mean that certain knowledge elements cannot be marketed separately. It may even be possible to reach new customer groups this way. Thanks to 365FarmNet, Claas was able to sell agricultural weather data to insurance companies. According to Wixom and Ross, such businesses represent the third stage of a company's development in the use of digital technologies.[28] The stage model of these two research scientists is shown in Figure 4.14.

For the majority of industrial companies, the third stage of this model is optional and not part of the core business. The focus on sales occurs during the second stage. This is because of the domain know-how advantage. At the same time, complex service solutions, which include much more than the sale of information, promise greater business potential.

Figure 4.15 outlines the typical gradual development of a traditional industrial company into a provider of complex service solutions. This

---

[28]B. H. Wixom and J. W. Ross, "How to Monetize Your Data," *MIT Sloan Management Review* 58, no. 3 (2017): 10–14.

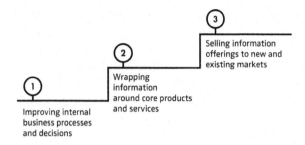

Figure 4.14: The stages of using digital technologies, according to Wixom and Ross.

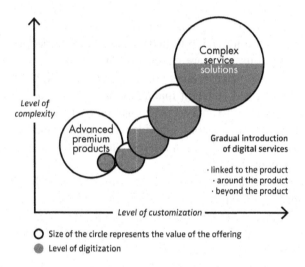

Figure 4.15: Gradual development from advanced premium products to complex service solutions.

process begins with the development of innovative digital services that are still closely related to an existing range of conventional advanced premium products, such as a digital dashboard to monitor machine data. After that, the offer is expanded to other areas of value creation. For example, as the supplier learns more about the customers' machine usage through the digital dashboard, they may eventually offer data-driven optimization of factory processes as a complex service solution.

A counter-example to such a typical evolution is provided by KBC (Kapsch BusinessCom), the leading B2B supplier of IT systems in Austria. KBC traditionally focused on integrating standardized hardware and software products and implementing them in their customers' organizations. KBC also offers the service of managing customers' IT systems. In the late 2010s, KBC realized a new opportunity in its markets: Customers grew increasingly interested in utilizing digital technologies to improve the effectiveness and efficiency of their value chain processes. To seize this market opportunity, KBC founded a separate unit and labeled it Digital Solutions. This unit offers customized projects to improve customers' value chain processes with the help of emerging technologies such as sensors, clouds, and artificial intelligence. KBC thereby leapfrogged to the highest level of difficulty, as shown in Figure 4.15: a complex service solution largely separate from the firm's traditional offerings.

To bring its digital solutions to the market, KBC follows a variation of the orchestrator approach outlined earlier. The salespeople in the traditional business units, who are called account managers, are tasked with gauging whether their customers are interested in a digital solution. If a customer is interested, account managers pass the opportunity over to a business developer, who analyzes the customer's processes and develops a solution concept. If a customer decides to purchase, the business developer collaborates with a solution architect and his team to implement the customized project.

As time went by, KBC realized that some of the individual complex service solutions which they had implemented offered the potential to be marketed as scalable digital offerings. To tap this potential, in 2020, KBC founded another business unit and labeled it Digital Platforms and Services. The business unit was tasked with identifying appropriate complex service solutions, turning them into scalable offerings, and bringing these offerings to market. An example of such an offering is the KBC Cyber Defense Center. As security attacks almost double every year, KBC decided to build up its own 7 × 24 Security Operation Center. The starting point was to cover their captive demand within the Kapsch Group. Shortly afterward, KBC launched this service on the market and Wienerberger — a leading international supplier of building materials with 200 production sites across 29 countries — was the first customer to join. Today, KBC is the Austrian market leader and analyzes trillions of security events with machine-learning tools to detect anomalies in the data traffic. This security platform gave KBC the opportunity to immediately turn what was once a complex service solution into a scalable service.

Note how KBC went through the process, from right to left, as we outline in Figure 4.15. Rather than start with simpler offerings and evolve toward more complex offerings, they successfully started with complex service solutions and evolved toward scalable digital services. KBC's success suggests that this approach is a viable alternative. However, it is important to consider KBC's unique position as a company with deep expertise in IT and digitization, which likely was a crucial driver of their success. For industrial companies with limited experience in this domain, following this approach seems riskier than a gradual evolution.

Bringing Digital Services to Market

No matter whether digital services[29] constitute the beginning or the end of a company's complex service solution journey, bringing such services to market is highly challenging in its own right. In order to overcome these challenges, market participants must first be able to recognize them correctly. Within this context, we conducted a research project in which we interviewed around 120 managers from 25 global industrial companies. The diverse set of individuals represented different hierarchy levels and regions. We interviewed people in roles ranging from CEO to sales representative, with a focus on the United States, Western Europe, and China. As it turned out, none of the participants were satisfied with the sales success of their digital service offerings. We were able to assign the causes to five areas: the customer, the product, the salesperson's lack of motivation, the salesperson's inadequate competence, and the company's inadequate framework factors. Participants were quick to mention elements in all five areas. Customers did not recognize the value of innovative offerings, because the level of reliability of digital services was low. There were no suitable incentive systems for sales managers, whose knowledge of digital technologies was inadequate. At the same time, the company did not invest enough in resource development.

Using in-depth analysis, we were able to identify more fundamental issues behind these initial arguments. It became clear that customers were merely using the missing customer benefit as an argument of convenience. In fact, customers shared a number of deeper underlying concerns. They were overwhelmed by the purchase decision and the many questions

---

[29]In the following, we use the term digital services rather than digital offerings or digital products. This is because these offerings are often brought to market "as a service", that is, on the basis of usage-based pricing.

it raised: Where are the data from production and operations stored, and how secure are they? How can and should user access rights be configured? How can the system be integrated with the machine park and legacy IT systems? How might an employer unduly monitor employee performance through the digital service? What will the supplier of a digital service learn about the customer company from the data they gain access to — and what is the implication? To evaluate these questions, buying centers grew ever larger to include representatives from the C-suite, operations, legal, IT, human resources, and even the works council. By and large, customers perceived great risks from the organizational changes required when buying and implementing a digital service and were hesitant to grant suppliers with insights into their processes. The latter issue points to a lack of customer trust in suppliers. As we discussed earlier, customer trust is a key prerequisite for eventually becoming successful with complex service solutions.

When it comes to the product, interviewees frequently attributed the low level of reliability to errors in the software code, but several underlying issues emerged as we dug deeper. The digital services were typically extremely complex and over-engineered, offering many functionalities that customers did not need. Other functionalities that were important to customers were missing, such as connectivity to other machines and systems. Respondents traced these issues back to the lack of customer integration in the development process. As we discussed earlier, customer understanding and focus are key when developing complex service solutions. Many industrial companies seem to lack such understanding and focus early on, even when taking the very first step toward such solutions. With the digital service business being small in size, many suppliers also did not have sufficient resources to quickly resolve customers' service cases and change requests.

The interviewees also lamented that the lack of suitable sales incentives impeded the motivation of sales teams. Indeed, although selling a digital service was more difficult and took longer than selling a machine,[30] its lower price entailed lower sales commissions. Again, the motivation of sales teams also fell victim to deeper issues. Many salespeople understood

---

[30]In a cross-sector study, for example, Steenburgh and Ahearne found that salespeople should expect to invest an average of 35 percent more time in this area. T. Steenburgh and M. Ahearne, "How to Sell New Products", *Harvard Business Review* 96, no. 6 (2018): 131–139.

their role as the one of a "machine seller", and thus focused their efforts on machines rather than digital services. They also feared that the low level of reliability of digital services would lead to customer dissatisfaction, to the extent that customers would stop purchasing industrial equipment, threatening suppliers' cash cow business. Some salespeople simply did not have time to deal with the new offerings, because their business was already at capacity.

When it came to salespeople's lack of competence, we found that the problem went beyond having too little IT knowledge. Although sales representatives stated that they knew their customers' companies well, they could not recognize any concrete improvement potential in customers' value creation processes. This is because salespeople neither had the experience nor the training to generate *deep* customer understanding. In addition, salespeople were overwhelmed by the changing buying centers they needed to interact with. For their traditional equipment sales, they usually sold to production managers or purchasing managers. When it came to digital services, the ultimate decider was usually a top manager, but salespeople lacked the contacts and communication skills required for selling at that level. Lastly, selling digital services required salespeople to engage in team selling as suppliers introduced new sales roles such as technical sales, implementation specialists, and customer success managers. However, many salespeople were unable to sell in teams, as they had built an entire career as a "lone wolf" who excelled at hunting and converting sales opportunities on their own.

When it came to framework factors within the company, it became clear that a lack of focus was largely to blame for inadequate investment in resource development. A small number of experts were confronted with too many inquiries regarding product development, sales, and service, leading to unreliable products and a slow resolution of customer complaints. However, again, the true challenges lay deeper. One of these challenges was the management's optimism, leading to unrealistically high sales targets when launching digital services. Respondents also called out their company's corporate culture and management style — as well as excessive influence from headquarters — as reasons for unsuccessful business development. Lastly, suppliers were still looking for the right channels through which to sell digital services. They had typically started out by assigning existing equipment salespeople the task of cross-selling these services. Few companies succeeded with this approach, while a few others sooner or later pivoted to team-selling approaches, in

	Customers	Product	Sales force willingness	Sales force ability	Corporate framework
Obvious reasons	Perception: Value too low and thus low willingness to pay	Product reliability too low	Incentives not attractive enough	Lack of IT competence	Insufficient pre-invest-ment in resources
Beyond the obvious	Organiza-tionally not prepared (buying center, legal, technical, social issues)	Product too complex/over-engineered (incl. unneeded functions)	Role perception as a "machine seller"	Do not understand value-creation potential in customer's processes	Overly optimistic revenue and profit expectations
	Perception of high risk concerning expected changes	Weak connectivity to other machines and systems, such as Enterprise Resource Planning (ERP)	Concerns about negative impact on cash cow business	Missing contacts and skills for consultative C-level selling	Lack of digital service culture and manage-ment style (e.g., speed, error culture)
	Resistance to share (further) insights	Insufficient support for trouble-shooting/ updates	Time constraints due to full pipeline (with cash cow business)	Lack of teamwork skills	Ineffective sales channels setup

Figure 4.16: Problem areas of industrial companies in the marketing of additional digital offerings.

which salespeople were supported by specialists in technical sales roles. Note how industrial companies thereby set the course for either the "hero" or the "orchestrator" approach outlined above. Most respondents in our study, however, were of the opinion that their company had not yet found the right channels and roles to bring digital services to the market. Figure 4.16 offers an overview of the most important problems identified in this research project.

These problems not only led to lower sales but they also put the core business at risk. Salespeople who do not properly understand new offerings — yet strongly promote them to customers — run the risk of making false promises out of ignorance. If customers are later disappointed because expectations have not been met, they may call the supplier's other product areas into question. A similar situation emerges if too few resources have been created to provide the service offerings.

Managers can overcome these problems by taking a number of actions. We already mentioned some of these above. Managers should proactively choose suitable customers only. As long as the new offering's complexity is limited, training can compensate for a lack of salespeople's expertise. As the level of complexity increases, traditional sales resources should only act as a door opener. This will help bring customers together with the supplier's team of appropriate experts.

This is how the previously mentioned truck manufacturer, MAN, pursues its own digital offering under the name RIO. The simpler set of digital offerings are designed to improve MAN's truck and operating costs, and they are marketed by existing trading partners. But for customers who need digital solutions to optimize an entire vehicle fleet, MAN engages a team of its very own experts. This becomes all the more important if the vehicle fleet is not exclusively made up of MAN vehicles, and if the customer has to establish digital connectivity to other partners. The customer does not enter into a contract for such a solution with a trading partner, but directly with MAN.

KBC follows a similar approach to marketing its digital platforms and services. The company created a new sales role — labeled sales experts — that focuses on selling digital services. Sales experts coordinate with existing account managers about which customers to target with which digital service. Once a digital service is sold, a customer success manager takes over to ensure customers receive high value-in-use. For account managers, this setup entails a further evolution toward becoming "orchestrators." Their job profile is shifting from *making* deals to *orchestrating* them.

To ensure that account managers are willing to orchestrate and collaborate with sales experts, KBC uses double-counting incentives. This means that the account manager and the sales expert do not have to negotiate incremental contributions and decide how to split commissions, because a digital service fully counts toward the quota of both. To solve the problem of unattractive incentives due to the lower one-off business of digital services, KBC calculates commissions on the basis of the predicted contract duration with a customer. Thus, account managers not only receive compensation for the immediate digital service revenue they generate with a customer but also for the expected revenue and profitability for the next three to five years. As a word of caution, incentives for complex service sales should be low to moderate, as high incentives can preoccupy salespeople's minds and hinder them from solving customers' problems.[31]

[31] S. Alavi, E. Boehm, J. Habel, J. Wieseke, C. Schmitz, and F. Brueggemann, "The Ambivalent Role of Monetary Sales Incentives in Service Innovation Selling", *Journal of Product Innovation Management* 39, no. 3 (2022): 445–463; see also J. Habel, S. Alavi,

Aligning the Company

When companies make everyday statements on why it is important to retain competent employees, it is often little more than lip service. Talented people can and do leave industrial companies with established products in the marketplace. Yet, it does not threaten these businesses' existence. For complex service solutions, the situation is different. That is why human resources (HR) management for these companies is a top priority. It is not enough to hire employees, develop them, and cultivate their loyalty. Managers must also terminate employees who are not suited for their role. Tom Miller's poignant quote from the first section of this chapter captures the challenges of human resources during the introduction of complex service solutions: "We underestimated how different our people's skills portfolio requirements would be. The people from the traditional business did not even have the right skills to interview the necessary candidates." That is why managers should provide training courses to employees who are directly involved in the value creation process of complex service solutions, as well as those who work in related administrative areas.

Good HR work includes freeing employees from activities to which they cannot add value. This includes the internal digitization of standard activities. On the one hand, this has an impact on internal processes. That is why HR managers should not only focus on saving resources in administrative areas but also ensure that employees in operational areas are actually given the proper amount of support. In addition, processes between customers and suppliers must be digitized, at least to the extent that customers are willing to accept it. This can include ordering hardware replacement parts or upgrading the necessary software after implementation of the solution. If the customer buys these elements separately, the supplier's sales staff or external sales partners no longer need to provide personal support. Instead, these purchase processes can be increasingly managed via e-business platforms. This generates cost savings for customers and suppliers alike.[32]

---

and K. Linsenmayer, "Variable Compensation and Salesperson Health", *Journal of Marketing* 85, no. 3 (2021): 130–149.
[32]P. Guenzi and J. Habel, "Mastering the Digital Transformation of Sales", *California Management Review* 62, no. 4 (2020): 57–85.

In order to optimize process digitization, customers will require the right IT systems. Suppliers must keep these IT landscapes up to date with the latest technology. Because these systems are in a constant state of development, this is not a trivial task. Additional complications come into play. For example, the new system must be compatible with the customer's existing IT landscape. After all, these two systems may operate under different technical standards or follow different national compliance regulations. This puts demands on the supplier's IT systems and employees that go well beyond the typical functions of an industrial company's IT department. In addition, complex service solution suppliers have the role of keeping their digital landscapes up to date — a task that is not reserved for the IT department alone. Digitization should involve all corporate business areas with responsibility for complex service solutions. Accordingly, a chief digital officer should be as dispensable as a chief profit officer. Digitization must come as naturally to everyone as making profits. Managers do not need to develop a separate "digital strategy", because technical development must be an integral part of all planning processes.

Transforming a traditional industrial company requires more than the necessary technical and organizational changes. Managers also have to transform their corporate culture. Critically, that culture must fit the business. If technical and market factors change quickly, agility is one of the most important traits a corporate culture can have. It becomes a tangible factor, both for the speed in which decisions are made and the willingness of employees to adapt to change. For leadership, agility means accepting changes in planning — a skill that is rarely found in industrial companies. "Established companies don't want just plans; they want managers who stick to those plans. They often reward people for doing what they committed to do and discourage them from making changes as circumstances warrant."[33]

In addition to agility, managers have to be able to openly handle failures and mistakes. Managers must be role models in this regard, in spite of the regional differences in this type of cultural expression. In Asian and Western European cultures, failures and mistakes are viewed as flaws. This has a negative impact on managers' careers. As a result, these leaders tend to keep their errors secret. In North America, people are more open.

---

[33] R. M. Kanter, "Innovation: The Classical Traps", *Harvard Business Review* 84, no. 11 (2006): 72–83.

This is the region where "f***-up nights" have actually been introduced, in which managers publicly showcase their errors and take responsibility for them so that others may learn. In this respect, it is not surprising that Tom Miller, who disclosed the missteps made during the launch of Soarian, is an American.

When managers deal with mistakes so openly, there is no excessive hierarchical-orientation. This does not match the organizational structures required for complex service solutions, which are characterized by flexible project teams. Instead of being fixated on instructions from above, the employees involved must be willing to take responsibility for corporate decisions themselves. In order to accelerate this, many industrial companies have held training courses on "entrepreneurship" over the past few years. In addition, companies need to establish a climate of psychological safety, that is, a belief that one will not be punished or humiliated for mistakes.[34]

Agility, entrepreneurship, and f***-up nights: These catchwords seem to offer industrial companies the very model that start-ups frequently use when they launch complex service solutions. Yet, it would be wrong to adopt this mindset wholesale. High start-up insolvency rates alone make them inappropriate role models. If industrial companies actually did succeed in enforcing entrepreneurship values among managers, there is a risk that these very employees might leave the company to start their own.

Instead, industrial companies that want to achieve solid growth with complex service solutions have to find the right balance. This cannot be based on corporate culture alone. Although it is true that these businesses will have to become more flexible and agile in some areas — and that managers need to be less risk averse in their investment decisions — industrial companies are different. They have greater social responsibility than start-ups because of the sheer number of employees. Managers need to understand that poor decisions may endanger their company's very existence. Quality management should reflect market requirements and not, as is usual among start-ups, receive secondary priority. Even if an industrial company took its new offerings to market with a "fake it till you

---

[34]A. Edmondson, "Psychological Safety and Learning Behavior in Work Teams", *Administrative Science Quarterly* 44, no. 2 (1999): 350–383; J. Hagen, *Confronting Mistakes: Lessons from the Aviation Industry when Dealing with Error* (New York, NY: Palgrave Macmillan, 2013).

make it" mindset (as it is known in the IT industry), it would impact their trustworthiness in other business areas. Such differences between traditional industrial companies and start-ups are primarily based on different business objectives. Whereas industrial companies are interested in solid growth and a sustainable existence, many start-up owners want to make a lot of money quickly by selling their company in the short and medium terms.

Industrial companies that want to market complex service solutions in addition to their established business must therefore find the right balance between modern digital culture and traditional industrial culture. A central question in this context is whether the new business should be an integral part of the existing organization or whether it should be managed separately. Under an integrative approach, there is a risk that the new business will not be able to develop and realize new ideas under the dominant, traditional structures of the parent. Yet, a detached model means that valuable synergy potential may remain unused. In Chapter 5, we readdress the topic of group strategy. In the meantime, we revisit Beumer Group, introduced in Chapter 2, and its approach to overcoming this dilemma.

Beumer Group is a medium-sized industrial company in Beckum, Germany. Its products include luggage conveyor belts for airports. This company recognized that digital technologies would change its traditional business. In order to not lag behind market developments, two new organizational units were created. The first is BG.evolution — a business unit that develops digital services to improve and gradually expand the company's traditional offerings. It is based in Dortmund, near the corporate headquarters. The teams at BG.evolution developed an application that allows airport personnel to find no-show passengers' luggage items in the aircraft hold more quickly. BG.evolution first developed a simple prototype (i.e., a minimally viable product that the company could demonstrate to interested customers). Subsequently, the development department of Beumer Group's traditional business division assumed responsibility for this digital innovation. It was then further refined and adapted to meet the application requirements of individual airports. Beumer was convinced that generating digital ideas requires a different cultural environment than when implementing them at scale. To this day, those responsible for the established business regard BG.evolution as a young, creative think tank for digital experts with the role of an internal supplier. At the same time, the parent company is not compelled to adopt every idea that BG.evolution develops.

However, Beam (formerly BG.challenge), a different unit of Beumer, provides an important counterweight to the internal supplier role. This legally independent unit develops complex service solutions that are designed to deliberately challenge Beumer Group's current business. The unit is working on logistics systems, for example, that allow passengers to drop off their luggage at home or in the shop around the corner. They only reclaim their bags once they arrive at their destination. This would either render airport luggage conveyor belts obsolete or cannibalize the existing business. A young, creative group was set up at Beam. It was located in Berlin, far from headquarters. Beam reports directly to the head of Beumer Group. By adopting this reporting structure, the senior executive is not seeking to avoid disruptive innovations in the company's core business market. Instead, he is seeking to proactively engage and influence them.

By establishing two new business units with different levels of independence from the parent company, Beumer Group is trying to find the right balance between its digital and established businesses. In doing so, the company is putting the O'Reilly and Tushman approach into practice. Accordingly, businesses in the "exploitation" phase are being pursued differently from those in the "exploration" phase.

Beumer Group regards this solution as a success but remains open to adaptations. Because of the rapid developments in markets and technologies, managers understand that organizational balance must be found again and again. Change is inevitable. Yet, companies often struggle with change. This is one of the reasons that complex service solutions do not always succeed. Consider the problems in the Soarian case mentioned above and Rolls-Royce's financial difficulties in its aircraft turbine business.

There is another side of the coin to these examples. Rolls-Royce has been generating losses with its power by the hour business over the past few years. GE, in contrast, has been posting profits. In 2014, Siemens was happy to be able to sell the Soarian loss-maker to Cerner, which made profits. In addition, despite the bad experience with Soarian, Siemens Healthineers now offers similar complex service solutions and has been successful. Rolls-Royce has recently introduced changes that will improve its business in the aircraft turbine sector again. These developments reveal two critical insights. First and foremost, complex service solutions are neither completely profitable nor loss-making in and of themselves. Instead, their success largely depends on how they are managed. Finally, despite bad initial experiences, traditional industrial companies see digital transformation as an inevitable strategy for the future. They approach this change with a strategic mix of caution and optimism. Their mindset is reflected in the prescient axiom "Digital is dangerous. But analog is deadly."

Chapter 5

The Bigger Picture: Managing Different Businesses within a Single Company

Abstract

In the following chapter, we present the fundamentals of corporate strategy — the strategy that reaches across all business units. We take an in-depth look at the opportunities for creating synergies among business units and the resulting challenges. This involves taking a particularly close look at the synergy effects of cross-border cooperation and its application in all three counter strategies (see Chapters 2–4). It also addresses the issues of intercultural cooperation as well as the leadership and organizational opportunities for overcoming them. Finally, we consider future developments in politics, economics, and technology, and the influence they have on corporate strategic decision-making.

The Fundamentals of Corporate Strategy

In February 2009, turbulence in the financial markets had reached industrial companies. Revenues sank dramatically. Basler AG, a hidden champion from Ahrensburg, Germany, was also impacted. Dietmar Ley — to whom the company's founder, Norbert Basler, had handed over management of the company — initiated a series of austerity measures. Salaries were frozen. Top executives took a 30 percent reduction in salary. Travel expenses were cut back, and advertising activity was reduced, but the cost savings did not compensate for diminished revenues. It was foreseeable that the company's financial reserves would soon be depleted. Yet, despite this painful insight, Ley was convinced that a significant staff reduction was unavoidable for maintaining the company's independence and saving it from bankruptcy.

At the time, Basler was divided into two divisions: the Solutions and Components business units. The latter produced and marketed digital cameras for industrial applications. Manufacturing industries used these cameras for product testing. Physicians used them to diagnose skin diseases. They were also used in ATM machines for facial recognition. The Components business unit offered a broad product spectrum, ranging from simple devices for €250 to advanced cameras for €1,500. In the premium segment, Basler was the global market leader, although the lower- and mid-price market segments were significantly larger. Basler shared these segments with other equally large medium-sized companies, most of whom still used analog technology in their cameras (see Figure 5.1).

The Solutions business unit offered complete quality-control solutions for industrial products. This is the business that had made Basler big; camera production had been added later. For customer-specific solutions, Basler cameras were implemented as components, which only represented a very small portion of the test system offerings. Basler purchased, configured, and installed all other components. This process was supervised by experts who were familiar with their customers' industries and related production processes. Among the customers that Basler focused on were optical media industries such as those that produced CDs and DVDs as well as suppliers of sealing inspection solutions and solar panel

Figure 5.1:   A Basler industrial camera (Components business division, photo left) and inspection system (Solutions business division, right) (© Basler AG).

manufacturers. Basler was also the market leader worldwide for product quality-control solutions for optical media and sealing inspection solutions. Over the long term, however, these industries offered few growth opportunities. When it came to solar panels, Basler assumed that production volumes would increase, particularly because of high growth levels in China. Chinese competitors, however, had established themselves in their home market, where they were increasingly gaining market share.

The Solutions and Components business units had approximately the same number of employees and had achieved comparable earnings in recent years. In order to reduce the amount of personnel, Ley saw no other way than to substantially reduce the activities of one of the business units. He planned to take a portion of the cost savings, invest it in the other business unit, and ultimately lead a strengthened Basler out of the crisis. Yet, which business unit should Ley scale down, and which one should he build up?

Ley's challenge extends across business units. It goes well beyond what we have discussed in Chapters 1–4, in which only the strategy options for specific markets are examined. Many companies are active in more than one market and have several strategic business units. These business units address different target groups with different products. Each takes responsibility for its own profits and losses. When we use the term "corporate strategy", we are referring to the strategies for managing several cross-divisional business units.

At launch, most companies are only active in one business segment. If there is success with the first business segment, other areas are explored. Existing financial resources can then be used to expand the company's activities into other business areas. As a result, the company's initial strategic issues are always growth-oriented (i.e., "in which new lines of business would we like to grow?") and are not — as Basler did during the financial crisis — focused on withdrawing from particular business segments.

The entry into new business segments is called diversification. We distinguish between vertical, horizontal, and lateral diversification. Companies use vertical diversification to extend their portfolio offerings upstream and downstream along the value chain. This was the case with Basler when the company entered the camera components business in addition to its system solutions. With horizontal diversification, companies broaden their range with products along the very same value chain. This occurs when a bulldozer manufacturer adds a backhoe to its offerings. Finally, with lateral diversification, the business units do not have any relationship to one another. For example, India's family-run company Tata operates steel factories and hotels in addition to offering software and telecommunications services. It is also India's largest automobile manufacturer. Lateral diversification is often used by companies to improve their risk position, because if a company depends on the success of a single business segment, its very existence is threatened if that part of the market experiences a crisis. If the company is operating in several market areas, it can compensate for such challenges. This aspect is particularly relevant if we think about the solidity of a company over a long period.

Analysts and investors are now taking a more critical view of the argument for risk reduction in modern capital markets, in which huge investment funds have become the most influential shareholders. This is because mutual funds provide investors with a risk-optimized business portfolio as their core competency. They invest not only in different companies but also in various sectors and regions. They expect companies to deliver high dividends and rising asset prices, not independent risk management through business diversification. We return later to explore the circumstances under which a fund might nonetheless invest in companies with diversified business portfolios.

Here we examine an industrial company's approach to dealing with the three central questions that executives must answer when designing their group strategy:

1. Which strategic business units should be part of the company? Should new ones be formed or purchased? Are there others that we should unload?
2. How should the company's resources be divided among the individual strategic business units? In which business units will we invest, and how much? Where will we cut back on funding or personnel?
3. To what extent should headquarters exert influence on the management decisions of strategic business units? Will they be granted broad autonomy? Or should we tell them which IT systems to use, which salary ranges are acceptable, and which travel policies apply?

With regard to points one and two, a matrix developed by the founder of the Boston Consulting Group (BCG), Bruce Henderson, has achieved wide recognition. It helped the BCG achieve its breakthrough into the

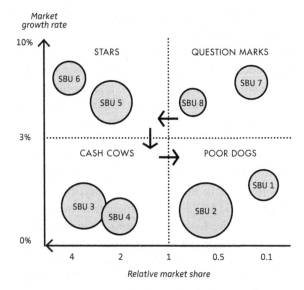

Figure 5.2: The BCG Matrix of a fictional company (SBU stands for strategic business unit).

international consulting market. This matrix provides an overview of a company's business divisions and simplifies the complexity of corporate strategic decisions (see Figure 5.2).

The circles in Figure 5.2 represent business units, and their sizes correspond to the extent of the units' respective revenues. The horizontal axis shows a business unit's relative market share: A value of one means that the business unit generates as much revenue as that market's largest competitor. If that unit's market share is greater than one, then it is the market leader for that business segment. If the relative market share is less than one, then the largest competitor is generating higher revenues. The vertical axis indicates the average market growth rate. In the example above, then, the business unit markets are growing. The positions in the lower part of the chart demonstrate below-average market growth.

In addition, the BCG Matrix provides business unit portfolio management recommendations. Accordingly, new units are only established in markets with above-average growth. They start out small, and in order for them to grow, the company must invest in them. Ideally, this should continue until it becomes the largest unit with the highest revenues in that respective market. Because all new business units do not achieve this level of market success, the circles in the upper-right quadrant of Figure 5.2 fall into the "question marks" quadrant. Units that attain market leadership are placed in the "stars" quadrant, which we see in the upper-left corner. Yet, no market's growth lasts forever, as any market is subject to cycles. At some point, growth rates will fall and the business unit will sink into the "cash cows" quadrant. Because of their leading market positions, cash cows still generate profits, which should be used to improve the question marks quadrant. The withdrawal of resources, however, reduces the cash cows' market share. They then become "poor dogs". Business managers have to find the right time to sell off poor dogs.

Basler used this matrix in 2009 as an analytical tool to evaluate its own situation. Using the BCG Matrix, managers not only conducted an exhaustive analysis of the Components and Solutions business units but they also broke down their analysis into its constituent customer segments. It turns out that managers did not anticipate any growth in the optical media and sealing inspection solutions market segments. They had been assigned to the cash cows quadrant even though they were not generating profits. Thanks to the Chinese market, the solar panels segment had grown, but Basler assumed that Chinese solar panel manufacturers would increasingly start buying the very testing systems sold by Basler from Chinese suppliers. This meant that Basler would not participate in that market growth. As a result, Ley decided to make significant reductions in the Solutions unit. The After-Sales Service unit would continue to exist, but Basler would not make further investments in new acquisitions and research. The Components unit benefited from the freed-up resources, particularly in the rapidly growing low-cost camera segment — a business that still occupied the question marks quadrant in 2009. Thus, Basler built up production capacity there and secured a quantity-based cost advantage vis-à-vis other medium-sized competitors. Among other things, Basler used its premium sector digital know-how, which analog-based competitors had yet to establish. Thanks to this cost advantage, Basler achieved market leadership in the lower price segment. Based on this 2009 strategic decision, Basler was able to triple its revenues by 2018 and quadruple its profitability.

The recommendations for action offered by the BCG Matrix are nonetheless controversial. Critics question the presumption that a business segment should always pursue market leadership. The PIMS study mentioned in Chapter 1 did indeed demonstrate that a large market share promises high levels of profitability. Yet, the same study shows that this equally applies to business units with a very small market share. Moreover, the BCG Matrix maintains that only companies with market-leading business units can have stars and cash cows. If a company does not have these types of business units, then it makes no sense for companies to work with the BCG Matrix, even if they are highly profitable.

In addition, the BCG Matrix does not specify how markets should be defined and how business units should be separated from one another. As a general rule, each division should have its own product–market combination and its own competitors. But what does this mean? If, for example, a vacuum pump manufacturer sold premium and no-frills products in China and Western Europe — and if that company's competitors had a regional or quality-related focus — how many business segments should the manufacturer create? Should it have one unit for vacuum pumps, two for advanced premium and no-frills products, or four for advanced premium and no-frills products in Western Europe and China? There are no fixed rules here, but answering this question is crucial for assessing market share. That is why decisions must be made here on a case-by-case basis, as in the Basler example. As it stands, the company's analysis did not examine strategic business units as a whole. Instead, it used sub-segments.

Regardless of how managers decide to differentiate business segments, corporate strategy logic always requires them to follow one rule: The whole must be greater than the sum of its parts. This means that cross-segment activity costs must always be outweighed by the benefits generated. The value of an individual unit must be lower than its value within the group. Figure 5.3 illustrates this connection.

The advantage that a corporate headquarters creates is known as the "parenting advantage." From a strategic business unit's perspective, this advantage involves using synergies created by linkage influence. This can be the result of growing cost savings ($1+1 = 1.8$, so to speak), as well as additional revenues ($1+1 = 2.2$, so to speak). The latter emerge when business unit A's customers, based on their good experience, show demand for business unit B's products and become B's new customers. Cost synergies exist when all business units procure the materials they need through a central purchasing department. This leads to discounts, which suppliers would not give to a single business unit. Additional cost savings can also be realized through the shared use of IT systems, M&A experts, and external finance instruments.

Synergies are among the reasons why investment funds, as mentioned above, buy shares of companies that are active in diverse business sectors.

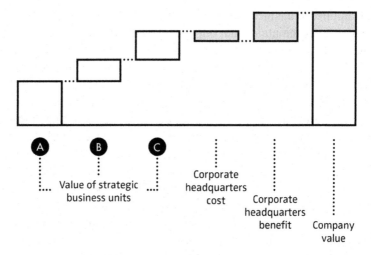

Figure 5.3: Financial logic for a corporate group's strategic advantage.[1]

Of course, each business sector should achieve success on its own and generate economic value, but a company can also create added value through synergies. In doing so, each business unit should contribute to the synergies of a corporation. According to financial market logic, the company should be able to create its added value better than other owners. In this context, we refer to the "best owner." This means that a strategic business unit should belong to the owner who creates the maximum amount of economic value. Against this backdrop, Siemens AG is examining its strategic business unit portfolio based on the following questions:

- Growth segment (*Does this business unit address a growth segment?*)
- Potential profit pool (*What is its profit potential?*)
- Competitive advantages (*What are its competitive advantages? Why Siemens?*)
- Synergetic value (*What should be the synergy contribution level?*)
- Paradigm shifts in technology and markets (*Should we expect paradigm shifts related to technology or the market that justify the existence of this business unit?*[2])

---

[1]Based on H. Hungenberg, *Strategisches Management in Unternehmen* (Wiesbaden: Gabler Verlag, 2014).

[2]Documents published by Siemens AG on the internet; Guidelines for the Group Strategy Vision 2020 (translation by the authors).

Siemens is a very good example of how large corporations have been scaling back — rather than building up — centralized structures in recent years. From a financial perspective, Siemens suffered under a so-called conglomeration discount for years. This meant that the stock market valued the company for less than the sum of its individual business units. As a result, several units have been spun off in recent years. For example, Siemens sold a portion of its household appliance and lighting businesses. The company spun off its wind turbine business into the publicly traded company Siemens Gamesa Renewable Energy and brought Siemens Energy onto the stock market in 2020. It transferred its medical business into a stand-alone company. Siemens also aimed to merge its rail business into a joint venture with the French company Alstom, but European antitrust authorities stopped this plan in 2019. Siemens' competitor GE has streamlined itself by selling off the divisions Consumer & Industrial and GE Capital. Several automotive groups are following the trend toward decentralization. Daimler AG and Volkswagen AG, for example, are spinning off their truck businesses to create separate publicly traded companies.

Many medium-sized companies try to avoid corporate structures in the first place, despite growth. We now refer back to the EOS example from Chapter 2. After launching in 1989, the company focused on what the emerging technologies were at the time for additive manufacturing (AM), including 3-D printing. It used them to cover its entire value chain. A billion-dollar market later emerged from this niche, with broad application across numerous industries. Instead of pursuing a corporate structure format, founder Hans Langer, together with other industrial partners, launched numerous new companies — each of which focused on profitable AM market niches. These companies were independent and not forced to cooperate with Langer. Under this scenario, Scanlab created new global market leaders, including today's leading manufacturer of Galvanometer scanners.

Thus, there are reasons for not combining multiple business units under one corporate roof. A corporate headquarters' influence on strategic management decisions plays a critical role here. It involves a higher level of authority in the decision-making process, which makes it more time-consuming. At the same time, it does not foster manager motivation within the business unit. The more that people interfere at the top, the more time that is lost and the greater the danger of bringing the business unit's entrepreneurial spirit to a grinding halt. A company or division owner must weigh the advantages and disadvantages to find the optimal business management balance. Approaches range from financial investors, who merely give direction regarding financial targets and reporting systems, to corporations, which want authority over operational decisions — such as which class of airline service business unit managers are allowed to book.

We now take a look at the topic of synergy generation and the challenges in implementing the three counter strategies — discussed in the previous chapters — simultaneously across a globally distributed value chain. Whether or not a company has formally created the relevant strategic business units or national subsidiaries is not important. We are interested in how synergies can emerge from country- and strategy-specific differences.

The Synergy Potential of Global Counter Strategies

In 2012, the Chinese company Weichai, the world's largest manufacturer of no-frills engines for trucks and the 11th largest truck producer, acquired a 25 percent minority stake in Kion AG, a German manufacturer of premium-segment forklift trucks. Weichai also acquired a majority stake in Kion's high-pressure hydraulic systems.

Weichai was the most profitable subsidiary of the company Shandong Heavy Industry Group (SHIG). The company's other divisions produced machinery and vehicles for the mining, agriculture, and construction industries. With the Shantui brand, the company was the world's largest manufacturer of bulldozers (see Figure 5.4), closely followed by the

Figure 5.4:   A forklift (left)[3]; a Shantui bulldozer (right, © Shantui).

---

[3] https://commons.wikimedia.org/wiki/File:Forklift_Truck-no_lines.svg.

American company Caterpillar. However, SHIG sold its no-frills products mainly in its home market. The company's few exports were still limited to China's neighboring countries, but SHIG wanted to change this over the medium term.

Weichai and the other SHIG companies produced most of their product components in-house, including axels, pumps, and gearboxes. High-pressure hydraulic systems were an exception. These expensive components were purchased from the Japanese company Kawasaki and other Western suppliers.

In 2011, Germany-based Kion AG was the world's second-largest forklift manufacturer after Toyota. It operated in more than 100 countries. The Kion premium-segment brands Linde and Still had leading positions in many countries, yet the company earned 80 percent of its sales revenue in Europe. In China, the company acquired the no-frills company Baoli in 2010, but it had a relatively weak presence in this region. Kion assumed, however, that the demand for forklift trucks would increase by 25–35 percent in China over the next five years. Among the many parts that Kion produced in-house were high-pressure hydraulic systems. Volkswagen AG supplied Kion with around 30,000 custom-made engines per year for forklifts. These engines were not powered by electric motors, but rather by internal combustion engines.

What would be the benefits of a collaboration between Kion and Weichai or SHIG?

- Weichai could help Kion gain a stronger foothold in China. Sales and service centers for trucks could be expanded to offer forklift trucks so that Kion would not have to build these centers on its own.
- Kion, in turn, could help Weichai build an international sales and service system. Emerging economies such as Brazil would be strong candidates. (Because of the emissions regulations in Western Europe and the United States, no-frills trucks were not yet being sold in these countries.)
- In addition, Kion would be able to help move Weichai's planned globalization forward. Kion could share its experiences with employee development and picking the right tax advisers in other countries.
- Kion could supply Weichai and other parts of the SHIG group with high-pressure hydraulic systems. The group, in turn, would retain the profits of these high-priced products. The demand for Shantui

bulldozers alone would be enough to boost production volumes, which would allow Kion to achieve cost-cutting economies of scale in production.

- By combining the technology skills of Kion development engineers and the no-frills experience of the SHIG group, a no-frills, high-pressure hydraulic system, which was not yet available on the world market, could be developed.

Since the early 2010s, Chinese companies have increasingly acquired equity stakes in German industrial companies or have purchased them outright. This was the case with Weichai, which increased its stake in Kion from 25 to 45 percent in 2018. In terms of the synergy potential, most of these Chinese companies follow a similar logic: The German companies offer their globalization and technology expertise, as well as their premium brand reputations, to the Chinese groups. This, in turn, helps (former) German companies gain access to China's large revenue potential and to improve their financial positions. The last argument, by the way, was also relevant to Kion. The company had previously belonged to US financial investors KKR and Goldman Sachs. During the years that they owned Kion, they managed the company with high levels of debt.

Looking more generally at the cost synergy potential that results from cross-border cooperation, most companies focus on economies of scale. Suppliers can bundle orders into greater quantities for larger discounts. A company can also use its know-how more efficiently to realize cost advantages. This is the case when the customer behavior changes in country A are relevant in country B, or when the business expansion knowledge gained in country A can be used in country B. One example is Facebook. Its initial experiences in the United States benefited the company as it built its business in Europe. Another example is the machine maintenance contracts in the industrial sector. In Western countries, this type of contract has been established for years. Demand for them in emerging-markets has yet to materialize.

In addition to cost advantages, cross-border cooperation can generate potential revenue synergies. They develop among customers who are active in country A and who want to collaborate with the same suppliers. For this reason, several medium-sized automotive manufacturers who supply major car companies have established subsidiaries abroad. This allows them to internationalize their sales while they develop their local customer base.

We have now examined the synergy potentials of cross-border cooperation. Next, we turn to the potential benefits of simultaneously pursuing the three counter strategies we discussed in the previous chapters. On the one hand, we assume that the three strategies demonstrate key differences within their product–market combinations. On the other hand, they share overlapping touch points. One example is Kion. Since Weichai became involved with the company, it has been able to push ahead with its no-frills forklift offerings. At the same time, it has entered the complex service solutions business. By purchasing Egemin in 2013 and Dematic in 2016, for example, Kion acquired two companies that offer software and consulting for intralogistics solutions. This, in turn, helped Kion optimize its warehouse processes. Here, then, we find overlaps between both the solutions-focused and the classic forklift businesses. In addition, the products share interdependencies despite their different technologies. Companies that implement intralogistics concepts often need forklifts to do so. The use of forklift trucks, in turn, requires many companies to develop a software-based operational concept.

Similar developments can be found across other companies' product and service portfolios. In addition to its premium products, Trumpf manufactures no-frills laser machines under the brand JFY. At the same time, it delivers consulting and software-based solutions to optimize its customers' manufacturing processes under the brand TruConnect. Claas, Europe's largest supplier of farm equipment, sells in both the high-price and low-price agricultural machine segments. Furthermore, the company operates 365FarmNet, as discussed in Chapter 4. This digital platform assists farmers in optimizing their resource efficiency while reducing back-office management tasks. Siemens Building Technology goes one step further by using its complex service solutions to handle office building management functions. For Swiss banking company Credit Suisse, this involves more than 1,000 real estate properties. At the same time, Siemens Building Technology continues to expand its range of premium and no-frills products.

None of these companies see themselves as financial investors that run independent business units. Rather, they are groups that want to create cross-divisional synergies. So, how can we pinpoint potential synergies when business units pursue different counter strategies?

If a company has already successfully marketed advanced premium products but would like to offer no-frills products, teams can rely on existing technical expertise for premium products. No-frills products provide even greater benefits if customers already know and appreciate the company's premium brand. This was the case with the Siemens no-frills fire protection systems, which were brought onto the market as Siemens Cerberus ECO, presented in Chapter 3. No-frills products can generate additional revenue synergies when customer contacts who have expressed an interest in significantly less expensive products can be leveraged. This is because these customers manufacture no-frills products in addition to advanced premium products.

Of course, the revenue synergies can go in the other direction. Even advanced premium products can receive synergy benefits through no-frills products. These advantages are particularly evident for customers in emerging and developing countries who, over time, will become interested in high-quality products beyond no-frills products. The transfer of technical know-how from the no-frills sector to the premium segment is also relevant. One example is GE's portable electrocardiographs. They were initially designed for emerging and developing countries. Over time, GE discovered that there was a need for portable electrocardiographs in industrial countries, too. Engineers used the no-frills product concept to develop corresponding premium products.

There are even mutual synergy benefits between advanced premium products and complex service solutions. When traditional industrial companies enter the complex services business, the new business sector benefits from the good reputations of established products. The same logic applies if a different brand name is used for both sets of offerings. Although Claas markets its data-driven platform under the 365FarmNet brand, most farmers know that Claas is behind this offering. As a result, the company is able to transfer the high-quality image of its agriculture machinery to its new service offerings. This image transfer is important, since — as presented in Chapter 4 — it plays an excellent role in mitigating the perceived risk in purchase decisions for complex service solutions.

The information gleaned from customers of complex service solutions can represent, in turn, valuable synergy effects for the advanced premium products business segment. This is how Claas, for instance, received valuable customer insights from 365FarmNet. The information gained from farmers' decision-making and usage patterns allowed Claas to provide its traditional equipment developers with product improvement ideas. In addition, insights can be derived from the customer information provided by complex service solutions. This information can reveal customer demand for new advanced premium products. Furthermore, to identifying synergy benefits, industrial company managers should ask themselves what would happen if they did not pursue both policy options. For example, if the data-based platform of a Claas competitor were to succeed in the market and if that competitor were to interfere with the interfaces between its platform and Claas's machines, Claas's traditional business could be threatened.

Until now, industrial companies have offered few examples of synergy effects between complex service solutions and no-frills products. In principle, we might expect benefits similar to those mentioned above by combining complex service solutions and advanced premium products. Information that comes from complex service solutions, for example, can also be used to develop no-frills products. Similarly, complex service solutions can be offered to no-frills product customers. It would be interesting to take the simplification idea of no-frills products into the design of complex service solutions. This would reduce them to the essentials and convert information complexity into simple rules. Opportunities like these are currently being tested under the term "simplexity".

Once managers fully envision the potential synergies that come from cross-border cooperation and the simultaneous pursuit of all three counter strategies, we begin to understand why industrial companies want to fully exploit this opportunity. The potential benefits, however, obscure the fact that transnational management and the simultaneous implementation of counter strategies are difficult. The three central questions, then, that have to be answered are as follows:

- How should we deal with cultural differences?
- How should the group structure itself organizationally?
- Which external factors should be considered?

The Greatest Challenge in Synergy Implementation

In the early 1990s, IBM ran into financial difficulties. In the past, the company had achieved success, particularly because of its high-quality IT hardware, such as PCs, servers, mainframes, and associated software products. However, competitors caught up with IBM. They developed a quality advantage in less sophisticated product segments. At the same time, they had a cost advantage over IBM. Lou Gerstner, the CEO who joined IBM in 1993, was forced to strategically realign the company.

He streamlined the traditional product portfolio and sold the PC unit to Lenovo in 2005. He then expanded IBM Global Business Services, which developed and implemented comprehensive IT solutions. In doing so, Gerstner had complemented IBM's premium products with complex service solutions.

For IBM customers, solution purchases had strategic importance. Top managers were usually in charge of the purchase decision. To serve this target group, IBM wanted to build a strategy consulting team that would compete with companies such as McKinsey and the Boston Consulting Group. The new group's strategic consulting expertise, combined with IBM employees' traditional IT expertise, promised to deliver sustainable competitive advantages.

In 1993, IBM began building the legally independent business unit IBM Consulting Group in Europe. To fill the new organization, IBM recruited a number of experienced managers away from other large consulting firms. They received salaries and bonuses similar to those they had received at their former consulting firms. As a result, their incomes were well above those of their colleagues in other IBM divisions.

Sustained success remained elusive for the IBM Consulting Group. It did not realize the expected collaborative synergies from consulting and IT specialists. By 1996, the IBM Consulting Group's independence was dissolved, and the group's resources were further reduced. According to former CEO of Europe Erich Clementi, this was largely because of the differences between the IT and consulting business cultures. Even later, he was still convinced that collaboration between both groups made sense from a strategic perspective. IBM had nonetheless not been able to bridge the cultural differences.[4]

By the term "culture", we refer to a system of rules and habits that influence human coexistence and behavior. These rules are based on values. They guide people from the same culture to approve certain behaviors and reject others. When we talk about different cultures in everyday life, we often refer to regional differences. For example, we might compare and contrast Chinese and American cultures, although within this framework, we want to examine the far-reaching cultural differences of people within a business context. This is how specific value systems have developed within certain industries. Likewise, individual companies can exhibit

---

[4]Interview of Mr. Clementi by one of the authors in 2006.

unique cultural characteristics. Individual value systems can even exist within certain groups in a company. Keaveney observed differences among employees in the development and sales departments of industrial companies. Within these very same groups, he also observed similar sources of misunderstandings and collaboration problems.[5] Our primary interest, however, is in cultural differences among employee groups whose work involves different counter strategies. Although there are no comprehensive empirical studies, the long-standing experience of the authors in cooperating with industrial companies supports the following statements:

- Business segments for advanced premium products represent the core values of quality and reliability. Product promises must be kept with customers as well as colleagues. Perfection is worth more than speed. Tradition is valued, and employee technical expertise is particularly well regarded. As a result, R&D departments are important.
- By contrast, the business units for no-frills products are infused with a focus on costs. Smooth processes play a vital role. The functional areas of purchasing and manufacturing have a high level of influence. Business employees who exercise control functions receive a high level of power and respect.
- The primary focus of complex service solutions is on the customer. Employees who work closely with customers and are successful in sales enjoy high status. Managers approach innovation with an open mind. Emphasis is placed on speed and flexibility in dealing with customers, as well as in managing internal processes.

Figure 5.5 illustrates the different value priorities of the three counter strategies.

Cultural differences are reinforced when a global company's employees come from different regional cultures. Hofstede's widely accepted conceptual framework illustrates this phenomenon.[6] Over the course of

---

[5]S. M. Keaveney, "The Blame Game: An Attribution Theory Approach to Marketer-engineer Conflict in High-technology Companies", *Industrial Marketing Management* 37, no. 6 (2008): 653–663.

[6]G. Hofstede, *Culture's Consequences: Comparing Values, Behaviors, Institutions and Organizations across Nations* (Tilburg: Sage Publications, 2001).

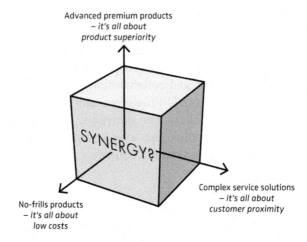

Figure 5.5:   The different value priorities of counter strategies.

his work from 1967 to 2010 — most of which is based on research at IBM — Hofstede defined six categories for identifying the major regional characteristics. Figure 5.6 shows these categories relative to China, the United States, and Germany.

In practice, Hofstede's systematic approach was well received, but he encountered opposition within the academic community, as he did not use representative samples. Meanwhile, other approaches were developed to address regional cultural differences.[7] Of particular interest are the studies of Brett, Behfar, and Kern, which shed light on cooperation within multi-cultural teams in global companies.[8] The authors identified the factors that create four major obstacles to multicultural collaboration:

- Language difficulties.
- Different ways of dealing with hierarchies.
- Different speeds in decision-making.
- Different forms of direct and indirect communication (i.e., the extent to which opinions are expressed).

---

[7]See, for example, the eight-dimensional approach of E. Meyer, "Navigating the Cultural Minefield", *Harvard Business Review* 92, no. 5 (2014): 119–123.

[8]J. Brett, K. Behfar, and M. C. Kern, "Managing Multicultural Teams", *Harvard Business Review* 85, no. 11 (2006): 85–91.

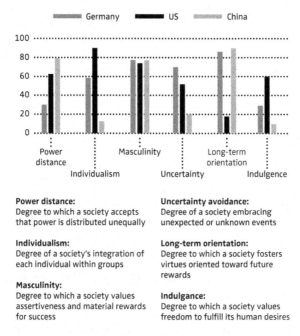

Germany   US   China

Power distance:
Degree to which a society accepts that power is distributed unequally

Individualism:
Degree of a society's integration of each individual within groups

Masculinity:
Degree to which a society values assertiveness and material rewards for success

Uncertainty avoidance:
Degree of a society embracing unexpected or unknown events

Long-term orientation:
Degree to which a society fosters virtues oriented toward future rewards

Indulgance:
Degree to which a society values freedom to fulfill its human desires

Figure 5.6: Cultural differences according to Hofstede.[9]

How Should Companies Handle Cultural Differences?

Brett, Behfar, and Kern offer suggestions on how to deal with these differences. First, managers should make differences transparent so that all stakeholders are aware of them and accept them as legitimate forms of diversity. Second, teams and tasks should be structured to avoid interpersonal conflicts as much as possible. This includes building sub-teams that harmonize well with each other, and whose work can later be brought together by using mediators or "network brokers."[10] Third, in the case of cultural conflicts, top management interventions are recommended that provide clear guidance based on the values that apply within the organization. As a fourth and last measure, the authors recommend an exit. This

---

[9]G. Hofstede, "Dimensions Data Matrix", (version 2015 12 08)." Retrieved from https://geerthofstede.com/research-and-vsm/dimension-data-matrix/. (Accessed May 4, 2020).
[10]The concept of "network brokers" can be found in R. S. Burt, "Structural Holes and Good Ideas", *American Journal of Sociology* 110, no. 2 (2010): 349–399.

means that employees who cope poorly in a multicultural environment over the long term should leave the relevant team.

To avoid an exit scenario, managers should take care in choosing the appropriate employees before forming multicultural teams. Managers can use the core evaluation criterion "cultural intelligence" (CQ) as a basis for identifying appropriate employees. This concept applies the earlier insights of Earley, Ang, and Tan.[11] According to these researchers, CQ reflects a person's ability to recognize the cultural characteristics of other people, and to interpret and adapt their own behavior accordingly. To illustrate, Earley and Mosakowski reported on how an American manager perceived the way that ideas were presented in an international team. Two German engineers criticized ideas clearly. American managers concluded from this that Germans are abrasive and rude. With the necessary degree of CQ, according to the authors, the American colleague would have recognized that Germans draw a distinction between expressing an opinion about an idea and about the people presenting it. They would have understood that the German colleagues did not want to hurt anyone's feelings. Moreover, a manager with a high CQ would have been able to estimate which portion of this behavior could be attributed to German culture and which portion to engineering-specific culture.[12]

Interestingly, CQ seems to be less pronounced among successful executives. They build their careers by first proving themselves within a less diverse cultural environment. This is where they gain their initial leadership experience. The successes they build here are often the foundation for receiving higher leadership positions with functional and transnational responsibilities. It is here that CQ deficits become apparent. Earley and Mosakowski discovered that the very executives who thrived in cultures with little diversity had enormous difficulties in leading intercultural teams. CQ is not innate, but it can be learned. Earley and Mosakowski have developed a method for measuring CQ as well as training methods for teaching them.

This approach is particularly relevant, as it is not just limited to regional cultural differences. It can also be applied to cultural differences across industries, companies, and business strategies, although the root

---

[11] C. Earley, S. Ang, and J. S. Tan, *Developing Cultural Intelligence at Work* (Stanford, CA: Stanford University Press, 2006).

[12] C. Earley and E. Mosakowski, "Cultural Intelligence", *Harvard Business Review* 82, no. 10 (2004): 139–146.

causes of existing cultural differences among employee groups cannot be readily determined. A CEO whose company was part of a German–Chinese joint venture in the truck industry summed up for the authors of this chapter his bewilderment over the organization's inability to collaborate: "I am well aware that the groups do not get along. Whether this is because of the German–Chinese cultural differences, the respective corporate cultures, the different business strategies, or simply the two bosses' personal idiosyncrasies, I don't know yet."

As mentioned above, supervisors should intervene when teams or employees are involved in an ongoing multicultural conflict. This is a sensitive matter if the conflict is based on underlying differences in ethical views — that is, when the decision has to be decided on moral grounds on the basis of right and wrong. Ethical differences happen less because of the pursuit of different business strategies, but rather when a company operates in several regions of the world. Imagine a Canadian manager who comes from a culture that considers customer gifts to be a form of attempted bribery. Imagine now that this very same manager leads a salesforce in a Middle Eastern country and forbids his employees from giving gifts to customers. The local employees will disagree with that direction, not only because they fear disadvantages in winning sales contracts but also because they feel that the direction discriminates against their culture. For them, gifts are an expression of politeness. To appear empty-handed is an affront. Alternatively, how should the sales director deal with this situation? How does his group supervisor (i.e., the member of the executive board who is responsible for sales) decide this question?

The problem can be assessed from two different dimensions that represent the polar attributes of a particular scope of action. To begin with, managers can pursue a policy of cultural relativism, in which the ethical values of other cultures are, in principle, accepted equally. Accordingly, a global corporation would follow the respective ethical norms of the culture in which it operates. The Canadian manager would have to respect the Arab gift-giving culture, and the ban on gifts would be lifted accordingly.

The second option would be to follow the dominant ethical code of a specific culture, usually that of the company's home country. For a Canadian company, all actions that are considered unethical in Canada would also be considered unethical in the foreign branch offices. The board would decide in favor of the new sales director and follow their lead. The literature refers to the second approach as ethical absolutism, sometimes referred to as ethical imperialism, because the home culture's ethics are viewed as superior and forced upon others.

In practice, companies should move flexibly between these two polar extremes. This is the approach that was developed by Donaldson[13] in the 1990s and based on three basic rules:

- Core values are defined as minimum standards that are binding for all regions of a company.
- Traditions are respected.
- Ethical decisions are made depending on the context.

Core values should be linked to ethical guidelines that already apply in most cultures, even if a violation is dealt with differently. There is a broad global consensus, for example, that employers must protect the health of employees and not allow them to come into contact with toxic substances.

North American companies, in particular, often document their ethical rules in a code of conduct that forms part of a compliance management system. Donaldson found that although this set of rules is repeatedly made known to employees, they are rarely familiar with it. In addition, policy guidelines in North American and European companies tend to emphasize the values of their home country. By doing so, they encounter misunderstandings and resistance, particularly among employees who work in other cultures.

Companies should keep a universal, basic rule definition to a minimum and give managers leeway to take unique, regional values into account when making business decisions. The amount of discretion managers can use depends on the context. Permissible gifts in the Middle East would, for example, depend on the gift's value, when the customer received the gift, and the nature of the gift giver's relationship to the customer. Even in the Arab world, some gifts go beyond generally accepted courtesy standards and are considered bribery.

Particularly in difficult-to-assess ethical conflicts, senior managers should include middle managers in the decision-making process and take their arguments into account. This is how one achieves broad internal acceptance. Managers can create case studies as an internal

---

[13]T. Donaldson, "Values in Tension: When Is Different Just Different, and When Is Different Wrong?", *Harvard Business Review* 74, no. 5 (1996): 48–62.

communications tool for particularly relevant decisions. These case studies can show the problem definition as well as the solution chosen by management. If a case study needs to be examined without actually identifying the people involved, the process can be anonymized. Such case studies should be made available to interested staff members, for example, via intranet or in internal publications. If similar problems arise, they can be discussed with the employees.

Openly communicating ethical issues in a company is especially useful in organizations that shift between cultural relativism and absolutism. This is because employees do not always understand positions that steer a middle course, particularly as they can change over time. These positions are marked by ambiguity, and inconsistencies have to be accepted. This requires everyone involved to be aware of the company's internal communication process. Managers who cannot negotiate the ambiguities of a global environment should ask themselves if they are the right fit for the role.

Does the World De-globalize?

Intercultural cooperation has always been a key challenge for internationally active companies and their managers. Now, in addition, they must adapt to new developments in global trade. Some of these are not conducive to global trade. Consequently, there has been much talk of de-globalization for some time.

But when it comes to data — we recall that in Chapter 1 globalization was defined as the cross-border movement of goods, services, people, money, and data — cross-border traffic has exploded in recent years. So, there can be no question of a general de-globalization. Nevertheless, cross-border transfers are reaching their limits. One example is the regulations of the Cyberspace Administration of China, which came into force in 2021 and has made it more difficult for car companies to transfer data generated in China to other countries. An increase in such restrictions can be expected in the future, both in China and in other countries. Managers of global companies need to be prepared for such changes. In the following sections, we present the most important changes and then discuss possible adaptation measures.

In terms of the cross-border movement of goods and services, there had been stronger growth than in global gross national product for decades.

Development of global export of **goods** and *services* (in USD trillions)

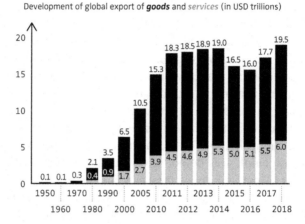

Figure 5.7:   Development of export of goods and services.

But the major growth rates have declined since 2011. Figure 5.7 illustrates this development.

Should companies continue to push their internationalization at all if the growth of international trade is declining? We expressly answer this question in the affirmative, because the business potential for globally active companies is still much greater than for those companies that limit themselves to national markets. However, globally active companies have to adapt. Global business operations function differently today than they did 10 years ago. In the following sections, we highlight the most important changes.

The significant decline in global trade in 2019 and 2020 was mainly due to the COVID-19 pandemic. After first appearing in China in late 2019, the virus spread globally in a matter of months, dwarfing even the decline in overall economic performance triggered by the 2009 financial crisis. The Chinese economy recovered from the economic impact by the fall of 2020, while other countries did not return to pre-pandemic economic performance until late 2021. In the wake of the COVID-19 pandemic, however, a trend intensified that has since had a lasting impact on cross-border trade in goods and services: Nationalism.

The first major media attention was given to this development at the start of Donald Trump's presidential candidacy in 2016, when he ran his election campaign with the slogan "America first". Similar nationalist tendencies can be found in countries such as China, India,

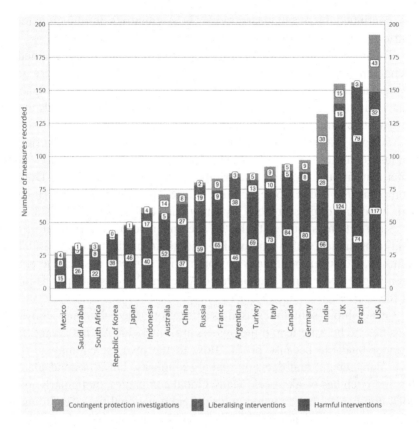

Figure 5.8:   G20 trade-related measures in 2020.[14]

Turkey, and Brazil. In Germany and France, like-minded parties have been launched by right-wing conservatives who turned away from global interests.

However, nationalistic measures directed against free global trade were already being implemented in the United States before Donald Trump's presidency. In the 1970s, for example, import restrictions were imposed on steel imports in the United States, as in other countries, to protect national steel companies from foreign competitors. Global Trade Alert statistics (see Figure 5.8) show that the trend toward protectionism

---

[14]S. J. Evenett and J. Fritz, *The 26th Global Trade Alert Report* (London: CEPR Press, 2020).

has continued in recent years, with G-20 countries introducing more restrictive trade measures than liberalizing ones in 2020.[15] The obstruction of imports runs parallel to other measures designed to strengthen domestic companies. For example, in 2020, the Japanese government allocated more than $2 billion in support for Japanese companies if they withdrew their operations from China. Government officials in the United States are also seeking to help domestic companies "to reshore." In addition, campaigns are being launched in a number of countries to encourage domestic consumers to buy products made domestically. "Buy American" is just one example. Both under the presidencies of Donald Trump and Joe Biden, corresponding campaigns were launched that have their historical origins in the "Buy American Act" of March 3, 1933.

Such actions should actually be accompanied by a definition of the conditions under which companies and their products are considered domestic. However, politicians do not provide concrete answers here. So, when might a company be considered American? Different options present themselves.

Ownership is sometimes used as a criterion: The public may consider a business to be American if the owners are American. At first glance, that is understandable because profits flow to the owners. Ultimately, they have management and decision-making authority, but at second glance, this approach has weaknesses. Many global companies, particularly joint-stock companies, have owners with different nationalities. According to this reasoning, Alibaba, which went public on the New York Stock Exchange in 2014, is not a Chinese company. In fact, a Japanese bank is currently Alibaba's largest shareholder; the second largest is the US company Yahoo!. Even Siemens would not be a German company using this standard, as not even one-third of its shareholders are German. Or, consider a winery in the Bordeaux region. It still produces the same wine, even though it has been bought by a Chinese businessman. Should we suddenly consider the company to be Chinese?

---

[15] It should also be noted that socio-political resistance to globalization is also on the rise on the left. Networks such as ATTAC (Association for the Taxation of financial Transactions and Aid to Citizens), for example, organize protest actions during international summit meetings. However, the critique focuses less on national interests than on the distribution of profits generated by global trade and the capitalist economic order as a whole.

Other criteria that are used for determining a company's nationality include the country in which the headquarters is located, as well as its corporate tax residence. In part, the nationality majority within the senior management team or the country in which the most value creation occurs also plays a role. In each of these cases, observers could argue for or against a company's national designation. From a political point of view, the value-added criterion is attractive, as it is linked to the creation of jobs and gross national product. When nationalism is on the rise, politicians are more likely than ever to emphasize the value-added criterion for this very reason.

Ultimately, however, there are no generally accepted definitional criteria for the question of national affiliation. Companies must therefore be prepared for the fact that their treatment in a country depends heavily on how they are perceived by the public there. We return to this in the section "Realigning external communications."

Resistance to global trade is faced by internationally active companies not only from the right-wing, national-oriented political spectrum. Left-leaning networks such as ATTAC, for example, also organize protest actions during international summit meetings.

Here, criticism is directed primarily at the distribution of profits generated by global trade. Criticism of international trade has even broader social support than ATTAC because of its impact on global climate change. The carbon footprint of cross-border flows of goods cannot be quantified precisely, but it is estimated that cargo shipping alone accounts for more than 3 percent of global CO_2 emissions. Because the issue of climate change is growing strongly in the social consciousness of many countries, the public will increasingly shift its criticism toward those companies that actually ship goods and blame them for creating emissions in the first place.

A challenge of a completely different kind is facing internationally active industrial companies in view of the increase in region-specific customer demand. For most suppliers, the days are over when they could develop and produce standard products in their home country and then ship them to their customers. Western companies in particular that sold their products in China had to adapt in this respect. In addition to low prices, customers there increasingly expected faster delivery times and customized product adaptations. This has resulted firstly from increased self-confidence on the part of Chinese customers, who are becoming progressively more aware of the sales significance of their market. Secondly, the rise of region-specific norms and standards, such as those introduced by China in the area of high-speed trains or cyber security, has played a role here. However, the introduction of new, region-specific norms and standards is not unique to China. For example, companies marketing digital offerings in Europe have had to adapt to the General Data Protection Regulation introduced there in 2018. They are significantly more restrictive than the rules currently in force in the United States and China.

Such differing regulations often run parallel to regionally divergent customer preferences. In recent years, for example, European B2B customers have been far less willing to use cloud technology than Chinese and American customers. This increasing regionalization of customer needs was a major reason for many industrial companies to relocate development and production to the most important target markets, especially as this shortened delivery times for customers there.

This trend has been favored by the alignment of salaries among the world's major economic regions. It is above all the salary increases for qualified employees in the emerging-markets that have ensured more balance here. China plays a prominent role here, with salaries doubling in real terms between 2008 and 2019.[16]

As a result, leveraging global shipping to achieve "wage arbitrage" cost advantages is not as rewarding as it once was. In parallel with the higher qualification levels of employees in the Asian region, numerous new companies have emerged precisely there, enabling the establishment of a regional supplier network, that is, so-called nearshoring. Accordingly, in 2019, the share of Asia's cross-border trade that took place only between Asian countries had already risen to more than 60 percent, with this share even exceeding two-thirds for European Union (EU) countries.

The EU is a prime example of how "intraregional trade" is politically launched through regionally focused trade agreements, yet the output of these countries accounts for only 18 percent of global gross domestic product. For the North American Free Trade Agreement (NAFTA), a trade agreement between the United States, Canada, and Mexico, this figure is

---

[16]International Labour Organization, *Global Wage Report 2020–21* (Geneva: ILO, 2020). Retrieved from https://www.ilo.org/wcmsp5/groups/public/---dgreports/---dcomm/---publ/documents/publication/wcms_762534.pdf.

28 percent, and for the Regional Comprehensive Economic Partnership (RCEP), which governs trade among 15 Southeast Asian countries, it is as high as 30 percent. More significant than RCEP for China, however, may be its "Belt and Road Initiative", launched in 2013 to strengthen trade flows with southwestern countries. It is estimated that China will invest around $1.4 trillion in this project,[17] which is scheduled to run until 2049 — the 100th anniversary of the founding of the People's Republic of China. The funds will mainly go to infrastructure projects financed by the Asian Infrastructure Investment Bank. As part of this initiative, China is demanding greater use of the yuan in trade and development agreements, progressively edging out the dollar and euro.

While regional and bilateral trade agreements are increasing, global agreements are losing importance. In the United States, there are even repeated calls across party lines to withdraw from the World Trade Organization. Even a long-established institution such as the World Health Organization is currently facing declining support from several member countries. This development indicates that global cooperation among nations is weakening and that the world is instead increasingly dividing into three strong economic blocs, dominated by the United States, Western Europe, and China. These zones are strengthening their own norms and standards, each orienting themselves to a different lead currency in the form of the US dollar, the euro, and the yuan, and attempting to strengthen their positions of power worldwide through further measures. At the same time, the formation of these economic blocs need by no means affect the overall global volume of cross-border trade in goods and services, insofar as it is compensated for by increasing trade with countries in these economic blocs.

Technological developments in the digital sphere are having an even greater impact on the processes of internationally active companies and on global trade as a whole than any of the trends mentioned so far. Digital applications can be used to verify deliveries in real time and automate document processing, artificial intelligence optimizes the choice of transport routes, and e-commerce platforms and blockchain accelerate sales and administrative processes. Therefore, according to a study by McKinsey, by 2030, transportation costs will be reduced by 16–28 percent, and global

---

[17]Q. Liu and L. Ke, *One-Belt-One-Road Policy Implication on Logistics Route Competition* (Hamburg: Hamburg Business School, University of Hamburg, 2018).

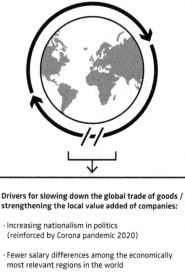

Figure 5.9:   Key developments impacting global trade.

trade will increase from 6 to 11 percent.[18] However, new technologies will make cross-border trade redundant in some areas. For example, products that previously had to be shipped can be manufactured locally with the help of 3-D printing.

Figure 5.9 summarizes the listed developments that are currently influencing global trade. An internationally active company has to analyze

---

[18]McKinsey Global Institute, *Globalization in Transition: The Future of Trade and Value Chain* (2019). Retrieved from https://www.mckinsey.com/featured-insights/innovation-and-growth/globalization-in-transition-the-future-of-trade-and-value-chains. (Accessed May 12, 2020).

these developments and decide to what extent it has to adapt to them. In the following sections, we provide guidance on three sets of questions:

- Where should what value be added?
- To what extent should organizational structures and decision-making processes be adapted?
- To what extent should external communication activities be adapted?

Does the Value Creation Process Regionalize?

In order to examine the impact of these trends on the value creation of an internationally active company, we are guided by Michel Porter's value chain model presented in Chapter 1. He distinguishes primary activities such as production and sales from support activities such as accounting and IT infrastructure. Changes in the respective value creation areas depend first of all on the industry in which a supplier operates. For example, a manufacturer of gas turbines will encounter completely different conditions than a manufacturer of gear units. The former manufactures few but very expensive products for which there is hardly any regional adaptation. They are extremely complex, knowledge of production processes is subject to the utmost confidentiality, and setting up a new production site is expensive. This is much less true for a manufacturer of numerous, relatively inexpensive industrial gear units, which have to follow the respective standards in different countries and for which setting up a production site abroad is inexpensive.

Despite these sectoral differences, overarching trends can be identified in the shifts in value creation. We do not agree with the currently popular statement that the de-globalization of the world economy generally leads to a regionalization of companies. Just like developments in global trade, the regionalization tendencies of companies must be viewed in a differentiated manner. The picture of regional decentralization and cross-national centralization movements varies depending on the value-added sectors. To this end, we conducted a research project that included interviews with more than 40 board members of international industrial companies. The results build the central basis of the following remarks.

With regard to production, it has been mentioned above that many industrial companies have relocated abroad in recent decades, either because of cost advantages, political pressure, or in order to be able to supply customers with their ordered products more quickly. Especially in the years around 2010, many Western industrial companies established factories in Asian countries. Due to the coronavirus pandemic, and now the Russia–Ukraine War, the establishment of regional production sites and the stockpiling of local inventories have been supported by the argument that globally distributed production should increase a company's resilience to local crises. It should be noted, however, that the regionalization of production in recent decades has been accompanied by the possibilities to centrally control and manage these processes using digital technologies. In this way, companies are moving in the direction of the vision of "Industry 4.0," in which data input takes place at countless globally distributed points — with just one production machine, hundreds of sensors report all that is happening — while the control of global production processes is managed by a central system.

A similar development of regionalization and centralization can be seen in the logistics processes of an industrial company. Typically, the relocation of production abroad has been accompanied by the establishment of regional supplier networks and the supply of customers there. In this respect, inbound and outbound logistics have become more regional, but here, too, control has become more centralized through the increasing use of IT. This trend is expected to grow further in the coming years, and half of the administrative staff in these areas can be saved through the automatic initiation and monitoring of purchasing and transport processes.[19]

Sales is usually the first area of value creation that an industrial company regionalizes if it does not want to leave marketing abroad to trading partners. Subsidiaries are then established in the target countries with their own sales staff, who are to build up and maintain relationships with the customers there. Traditionally, they were given sales and profit targets, and otherwise worked relatively detached from headquarters. But the increasing automation of supplier and customer transaction processes is changing these relationships as well. For example, when a customer orders a standard spare part via a platform, there is no need for value creation by a sales representative on site. The order can be processed

---

[19]See O. Knapp and S. Marlinghaus, *Procurement Endgame* (Munich: Roland Berger, n.d.). Retrieved from https://www.rolandberger.com/en/Insights/Global-Topics/Procurement-Endgame/.

centrally. In addition, modern CRM systems increase the transparency and central control of regional sales activities.

However, this centralization process in sales contrasts with a trend resulting from the regionalization of customer needs. It requires closer customer support and input from the respective regions in product development and design. In addition, we saw in the chapter on complex service solutions that these involve a high degree of customer individuality and that the customer has a high need for advice before making a purchase decision. Regional sales and project staff who know the customer well and are trusted by the customer can make significant contributions here. In all these cases, the regional value added of a company increases.

This also applies to the phase after a transaction, that is, for after-sales services. In particular for complex service solutions, continued cooperation with the customer and long-term relationship management are required. Even in the case of the traditional after-sales services of industrial companies, that is, maintenance and repair, resources have often been built up in the respective regions in recent decades. Among other things, this was related to the fact that obtaining visas and the tax treatment of incoming service employees became more difficult in several countries. But this greater regionalization of value creation in after-sales services is also being countered by a trend shaped by the development of digital technologies. In Chapter 2, we saw how the Voith Group uses camera systems and "remote control" to check paper machines at the customer's site remotely. These technologies are now used by numerous industrial companies and reduce the regional value added of the supplier. This is even more true when the functionality of a product is software-based. For example, Tesla has shown traditional competitors in the automotive sector how to change the functionality of a car remotely through a software update.

Digital technologies have also led to increasing centralization in accounting. The fact that business units that are managed as legally independent entities in one country must comply with the respective national regulations in their reporting is nothing new. When it comes to managerial accounting, such as the calculation of contribution margins or internal profit figures, modern systems such as those offered by SAP provide uniform calculation systems centrally. This desire for uniform specifications or the reduction of regional special paths applies to the entire IT infrastructure. It plays a special role when a company wants to exploit the potential of big data. If the data supplied by machine sensors are incompatible due to different formats in the respective countries, it is hardly possible to gain valuable insights from its evaluation. In statistics, the larger the volume of data analyzed, the more valid the findings that can be derived from it.

Nevertheless, modern IT systems promote the regionalization of value creation. They make it possible so that if the specifications of a particular machine have been defined in, say, Thailand, this information is immediately accessible to colleagues in other countries. Perhaps the specifications fit the needs of a customer in Ecuador and the employees there can use them. So, the IT system strengthens the exchange between regions and the value added there. However, a transnational IT department should have defined the rules of data exchange beforehand.

In summary, it can be said that political, social, and technical developments are currently making adjustments necessary in the regionalization of value creation, but the effects vary. Oftentimes, value-adding activities are carried out in individual countries, while their control is increasingly transnational. This leads to the question of who should take over this control within which organizational structures.

Realigning Corporate Structures

The classic industrial company has a headquarters. Firstly, it is the place from where organizations manage their corporate activities, such as accounting. Secondly, the top managers of the lines of businesses are frequently located there. They are divided into organization units by function and — if foreign market activities have reached a significant size — by region. This type of organizational level may be aligned with more than one characteristic. This results in a matrix organization or an even more complex organizational structure, as shown in Figure 5.10.

All organizational structures address the key questions of who makes which decisions and who has the authority to enforce them. In global industrial companies, there is a classic area of conflict in internal decision-making authority. It exists between the core function and product divisions on the one hand, and foreign regional subsidiaries on the other. The former tend to favor standardization to save costs; the latter want to take their local country-specific market characteristics into consideration. Regional managers often complain that centralized product decisions do not meet region-specific customer requirements. The national subsidiaries

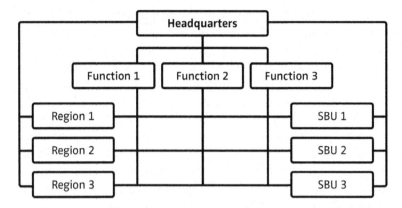

Figure 5.10: Multidimensional organization chart of an industrial company.

of several companies in the mechanical engineering industry complain that centralized development creates products that are too complicated and oversized. In other mechanical engineering companies, regional managers complain that quality and safety standards for their markets are not being sufficiently met. Many also object to the detailed process design guidelines or find that the amount of internal reporting that is expected by headquarters is exaggerated.

Yet, if country-specific products and processes were developed for all countries, a company with global operations would lose transparency. It would also make the cost of complexity too high. Managers must follow certain international standards because of legal requirements in the country where the corporate headquarters is located. In this respect, the right balance between global standardization and local adaptation must be found for both product management and process guidelines. The following rule generally applies: Globalize as much as possible, localize as much as necessary. But what type of organization should managers use to best implement this rule in practice?

Management professor Peter Li proposes the idea of the "second home".[20] In his view, two core criteria are important for finding a balance

---

[20]P. Li, "The Second-home Model toward the Dual-Core Paradigm: The Implications of ISE for MNEs from Advanced and Emerging Economies", Proceedings of the 2015 Annual Meeting of the Academy of International Business, Bangalore, India, June 28–30, 2015.

between standardization and regional adaptation. The first criterion addresses the cultural differences between industrialized and developing countries. Industrialized countries are characterized by very formal institutions in terms of market, law, and politics. Emerging-market institutions are often informal and rely, to a large extent, on personal relationships. The second criterion — and one that plays a key role for Li — deals with challenges in the higher and lower price ranges for a customer segment. We previously discussed no-frills products and advanced premium products in this context. Based on his two core criteria, Li proposes that global companies establish two headquarters. The first should be responsible for no-frills products and located in an emerging-market; the second should be responsible for advanced premium products and complex service solutions and be headquartered in an industrialized country. If only one corporate headquarters exists for both market segments, Li is concerned that the culture in the home market will be too dominant and impede the creation of alternative business approaches.

If there are two corporate headquarters, the one in the emerging-market should react flexibly to changes in requirements. The other headquarters should provide better efficiency and economies of scale in an industrial country. Li believes that the similarities between markets are so great in emerging economies, where no-frills products are sold, that a corporate headquarters located there can benefit from the resulting synergies. He sees similar potential synergies in the corporate headquarters of industrialized countries, which are responsible for advanced premium products and complex services solutions. If there are premium customers in emerging-markets and no-frills customers in industrialized countries, then managers should categorize customers based on their willingness to pay, not by their region.

Li uses the principle of yin and yang to explain the relationship between the two corporate headquarters. That is, both corporations recognize each other's identity, consider it complementary to their own, and join together in what Li calls a "holistic oscillation". To achieve oscillation, the senior management of the two corporate headquarters should each consist of about one-third of the executives from the other culture (see Figure 5.11).

The idea of distributing the tasks of headquarters among strong regional units is not new. Kenichi Ohmae's approach of "regional hubs" became well known in the 1980s. Ohmae recommended that internationally active companies set up three regional hubs within the so-called

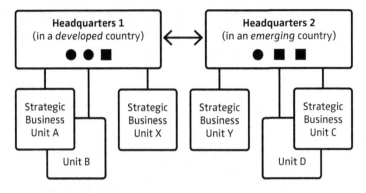

● Share of board members from an *emerging* country
■ Share of board members from a *developed* country

Figure 5.11: The "second home" concept according to Li.

power triad, that is, Western Europe, the United States, and Japan. This was intended to bring companies in these regions closer to the market and, above all, to enable them to better grasp the development of innovations and new competitors there. On this basis, Toyota expanded its sites in these three economic regions in the 1990s and also produced vehicles there that addressed regional differences in customer needs. But the differences were more about details. In essence, the number of vehicle platforms was actually reduced in order to achieve greater cost synergies. With the help of the "Toyota Production System", Toyota endeavored to achieve the same high-quality standards everywhere. In this respect, this example does not quite match Peter Li's second headquarters approach.

This is similarly true of the more recent example of Irdeto, a Dutch IT security company that set up a second headquarters in Beijing in 2007. Despite great efforts, sales outside Europe had lagged behind the company's expectations for years. The CEO, Graham Kill, attributed this primarily to the fact that European employees dominated key decisions at the Dutch headquarters and that his company suffered from "headquarters knows best syndrome". He therefore wanted to increase the cultural and regional diversity of the decision-makers. In addition to establishing the second headquarters in China, he decided, among other things, that half of the board members, including himself, would move to China. Half of the company's internal conference calls were scheduled to take place during core working hours in the Chinese time zone, the other half in the Central

European time zone. For every European manager who went to one of the Asian offices, a colleague from Asia was transferred to Europe. Internationally diverse committees determined the redistribution of administrative tasks.

As a result of these changes, the motivation of non-European employees increased, as did their acceptance and trustworthiness within the company as a whole. Sales in Asia increased strongly. Employees there no longer felt like "a prisoner of their home base" in terms of career development. To further push the international diversity of decision-makers, Kill established another headquarters in San Francisco after an acquisition in 2012. In 2014, however, the two non-European headquarters lost their status as headquarters, but this did not counteract the decisions to establish them. Rather, the goal of the organizational changes had been reached, that is, to achieve cross-cultural thinking with a regionally diversified team. Key management decisions were now made centrally by a team whose internationally diverse members were located in different parts of the world.

Here, there is a difference to Peter Li's second headquarters approach in that he does not want to give greater effect to cross-cultural thinking, but rather to culture-specific thinking. Although his approach limits the power of national units in favor of a regional headquarters, cultural differences are deliberately allowed among the global headquarters with the aim of being able to better serve the strategically different target markets.

Wilo is currently restructuring its organization along these lines. We introduced this medium-sized company in Chapter 1. Wilo manufactures pumps and pump systems for the building services residential water management and industrial segments, and it generates annual sales of €1.5 billion in 50 countries. Based in Dortmund since 1872, the company established its "second home" in Beijing in 2019 and a third headquarters in the United States in 2021 with the aim of addressing the entire US market. The starting point was the belief of CEO Oliver Hermes that the world is increasingly dividing economically and politically into three dominant economic blocs. Hermes speaks of three "tectonic plates" that are drifting apart in terms of economic policy. He saw indicators for the formation of these tectonic plates in the framework conditions for financial transfers, data protection, and standardization, among other things.

Since customer requirements in terms of pump quality and functionality differ from region to region, Wilo increasingly organizes product development and production separately in these three tectonic plates.

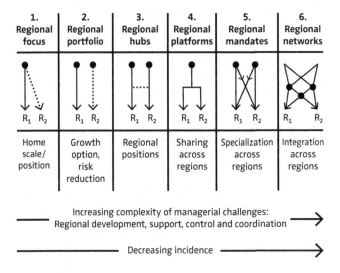

1. Regional focus	2. Regional portfolio	3. Regional hubs	4. Regional platforms	5. Regional mandates	6. Regional networks
Home scale/ position	Growth option, risk reduction	Regional positions	Sharing across regions	Specialization across regions	Integration across regions

Increasing complexity of managerial challenges:
Regional development, support, control and coordination ⟶

──────── Decreasing incidence ─────────⟶

Figure 5.12: Options for the organizational embedding of multiple headquarters.

However, some areas of the company continue to be managed centrally worldwide, for example, Controlling, which is based in Germany, and the newly established area for e-commerce applications in China. This shows that the organizational embedding of a second or third headquarters does not necessarily have to take place in the way suggested in Peter Li's approach, but that management responsibility can also be distributed differently.

Following Ghemawat,[21] the five organizational options presented in Figure 5.12 can be distinguished. In the "regional focus" approach, the second headquarters is a subordinate unit of the traditional corporate headquarters. In the case of the "regional portfolio," the headquarters act completely independently of one another, whereas in the "regional hub" form of organization, there is coordination among the individual regions. In the case of "regional mandates", certain areas of responsibility are assumed by one headquarters in each case with global responsibility for the others. In the case of "regional networks", the headquarters merely coordinate the assumption of such tasks by other corporate units.

The example of Wilo shows that these approaches can also be applied in mixed forms and adapted over time. The latter makes sense for Wilo,

---

[21] P. Ghemawat, *The Laws of Globalization and Business Applications* (Cambridge University Press, 2017).

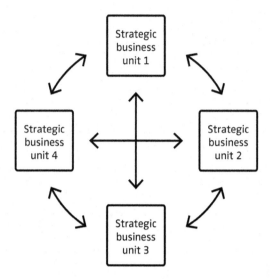

Figure 5.13: Schematic representation of a polycentric corporate organization.

firstly, because the formation of the three tectonic plates is slow and raises unresolved questions: Where should India — soon to be the world's most populous country — be placed in this grid? Where should Russia and Africa be placed? Secondly, phasing in these fundamental organizational changes makes sense if Hermes wishes to build support for them among the workforce. He wants to convince the vast majority of the workforce that these changes are right. He accepts that the process will take time.

Such consideration for employees' interests is less of a priority for other companies. Haier is an example of this. It is the world's largest manufacturer of household appliances, including washing machines and dishwashers. Instead of creating a second or even third headquarters, the company largely dissolved its headquarters in China in 2017, and as many as 10,000 managers with key functions were fired. Instead, there are now about 200 independent business units that compete with each other on the market, and they are even allowed to acquire one another. The headquarters only plays an investor role with a few core internal functions. They include the maintenance of a group-wide platform that shows employee availability and previous performance reviews. For CEO Zhang Ruimin, the restructuring was necessary to meet the demands of new information and communication technologies, increase customer proximity, and accelerate decision-making processes.[22] The decision to radically decentralize was, therefore, primarily because of the speed of change in the market. This, in turn, came in the wake of technical developments that in Haier's industry are referred to as a "smart home". As Zhang envisions it, a company is a polycentric group of networked business units. Its organization is more akin to that of a financial holding company than a traditional industrial company (see Figure 5.13).

Realigning External Communications

Whereas Haier's corporate organization has become more focused on individual business units, the organization of most industrial companies is currently tending toward regional shifts in emphasis. As shown above, this follows political and social developments in which nationalism has taken on growing significance. Accordingly, internationally active industrial companies are not only relocating more value-added processes abroad but they also want to present themselves in the respective country as a local partner rather than as a foreign company.

That was not always the case. Founded in 1600, the British East India Company — at the time still called the English East India Company — was proud of its national roots. It worked closely with its home country's political institutions and even developed its own corporate flag, which was designed to demonstrate the company's close relationship to the homeland outside of the United Kingdom (see Figure 5.14). Today, only a handful of companies still celebrate their national origins. Among the exceptions are Harley-Davidson and Victorinox.

German companies have long labeled their export products with the label "Made in Germany". Many companies are now dropping this explicit reference. At Mercedes, the label now reads "Made by Daimler". One reason for this is the fact that vehicle production for the global market would be too inefficient — and probably no longer possible — if manufacturing were limited to Germany. The company has also taken the aforementioned socio-political developments into account. If Germany were to lose worldwide favor, Mercedes would have to fear losing sales abroad if the company emphasized its German origins. An example is the French

---

[22]P. Michelman, "Leading to Become Obsolete", *MIT Sloan Management Review* 59, no. 1 (2017): 80–85.

Figure 5.14:   Flag of the East India Company (1801–1851).

supermarket chain Carrefour, which was boycotted in China in 2008 in the wake of political tensions between France and China.

The entire range of communication policy measures can be used to profile a company as a regional partner in a particular country. An example of the use of classic advertising media is provided by Siemens, a company that presents itself both in China and in the United States as a nationally active partner with close ties to the government.[23]

It becomes difficult for internationally active companies to profile themselves as national partners when a country's political institutions demand solidarity from them in conflicts with other countries. For example, China expects foreign airlines to designate Taiwan as part of China, and the US government demands that companies refrain from doing business with Iran. In these cases, the interests of two countries with which a company does business may be at odds, because the company can only comply with the wishes of one side. A delicate balancing act is required to ensure that good business relationships are not destroyed in the long term in such cases.

Excellent local knowledge and diplomatic skills are required to convey relevant messages in the appropriate tone and at the right moment. Against this backdrop, John Chipman, director of the International Institute for Strategic Studies, advises global companies to establish a professional foreign policy post similar to those used by national governments.[24] Using "corporate diplomacy", companies can better build bonds with a country's government and society.

---

[23] See Siemens homepages, https://new.siemens.com/us; https://siemens.com.

[24] J. Chipman, "Why Your Company Needs a Foreign Policy", *Harvard Business Review* 94, no. 9 (2016): 36–43.

In addition, such "corporate diplomats" should be active on a transnational political level and, among other things, use their diplomatic influence with international institutions. The spectrum of issues to be addressed is diverse and ranges from the protection of intellectual property to the regulation of environmental standards and the observance of fair competitive conditions. One of these issues should be highlighted here: the problem of IT security. Although many managers currently see this as the greatest threat to their business, we emphasized the opportunities offered by the use of IT in the preceding chapters, but the downsides should be mentioned as well.

Cybercrime can have several facets. Know-how can be stolen and IT systems can be manipulated by hackers in such a way that a company's processes are either impaired or brought to a standstill altogether. In the case of so-called ransomware, hackers inform the affected companies that their networks have been attacked and that they must pay a fee to unlock and reclaim their corporate data. This form of crime has increased worldwide in recent years. Companies have increasingly invested money to protect themselves against it, and spending on this is expected to rise in the future.[25] It is therefore all the more important that these measures are flanked by legal framework factors on the part of policymakers. However, such steps are largely ineffective if they are limited to one country. They must have a transnational impact and be based on cooperation between policymakers and companies at the international level.

Another threat from the IT sector arises from the current development of market structures. Some groups — including Google, Alibaba, Amazon, and JD — are gaining ever greater market power with the help of their IT-based offerings. There is a danger that they will exploit their oligopolistic or monopolistic situation against other companies. Even more threatening for many industrial companies is that deep-pocketed internet companies could enter product manufacturing themselves, making them new competitors. In 2018, for example, the European Commission's Directorate-General for Competition investigated Amazon. The e-commerce giant had allegedly used some of the data services it offered to its industrial customers to identify attractive business opportunities and then launched its own product offerings. Amazon has indeed brought dozens of its own brands onto the market over the past few years, which is a problem mainly for smaller product manufacturers. It is nearly impossible for companies of this

---

[25] PwC's 2018 Global Economic Crime and Fraud Survey. Retrieved from https://www.pwc.ch/en/insights/risk/global-economic-crime-survey.html.

size to seek protection from antitrust authorities; such cases are expensive and take years to resolve. By the time smaller companies can prove the abuse of a competitor's dominant market position, many of them have often already disappeared from the market. As a consequence, these small companies can no longer benefit from official intervention.

Cybercrime and the development of monopolistic market structures in the IT sector are just two examples of the current challenges that are of central importance to industrial companies and can only be tackled effectively at the international political level. Just as the influence of politics on corporate decisions has begun to increase recently, industrial companies should make greater efforts to influence political decisions.

Index

Printed in the United States
by Baker & Taylor Publisher Services